Praise for *Lamentations Throu*

"In this engrossing investigation of Lamenta
Wiley-Blackwell Bible Commentaries series
draw on a fascinating array of visual, literary
secular responses. The authors' adoption of
and emphasis on the contribution reception can make to exegesis, together
with the range of material surveyed and discerning critical treatment, make this
volume an indispensable resource for scholars and students of the book of
Lamentations, for those interested in the manifold ways it has been interpreted
and appropriated, and for anyone curious about reception history in general
and what it can teach us not only about the Bible's influence but also about the
biblical text itself."

J. Cheryl Exum, University of Sheffield

"Mourning the physical Jerusalem is the business of the biblical Lamentations.
Showing us how this is done in the book and in its reception history, over the
ages, is the business of the present volume. The volume's value as guide through
mourning is greatly enhanced by its inception as a Jewish-Christian authorly
cooperation. Jerusalem the symbolical is thus well served; and we, the readers,
those who nurture our own Jerusalems, gain a guide to mourning – as much
necessary, perhaps, as any guide for joy."

Athalya Brenner, University of Amsterdam

"I thoroughly enjoyed this book. It is informative, thought-provoking, and –
despite being a commentary – holds the reader's attention. It made me appreci-
ate Lamentations in a new way. To be recommended."

The Swedish Exegetical Yearbook 2014, 1 October 2014

Wiley Blackwell Bible Commentaries

Series Editors: John Sawyer, Christopher Rowland, Judith Kovacs, David M. Gunn
Editorial Board: Ian Boxall, Andrew Mein, Lena-Sofia Tiemeyer

Further information about this innovative reception history series is available at
www.bbibcomm.info.

Lamentations
Through the Centuries

Paul M. Joyce
and Diana Lipton

WILEY Blackwell

This paperback edition first published 2020
© 2013 Paul M. Joyce and Diana Lipton

Edition history: John Wiley & Sons Ltd (hardback, 2013)

Registered Offices
John Wiley & Sons, Inc., 111 River Street, Hoboken, NJ 07030, USA
John Wiley & Sons Ltd, The Atrium, Southern Gate, Chichester, West Sussex, PO19 8SQ, UK

Editorial Office
The Atrium, Southern Gate, Chichester, West Sussex, PO19 8SQ, UK

For details of our global editorial offices, customer services, and more information about Wiley products visit us at www.wiley.com.

Wiley also publishes its books in a variety of electronic formats and by print-on-demand. Some content that appears in standard print versions of this book may not be available in other formats.

Library of Congress Cataloging-in-Publication Data

Names: Joyce, Paul M., 1954– | Lipton, Diana.
Title: Lamentations Through the Centuries / Paul M. Joyce and Diana Lipton.
Description: Chichester, West Sussex : Malden, MA : Wiley-Blackwell,, 2013. | Series: Wiley-Blackwell bible commentaries. | Includes bibliographical references and index. | Description based on print version record and CIP data provided by publisher.
Identifiers: LCCN 2012048004 (print) | LCCN 2013006514 (ebook) | ISBN 9781118332641 (ePub) | ISBN 9781118320693 (MobiPocket) | ISBN 9781118320709 (Adobe PDF) | ISBN 9780631219781 (hardback) | ISBN 9781119673873 (paperback)
Subjects: LCSH: Bible. Lamentations–Commentaries.
Classification: LCC BS1535.53 (ebook) | LCC BS1535.53 .J69 2013 (print) | DDC 224/.3077–dc23
LC record available at https://lccn.loc.gov/2012048004 LC record available at https://lccn.loc.gov/2013006514

Cover Design: Wiley
Cover Image: Life of William Blake (1880), Volume 2, Job illustrations by Cygnis insignis is licensed under CC BY-SA

Set 10/12.5pt Minion by SPi Global, Pondicherry, India
Printed and bound by CPI Group (UK) Ltd, Croydon, CR0 4YY

10 9 8 7 6 5 4 3 2 1

For Sinéad and Olivia
and
For Jacob and Jonah

Contents

The Wiley-Blackwell Bible Commentaries series, the first to be devoted primarily to the reception history of the Bible, is based on the premise that how people have interpreted, and been influenced by, a sacred text like the Bible is often as interesting and historically important as what it originally meant. The series emphasizes the influence of the Bible on literature, art, music, and film, its role in the evolution of religious beliefs and practices, and its impact on social and political developments. Drawing on work in a variety of disciplines, it is designed to provide a convenient and scholarly means of access to material until now hard to find, and a much-needed resource for all those interested in the influence of the Bible on Western culture.

Until quite recently this whole dimension was for the most part neglected by biblical scholars. The goal of a commentary was primarily if not exclusively to get behind the centuries of accumulated Christian and Jewish tradition to one single meaning, normally identified with the author's original intention.

The most important and distinctive feature of the Wiley-Blackwell Commentaries is that they will present readers with many different interpretations of each text, in such a way as to heighten their awareness of what a text, especially a sacred text, can mean and what it can do, what it has meant and what it has done, in the many contexts in which it operates.

The Wiley-Blackwell Bible Commentaries will consider patristic, rabbinic (where relevant), and medieval exegesis as well as insights from various types of modern criticism, acquainting readers with a wide variety of interpretative techniques. As part of the history of interpretation, questions of source, date, authorship, and other historical-critical and archaeological issues will be discussed, but since these are covered extensively in existing commentaries, such references will be brief, serving to point readers in the direction of readily accessible literature where they can be followed up.

Original to this series is the consideration of the reception history of specific biblical books arranged in commentary format. The chapter-by-chapter arrangement ensures that the biblical text is always central to the discussion. Given the wide influence of the Bible and the richly varied appropriation of each biblical book, it is a difficult question which interpretations to include. While each volume will have its own distinctive point of view, the guiding principle for the series as a whole is that readers should be given a representative sampling of material from different ages, with emphasis on interpretations that have been especially influential or historically significant. Though commentators will have their preferences among the different interpretations, the material will be presented in such a way that readers can make up their own minds on the value, morality, and validity of particular interpretations.

The series encourages readers to consider how the biblical text has been interpreted down the ages and seeks to open their eyes to different uses of the Bible in contemporary culture. The aim is to write a series of scholarly commentaries that draw on all the insights of modern research to illustrate the rich interpretative potential of each biblical book.

John Sawyer
Christopher Rowland
Judith Kovacs
David M. Gunn

Abbreviations

ATD	Das Alte Testament Deutsch
BCE	Before the Common Era
BEATAJ	Beiträge zur Erforschung des Alten Testaments und des Antiken Judentums
BKAT	Biblischer Kommentar, Altes Testament
BZAW	Beihefte zur Zeitschrift für die alttestamentliche Wissenschaft
CE	Common Era
Eng. tr.	English translation
Heb.	Hebrew
ICC	International Critical Commentary

JBL	*Journal of Biblical Literature*
JSOT	*Journal for the Study of the Old Testament*
JSOTSup	Journal for the Study of the Old Testament Supplement Series
KAT	Kommentar zum Alten Testament
KJV	King James Version
LXX	Greek Septuagint
LHBOTS	Library of Hebrew Bible/Old Testament Studies
NCB	New Century Bible
NEB	New English Bible
NJPS	New Jewish Publication Society Version
NRSV	New Revised Standard Version
OBO	Orbis Biblicus et Orientalis
OBT	Overtures to Biblical Theology
OTL	Old Testament Library
RSV	Revised Standard Version
SBL	Society of Biblical Literature
SBT	Studies in Biblical Theology
VT	*Vetus Testamentum*
VTSup	Supplements to Vetus Testamentum
WBC	Word Biblical Commentary
ZAW	*Zeitschrift für die alttestamentliche Wissenschaft*

List of Figures

The Book of Lamentations

The book of Lamentations stands in a long tradition of ancient Near Eastern city-laments, and responds to the destruction of Jerusalem and its Temple by the Babylonians in the sixth century BCE. In the Hebrew Bible, Lamentations is found among the five *Megillot* ('small scrolls'), in the third category of the canon, the *Ketuvim* ('writings'). Lamentations is traditionally attributed to the prophet Jeremiah (for more on Jeremiah as author see below and

Lamentations Through the Centuries, First Edition. Paul M. Joyce and Diana Lipton.
© 2013 Paul M. Joyce and Diana Lipton. Published 2020 by John Wiley & Sons Ltd.

commentary sections on Lam 1:1–3, 6, 17, 21; 2:14, 18; 3:1, 25–30, 31–3, 41–2; and 4:20), and in the Christian canon it appears just after Jeremiah, among the books of the Prophets. It consists of five poems, four of which are acrostics based on the twenty-two letters of the *alef-bet*, the Hebrew alphabet (for more on acrostics see commentary sections on Lam 1:1, 6, 10, 12, 17; 2:18; 3:1, 7–9, 34–36; 4:1; and 5:1). Excellent introductions to the standard historical-critical questions may be found in the commentaries of Provan (1991), Hillers (1992) and Berlin (2002).

Who Wrote Lamentations?

The biblical book of Lamentations is anonymous: the identity of the author or authors of this book is unknown. However, the early and long-standing tradition, within both Judaism and Christianity, is that it comes from the prophet Jeremiah. This was encouraged by the probability of a sixth-century BCE setting, by a reference in 2 Chro 35:25 ('Jeremiah also uttered a lament for Josiah, and all the singing men and singing women have spoken of Josiah in their laments to this day. They made these a custom in Israel; they are recorded in the Laments'), and by some affinities with the so-called 'Confessions' in the book of Jeremiah. The Babylonian Talmud (*Baba Batra* 14b–15a) reports that 'Jeremiah wrote the book that bears his name, the book of Kings and Lamentations', and the Targum of Lamentations opens with the words, 'Jeremiah the prophet and high priest said …'. The tradition is reflected also in the headings of the Greek Septuagint and the Latin Vulgate (a practice carried over even to the English RSV, where an introductory heading reads: 'The Lamentations of Jeremiah'), and in the location of Lamentations in the Christian canon immediately after the book of Jeremiah.

This view is rarely defended by historical critics today, since overall the style and thought are somewhat different from the book of Jeremiah – indeed many positions in Lamentations appear to contradict Jeremiah's stance (Hillers 1992: 13–14). Nonetheless, the suggestion of Jeremianic authorship, while perhaps historically inaccurate, demonstrates readerly discernment of resonances between the books of Jeremiah and Lamentations regarding historical context and the anguished timbre of the authorial voice, and some who follow the modern critical consensus still choose to treat Jeremiah as the author of Lamentations in a symbolic sense.

That the association with Jeremiah has dominated the long view of Lamentations cannot be doubted, and not surprisingly the reception of the book in the visual arts is, by and large, characterized by association with the prophet. The Sistine Chapel ceiling painted between 1508 and 1512 by

Michelangelo, *The Prophet Jeremiah*, from the Sistine Chapel ceiling, Vatican (1508–12).

Rembrandt van Rijn, *Jeremiah Lamenting the Destruction of Jerusalem* (1630).

Gustave Doré, *The People Mourning over the Ruins of Jerusalem* (1866).

Michelangelo (born Caprese, Tuscany, 1475; died Rome, 1564) features a famous image of *The Prophet Jeremiah*, looking down disconsolately, his head supported by his hand; but though its viewers would have assumed that this was the author of Lamentations, there is no distinctive allusion to the book. However, a well-known picture by Rembrandt van Rijn (born Leiden, Netherlands, 1606; died Amsterdam, 1669) may well have the book more centrally in focus. It has been said of *Jeremiah Lamenting the Destruction of Jerusalem* (1630), from Rembrandt's early Leiden years, that 'this work remains unique in that it represents a major reception that focuses upon Lamentations'; the picture and its links with Lamentations are discussed in detail by Heath Thomas (Thomas 2011b: 154). Gustave Doré (born Strasbourg, France, 1832; died Paris, 1883) produced a very popular and influential illustrated Bible, published in 1866. This includes a striking image with a central figure who is

Marc Chagall, *Jeremiah's Lamentations* (1956).

presumably meant to represent Jeremiah; it is variously referred to as *The People Mourning over the Ruins of Jerusalem* and *Jeremiah Laments the Desolation of Jerusalem*. Finally, Marc Chagall (born near Vitebsk, Russia, 1887; died Paris, 1985) painted several famous pictures of Jeremiah, including *Jeremiah* (1956) and *The Prophet Jeremiah* (1968). Two other Chagall images, however, can be associated more particularly with Lamentations. *The Capture of Jerusalem* (1956) is discussed in some detail in our commentary at Lam 3:41–2; and special mention should also be made of *Jeremiah's Lamentations* (also 1956). In the latter Jeremiah clutches to his bosom what seems to be a scroll, in a pose that is very evocative of mother and child. Heath Thomas writes: 'One may note suggestions of a motherly metaphor at work, imagining Jeremiah the prophet as a "mother" for his children, the people of Jerusalem', and he speculates that this representation moves in the direction of emphasis upon 'the persona of Daughter Zion' (Thomas 2011b: 154).

The Language of Lamentations: Translations and Versions

The book of Lamentations was written in Hebrew, and some of the earliest instances of its reception history consist of translations, including the Greek Septuagint (see on Lam 1:3; 4:20), the Aramaic Targum (see on Lam 2:15–16; 4:20; 5:8), and the Latin Vulgate (see on Lam 1:2, 3, 6; 3:7–9; 4:20; 5:22). Most of the examples of reception history that we have examined here were based on translations into other languages. Our musical settings, for example, were based mostly on the Latin of the Vulgate, and the patristic readings we discuss were based predominantly on the Greek Septuagint. Some more recent interpreters knew the biblical text primarily as translated into their own vernacular, perhaps French or English. The poetic form of the Hebrew original has its own multivalency, and this is compounded by the phenomenon of translation. The language used, whether the original Hebrew or a translation, has its own particularity, and the capacity to reveal and conceal, to illuminate or to obscure.

What Makes Lamentations So Generative and Fertile?

What is it about Lamentations that has produced such a rich and diverse reception? It must be significant that the central themes of the book bear directly on central human questions. The experience of loss, bereavement and mourning is perennial. From the start, the book evokes the deepest and most personal of individual human losses ('like a widow', Lam 1:1) and moves on to confront the loss of children (Lam 2:12). Destroyed cities and displaced people: these have been all-too-common features of the human lot over the past two and a half millennia. And, as with the Psalms, these hard realities and the questions they pose for belief are explored in Lamentations with searing honesty (for example, Lam 1:12–16). Again, Lamentations is one of relatively few biblical books that give a voice to a woman, in this case personified Zion (Chapters 1–2). Some discussions of the impact made by biblical books such as Job cite the large size of the work, but it is worth reflecting whether it is precisely the small scale of Lamentations that has encouraged so many readers to turn to it. Finally, the poetic nature of the work should not go unmentioned. As Robert Alter has influentially emphasized (Alter 1985), the multivalent nature of poetry means that it is an effective vehicle for a wide range of emotions; this combined with its subject matter is surely of significance in accounting for the rich reception of Lamentations.

Timely Lament: Why Is Lamentations Read and Studied Now?

One answer to this question must surely be that our age is not short of occasions of radical loss that have so often, through the centuries, been the context for reading Lamentations. Examples that feature in this commentary include the Shoah (the Holocaust) (see on Lam 2:1–2, 11–12, 13, 20; 3:10–14, 41–2; 4:9–10, 13–15; and 5:22), the events in the Balkans in the 1990s (see on Lam 4:5), and 9/11 and its aftermath (see on Lam 1:1 and 3:43–8). Images of destroyed cities and dying children are all too familiar. It might be suggested, in addition, that the profound engagement of Lamentations with the human condition resonates with certain features of the modern mindset, including perhaps the lingering influence of existentialism (passé perhaps in many quarters but still a persisting influence on many Christian and Jewish preachers and teachers).

Within the guild of biblical studies it would seem that Lamentations is a book whose time has come. One catalyst for this was an influential essay by Walter Brueggemann, bewailing the 'Costly Loss of Lament' and calling for fresh attention to the biblical lament materials (Brueggemann 1986). We have seen a rich time in Lamentations study, with important contributions from, among others, Provan (1991), Hillers (1992), Dobbs-Allsopp (1993), Westermann (1994), Linafelt (2000a), Berlin (2002), Lee (2002), O'Connor (2002), Middlemas (2005), Mandolfo (2007), Salters (2010), Parry (2010) and Thomas (2013). The Society of Biblical Literature has provided an important forum for discussion, as is reflected in the essays edited by Lee and Mandolfo (2008). Moreover, there has been a comparable but largely independent revival of interest in this book within the context of Christian systematic theology in continental Europe (see Harasta and Brock 2009).

The Contexts in Which Lamentations Has Been Most Often 'Received'

A brisk sketch of the reception history of the whole book reveals the vast range of contexts in which this small book has made a big impact. The Hebrew Bible itself provides evidence of the reception of Lamentations, for example in Isaiah (see on Lam 1:21) and Qohelet (Lam 5:11–14). And, indeed, the reading of Lamentations in the light of older material such as Mesopotamian city laments (see on Lam 2:7–9) and the Egyptian cult of the dead (see on Lam 4:3–4) can be shown to have played a significant role in the reception of book. Allusions are found in the New Testament, for example in Matthew (see on Lam 2:15–16), and the Dead Sea Scrolls provide further scope for discussion (Lam 1:4). The fate of Jerusalem at the hands of the Romans drove many Jews back to the book of Lamentations, as may be seen in the Targum (Lam 5:8, 10), *Lamentations Rabbah* (see, for example, on Lam 2:18; 3:20–1), and the *Avot de Rabbi Natan* (Lam 3:16), as well as in the *Jewish War* of Josephus (Lam 2:22). In Jewish liturgy, it has been recited through the centuries on Tisha B'Av, the annual fast day commemorating the destruction of the two Temples and subsequent Jewish disasters such as the expulsion of Jews from Spain in 1492 (Lam 4:14–15; 5:21).

The Church Fathers made use of the book (see, for example, Irenaeus and Gregory the Great on Lam 3:1 and Justin Martyr and Origen on Lam 4:20), while medieval Jewish rabbinic interpreters such as Ibn Ezra (Lam 3:49–50), Yehuda Halevi (Lam 3:22–4), and Ibn Verga (Lam 5:7) engaged with the book in periods of dislocation and dispersion. In Christian tradition it came to be sung as part of the liturgy of Holy Week, the days leading up to Easter, from the Middle Ages on and through to the modern era, in the settings of, for example, Tallis (see on Lam 1:2), Palestrina (Lam 1:6), Couperin (Lam 1:10), and Frescobaldi (Lam 1:12). And other musical settings abound, from Handel (Lam 1:12) to Krenek (Lam 3:7–9) and Lovett (Lam 1:1).

Christian writers of the Reformation era such as Calvin (Lam 1:17) and Peter Martyr Vermigli (Lam 4:12) wrote on the book, as did mystical and devotional writers from St John of the Cross (Lam 3:1) to John Keble (Lam 3:22–3). And Jewish thinkers in modernity, not least in Eastern Europe, found the book a vital resource in adversity, for example the so-called K'li Yakar, Rabbi Shlomo Ephraim Luntshitz (Lam 2:14), and Nathan of Hanover (Lam 2:1–2). The role of Lamentations in various social contexts in Western Europe makes for a fascinating story, for example in England in response to the execution of King Charles I (Lam 4:20) or to the Great Fire of London (Lam 2:3–5), and in France both in high society and in literature (see on Lam 1:10).

Responses to the Shoah and its aftermath often feature Lamentations, for example, Cynthia Ozick's *The Shawl* (Lam 2:11–12), the Yiddish poet Abraham Sutzkever in the Vilna Ghetto (Lam 4:9–10) and Abraham Joshua Heschel (Lam 3:10–14). It has also been used to respond to more recent tragedies – such as the traumas of the Balkans in the 1990s (Nancy Lee on Lam 4:5, 7–8) and of South Africa in the late twentieth century (Johanna Stiebert on Lam 1:15–16), and the epoch-making events of 9/11 and their aftermath (David Shatz, on Lam 1:1; Daniel Berrigan, on Lam 3:43–8).

In various ways the scenes described in Lamentations have been represented in art, for example by Marc Chagall (Lam 3:41–2), or else have prompted reflections in relation to works of art, for example that of Samira Abbassy

(Lam 2:10) or the junk art of Zimbabwe (Lam 3:52–7). Modern novels, for example André Schwarz-Bart's *A Woman Named Solitude* (Lam 2:20), come into the story, as does autobiography, such as Lucette Lagnado's *The Arrogant Years* (Lam 3:4–6). Political philosophers such as the Italian Giorgio Agamben provide material to illumine the book (Lam 1:18), while the ongoing impact of Lamentations in the life of modern Israel is seen in the film *Eicha* (Lam 4:1), in novels such as Aharon Megged's *The Living on the Dead* (Lam 1:7), and even in the death notices of important figures in ultra-Orthodox Jerusalem (Lam 5:16).

Modern psychology interacts with Lamentations, especially in response to radical experiences of loss (Lam 3:17–18) and in relation to body language about emotional distress (Lam 1:19–20), as well as in Alice Miller's work on child abuse (Lam 3:25–30). In modern times the book has been much discussed by feminist critics, such as Deryn Guest (Lam 1:1), Johanna Stiebert (Lam 1:15–16), Carleen Mandolfo (Lam 2:21), and Naomi Seidman (Lam 4:14–15). And it has also been considered in the context of queer reading (Lam 4:16–19).

Finally, it is not just that reviewing all this fascinating material from the centuries after the writing of Lamentations provides a complement to the historical-critical study of the book. Historical criticism does not stand above the tide but is rather very much part of the story of the reception of the Bible. Questions of sources, date, authorship, and original intention – 'All these', as Roberts puts it, are 'part of the history of interpretation and not the foundation upon which other forms of interpretation may be built' (Roberts 2011: 3).

Reception History

'The study of postbiblical readings and artistic representations is known as reception history or *Wirkungsgeschichte*, that is, the history of the effect the Bible has had on its readers.' In this way John Sawyer offers a positive definition of reception history (2009: ix). Elsewhere he indicates the approach that it is attempting to remedy or complement: 'After more than two centuries of focusing almost exclusively on the quest for original meanings, it seems that finally biblical scholars are admitting that what people believe the Bible means is often as interesting and historically important as what it originally meant' (Sawyer 2011: 2). Jonathan Roberts distinguishes the reception of the Bible, which he takes to include every act or word of interpretation of the Bible, from reception history, which he understands to refer to 'a scholarly enterprise, consisting of selecting and collating shards of that infinite wealth of reception material in accordance with the particular interests of the historian concerned, and giving them a narrative frame' (Roberts 2011: 1).

Reception history is grounded in the philosophical hermeneutics of Hans-Georg Gadamer (born Marburg, Germany, 1900; died Heidelberg, Germany, 2002) (see especially his *Truth and Method*, first published in 1960: Gadamer 2004). Another seminal influence, generally in a more conservative direction, is that of Gadamer's pupil Hans Robert Jauss (born Göppingen, Germany, 1921; died Constance, Germany, 1997) (e.g. Jauss 1982). Accessible critical introductions to reception theory may be found in Holub 2003 and Parris 2009. One of Gadamer's accomplishments as a philosopher was to draw attention to the situated nature of all interpretive acts: as interpreters we always work from within our historical locations; our very consciousness exists within that context. Another crucial insight emphasized by Gadamer and others is that the reader is not the passive recipient of a text, but plays a creative part in constructing its meaning. Gadamer argued that as we encounter the past we must enter a dialogical relationship with it, gradually coming to recognize the otherness of the past, and in the process coming to acknowledge our own prejudices through that difference. Gadamer was concerned with the rehabilitation of tradition as something that may embody truth. But, as Roberts points out, for those seeking certitudes from the past this is a double-edged sword, for the reclamation of tradition as a dialogue partner also demands the relinquishment of the dream that the meaning of biblical (or indeed any) texts can be settled once and for all (cf. Roberts 2011: 3).

Margaret Davies indicates another significant influence when she notes the debt of reception theory to Gestalt psychology (Coggins and Houlden 1990: 579). Reception theory expects the reader to form the received text into a coherent whole; it is the task of the reader to discover an overall pattern in what is read. But different readers will create different unities, for texts are open to more than one meaning and readers may be more competent at construing some kinds of texts than others.

Until recent years, reception work on the Bible was principally a German-language phenomenon. The best-known German-language theologian working in reception history is Ulrich Luz, noted for commentaries on Matthew's Gospel within the ecumenical Evangelisch-Katholischer Kommentar (EKK) series, which pays particular attention to reception. In the English-speaking world Coggins and Houlden's *Dictionary of Biblical Interpretation* represented a pioneering venture (Coggins and Houlden 1990). It featured articles on 'history of interpretation' (John Sawyer), 'inner-biblical exegesis' (Rex Mason) and 'reader-response criticism' (Margaret Davies). Many of its articles dealt with the reception of the biblical books discussed, though it would seem that some contributors in 1990 did not really know what was expected of them and provided articles that could have been written much earlier or for a different volume.

In an important work entitled *A Biblical Text and Its Afterlives: The Survival of Jonah in Western Culture* (2000), Yvonne Sherwood charts the voyage to the present day of the biblical book of Jonah. Without wishing to claim that the relative choices of the terms 'reception history' and 'afterlife' necessarily signify radically different approaches to the same basic project, it is worth commenting briefly on how they might relate to each other. Generally speaking, afterlife refers to an unlimited period of time that commences when the duration of a normal lifespan has been closed. For humans, such closure would usually occur at the point of death. In the case of a book, it might coincide with publication or canonization, the moment at which a version exists that is in some sense complete. As indicated by her use of the phrase 'the survival of Jonah', for Sherwood it is as though the book of Jonah, whose afterlives she traces, is still alive and active, responsive and responding.[1] Reception history as a sub-discipline of biblical studies is still evolving, and it is clear from recent discussions that its various exponents have diverse views of what it entails (cf. Boer 2011; Rowland and Boxall 2013). As often understood, the notion of reception history is somewhat different from the notion of a textual afterlife. Unlike scholars who write afterlives, reception historians often distinguish sharply between the biblical text on the one hand and, on the other, the multiple manifestations, uses, appropriations and applications of the Bible, in which readers make new things of the biblical text. In addition, reception historians tend to exclude academic biblical scholarship from reception history, distinguishing between readers whose aim is to elucidate the biblical text, usually in its ancient context, and readers who, although they may well illuminate the Bible, are motivated by other interests.

In these respects, our volume falls somewhere between an afterlife of the book of Lamentations and a reception history. For us, as is clear from what we have chosen to include in this volume, all translations, interpretations and exegesis, however motivated and however much or little they elucidate the biblical text, belong together with music, art, literature and so forth in a reception history. In other words, we regard the historical-critical study of the Bible as a relatively recent phase in the long story of its reception, rather than as a kind of foundation on which reception history might be built as a second-stage superstructure. Following from this, we make no absolute distinction between readers whose starting point is the book of Lamentations as rendered in the Hebrew Masoretic Text and readers who are responding indirectly to

---

[1] Even the text on the back of the book makes this clear: 'This book charts the mutations of … the book of Jonah as it latches onto Christian and Jewish motifs and anxieties, passes through highbrow and lowbrow culture, and finally becomes something of a scavenger among the ruins, as, in its most resourceful move to date, it begins to live off the demise of faith.'

Lamentations as already translated, interpreted and even transformed in a new context such as liturgy or a work of art. While clearly we have selected the material included in this volume, and thereby created a pattern of some sort, we have not attempted to give them a 'narrative frame' (cf. Roberts 2011: 1).

Reception historians have worked hard to establish the credentials of their discipline and to persuade the guild that 'what people believe [the Bible] means and how they actually use it – in everyday situations, in the liturgy, in preaching, in the media, in literature, in art, in music, in film – can be studied with the same degree of scientific sensitivity and rigor as the original' (Sawyer 2011: 2). Nonetheless, its value and scholarly integrity are increasingly widely recognized, as indicated by several current major projects. One of these is the Wiley-Blackwell Bible Commentary series in which this volume appears; all four series editors have been champions of reception history in biblical studies over many years. Other examples include the *Oxford Handbook of the Reception History of the Bible* (Lieb, Mason and Roberts 2011), which combines surveys of particular biblical books with wide-ranging thematic essays; De Gruyter's large and ongoing multi-volume project the *Encyclopedia of the Bible and its Reception* (*EBR*); and a new annual journal, *Biblical Reception* (Sheffield Phoenix, from 2012).

Who Writes Reception History?

The field of reception history is, of necessity, one in which all its experts are at the same time amateurs. In the case of the Bible, reception history requires its practitioners to survey a vast sweep of history (extending in our case from the sixth or fifth century BCE to the present day), and to engage with a broad range of media (from classical to popular culture, from music through visual arts to all forms of the written word, and across the academic spectrum), in contexts religious (Jewish and Christian) and secular, from selected countries throughout the world. Even though we have the benefit of collaboration – our combined knowledge far exceeds what we know individually – we are both trained as biblical scholars and lack formal training in most of the areas and periods of reception that we analyze in this volume. This means that our success depends upon our willingness to engage in interdisciplinary research and to relate to a range of experts in fields other than our own. We need to be at once vulnerable, dependent and humble as 'non-experts' and also bold in moving beyond our specialized comfort zones. And we need to re-apply our academic training in biblical studies to other fields, ever-conscious of its gaps and limitations. This raises an important point. Most biblical reception histories to date have been written by biblical scholars. There is a strong case to be made for placing this task instead in the hands of cultural historians, a group more likely to include experts in a wider range of the areas mentioned above. In defense of biblical scholars, however, one can point out that – given the place of the Bible in Western religious and secular cultures – only the most blinkered or isolated student and teacher of biblical studies can avoid being exposed on a daily basis to some form of use and abuse of the Bible. Biblical scholars are usually, by necessity, looking at the Bible through more than one lens (expert and non-expert, religious and secular, academic and popular) and – given their professional preoccupations – seeing the Bible as it appears in a vast array of guises beyond their studies and libraries. At any rate, while emphasizing our limitations, we hope that our 'located' voices – reflecting two geographic regions, two religions, and two genders – will succeed in bringing a distinctive perspective to the study of reception.

Who Reads Reception History?

Numbered among the readers of reception histories are, of course, those who usually write them: scholars in the field of biblical studies. One reason for this is that reception history represents a significant sub-section in the field and researchers want to 'keep up'. Another is the value of what we term 'reception exegesis', which can make a genuine contribution to biblical exegesis as traditionally practiced. Yet another is that university courses in biblical studies are increasingly multi-disciplinary, investigating what happened to the Bible after it was written, sometimes as an end in itself and often as a way of making the Bible accessible. Reception histories are important resources for teachers and students of such courses. An arguably more significant group of readers of reception histories, however, are members of the faith communities that hold the Bible sacred. Ours is a world where religious differences seem to lie at the base of many of the most pressing political problems (in the Middle East, for example), and in which dealing appropriately with religious differences is a challenge even in countries (such as Britain) where they are not the occasion of extreme violence and upheaval on an almost daily basis. Ours is also a world in which politicians often invoke religious ideas and biblical language in their rhetoric and even in their decision-making processes. It is incumbent upon members of religious communities to achieve a more nuanced and sophisticated understanding of how the Bible has been used through the centuries, religiously and politically, for good and for ill, if only to help them to see more clearly how the Bible is being used now.

A third group of readers of reception histories could include those who turn to the Bible in times of trauma, individual and collective, whether to be comforted or to comfort others. A deeper appreciation for how the Bible has been used in the past, and is still being used, by others in similar circumstances, can enrich significantly the use of Scripture to console and heal (see on Lam 3:1, 17–18, 31–3). Needless to say, Lamentations is an especially valuable book in this respect. Finally, readers of reception histories such as this one should also include all those who enjoy being taken on a journey, through time and space, in the company of a text that has spoken to an astoundingly varied audience, and continues to speak.

The Ethics of Reception

It has been said: 'Texts, like dead men and women, have no rights, no aims, no interests. They can be used in whatever way readers or interpreters choose' (Morgan with Barton 1988: 7). Are we then, as readers, sovereign to do as we will with the texts we read? A growing literature has argued that there are in fact important ethical dimensions to reading texts. (Within the world of biblical studies, two important contributions are Schüssler Fiorenza 1988 and Young 1993.) Ethical issues are relevant, not least, to reception history, and a good many are encountered in the study of the reception of Lamentations. Some of the more important are highlighted here and will be revisited in the course of the commentary.

We saw earlier that selectivity is an intrinsic and inevitable feature of reception history. Whose responses are deemed to be of importance? How is the choice of material to be justified? We have tried to be attentive to feminist issues and to sensitivities in the relationship between Christians and Jews, and where possible also to questions bearing on race. But there are, no doubt, many issues we have failed to see, let alone address. Is it sufficient to acknowledge that we are located readers with limitations and prejudices, or is that to lapse into a failure of responsibility?

The subject matter of Lamentations is grim indeed. But there is much beauty in the poetry of the book and certainly artifice in the elaborate acrostic patterning. It could be argued that even in the original there is a certain glamorization of suffering, and this may justifiably cause some concern. Then we might consider later uses, such as the performances of Couperin's musical setting for Parisian high-society gatherings (see on Lam 1:10). The use of material that alludes to rape and torture for such entertainment may seem distasteful. We may be disturbed by the use others make of texts, but should we also feel morally uncomfortable about our own use of such material for aesthetic pleasure, as when relaxing to listen to the musical settings on a sound system?

We have noted that feminist critics have exposed the problematic nature of the language about women in Lamentations. For Guest the text must be ejected from Scripture (see on Lam 1:1). Others may comment critically on the language while remaining in dialogue with it (see Mandolfo on Lam 2:21), but what of our own complicity as readers? Pyper helps us see how the poet is complicit in compounding Zion's humiliation. And more – as readers we too are now implicated; we too have seen her nakedness, and witnessed the uncleanness in her skirts; and we find ourselves among those who have failed to comfort her' (cf. Pyper 2001. See on Lam 1:8–9). And it may not only be a matter of joining those who fail to comfort: what if the reader were to be sexually aroused by the material? Some scholars of the prophetic literature describe the most sexually explicit material there in terms of 'pornoprophetics' and perhaps similar concerns are in order here.

When considering ethical aspects, we must not fail to note the fundamental theological question of the appropriation of the Hebrew Bible as the Old Testament of the Church. In one sense it may seem entirely reasonable that the scriptures that formed Jesus and Paul should be treasured and made accessible by their followers. But the supersessionist manner in which Christian identity has so often been articulated (asserting the superiority of Christianity as a religion that has replaced Judaism) complicates considerably the phenomena of decontextualization and re-use.

Linafelt raises an ethical issue when he spells out what is problematic, from a modern, psychologically informed perspective, when victims appeal for comfort to the perpetrators of the violence committed against them, as Zion appears to do in Lamentations. He highlights the complexity of Lamentations and the fact that in many respects it resists systematic explanation of the original disaster and its implications (Linafelt 2000a). He is at pains to emphasize the danger of for-mulating too benign a characterization of the divine perpetrator and rushing on to resolution and hope, as he argues both Jewish and Christian interpreters of Lamentations have done through the centuries. In short, for Linafelt, to explain the unacceptable would itself be a crime.

'Is there any agony like mine?' asks Zion in Lam 1:12; 'To what can I liken you, that I may comfort you, O virgin daughter Zion?' we read in Lam 2:13. These verses articulate well the issue of the incommensurability of pain suffered by different individuals and groups. Many authors of Shoah literature resist comparisons for fear of compromising the Shoah's unique status, and in sifting the uses of Lamentations in different eras we too need to remain sensitive to this difficult issue.

Lenses for Lamentations: Types of Media and Their Implications for Reception History

In the world of biblical scholarship as it was about a generation ago, the range of relevant media was limited. Most biblical scholars would not have considered analyzing films or art, or even poetry, novels, liturgy or musical settings – whether from the perspective of what the Bible brought to these media or what they brought to the Bible. Even scholarship from other disciplines, such as philosophy, psychology or anthropology, interested biblical scholars primarily – if at all – from a theoretical point of view, for the interpretative frameworks these disciplines might offer for biblical scholarship. The spread of reception history has changed all this. Now biblical scholars look not only to the arts but also to other humanities subjects and, especially, the social sciences, for help in interpreting the Bible, and to see how their practitioners – non-professionals from the perspective of biblical scholarship – have interpreted the Bible in their own work. The professional borders have been blurred, if not erased, and it is no longer straightforward to determine who is the teacher and who the learner, who the expert and who the amateur. The present volume aims to showcase the book of Lamentations as it has been interpreted, alluded to and used in as wide as possible a range of media. It is important to be aware at the outset, however, that the nature of the medium in question will have a significant impact on how the Bible is being used. A poem or novel, for example, might be expected to cite explicitly words or even entire verses from the biblical text, while musical settings might often reference entire chapters. In these cases, it is usually relatively easy to see what is being used and how. Paintings or sculptures, on the other hand, are less likely to be explicit in this way, and it can be difficult or even impossible to isolate the single verse or image from the Bible that the artist had in mind. Following our decision to work through the biblical book verse by verse or unit by unit, we link all artistic, musical or other representations to a particular verse or unit that illustrates well the particular usage, even when we are aware that their artists or composers were likely to be thinking about the book in more general terms. We make this clear wherever it occurs, and try to spell out the benefits of this strategy.

In the case of representations of the book of Lamentations in various media, two factors in particular require special consideration. First, as noted above, the biblical book has long been attributed to the prophet Jeremiah. Indeed, the association between the two is so strong that images of Jeremiah are as likely to allude to Lamentations as to the book of Jeremiah itself. If a painting or sculpture depicts Jeremiah holding a scroll, for example, it could be the book of Lamentations, and if Jeremiah looks downcast, it may well be because he is contemplating the destruction of Jerusalem as described in Lamentations rather than as described in the book of Jeremiah. It is thus no straightforward matter to decide to what extent images of Jeremiah involve allusions to the book of Lamentations. Even less straightforward to answer is the question of whether or not it is significant that many translations, versions and musical settings of Lamentations follow the name by which the biblical book came to be known: 'The Lamentations of Jeremiah'. Does this identification with a specific author, about whom we know a certain amount from another source, namely the book of Jeremiah, affect the way that the translators and composers in question interpreted the book of Lamentations, or is the association with Jeremiah little more than a matter of a label for them? This brings us to our second factor relevant to the representation of Lamentations in various media – the very word 'Lamentations'. While 'lamentation' (in its singular or plural form) is far from falling into the category of 'Deuteronomy', a non-English term that is hardly ever used without reference to its eponymous biblical book, it is also far from 'Numbers', a word that by no means evokes the biblical book when used in a different context. This means that if an artist chooses to call his or her work 'Lamentation(s)', it is difficult to be sure whether or not he or she has in mind, consciously or unconsciously, the biblical book. In the present volume, however, we have taken the view that such a choice of title invites at the least further consideration.

We mentioned above that the increasing influence of reception history has blurred the borders between biblical scholars and others when it comes to representing and interpreting books of the Bible. Depending on exactly what it is one wants to learn about a biblical book, it might be as helpful to look at how it has been used in art or liturgy as to consult traditional scholarly commentaries. It is important to note, however, that the welcome expansion of the field of interpreters of the Bible does not entail the exclusion of biblical scholars, and we have tried in this volume to give them an appropriate place within the reception history of Lamentations (see, for example, on Lam 5:1–5 in relation to Hermann Gunkel). Finally, at the other end of the chronological scale, we, like others before us, have committed ourselves here to including the Bible itself in the history of interpretation of the book of Lamentations (see, for example, on Lam 1:21 in relation to Isaiah, or Lam 5:11–14 in relation to Qohelet). This decision is not uncontroversial, since it involves in particular judgements about the relative dating of Lamentations and biblical books that might allude to it; nonetheless, we believe it to be legitimate and have often found it illuminating.

Reception Exegesis

For a variety of reasons it seems to us that alongside the reception history we set out to write, we have generated a distinctive type of commentary that we have come to term 'reception exegesis'. According to John Sawyer, '[Reception history] also involves collecting and analyzing the many meanings that each text has had in different contexts, in a way that often gives us new insights into the language and imagery of the Bible' (Sawyer 2009: ix). We believe that such study of how the Bible has been received may provide assistance in the exegetical task. Our term 'reception exegesis' shares common ground with 'reception criticism', favored by some over 'reception history' because it signals that the enterprise involves not merely cataloguing cases of reception but also critical analysis (cf. Exum 2012: 473–6).

A significant part of this volume proceeds according to a structure that, although we had not intended it, functions remarkably similarly to rabbinic midrash. But whereas midrash typically brings into the discussion a verse from the Psalms or other Writings (especially Proverbs, Job, or the Song of Songs), our volume brings an interpretation or a use of the Lamentations verse that is our focus. Needless to say, this difference is significant. In the vast majority of cases, the verses from Psalms, Proverbs and so forth that midrash brings to interpret a verse from the Pentateuch do not relate to the pentateuchal verse in their original context. They are brought together in the mind of the interpreter. In our case, by contrast, the text or other medium that we are bringing was usually (though by no means always) created explicitly in response to Lamentations. In most cases, however, the secondary text or, better, the 'receiving text' that we bring to bear was not intended to *interpret* the biblical text. Our particular contribution is not, as in the case of midrash, to bring together two texts that were not originally connected, but rather to show that biblical scholars bent on interpretation do not have a monopoly on explicating the ancient text. Illumination can also be derived from textual and other media that are better characterized as responding to or using Lamentations, rather than interpreting it. Reception exegesis can shine a spotlight on biblical verses that have been dulled by familiarity; it can foreground biblical concepts and concerns that have faded over time into the background; and it can even give rise to radical new readings of difficult Hebrew terms and texts.

This does not mean, of course, that examples of reception history that do not enrich our understanding of the core biblical text are less valuable than those that do. In other words, the legitimacy of reception history as an enterprise by no means depends upon its having to yield exegetical fruit. Reception exegesis merely offers an additional dimension to reception history as usually understood. Having said that, though, it must be confessed that there is a sense in which the reception exegesis dimension helps to justify the choice of two biblical scholars (in our case) rather than, say, an art historian and a historian of music to write this book and others like it. As biblical scholars, we are not trained to analyze novels, paintings, music, psychology and so forth, and must inevitably approach them as amateurs. We embrace that challenge because we are committed to the view that interdisciplinary work requires that those who engage in it make themselves vulnerable in this way. If, in the end, we are also contributing to a greater understanding of the underlying biblical text, then at least we are achieving something that we were trained to do! Finally, for now, a further comment on how reception exegesis may be helpful in showing how biblical scholars can interact with others in an interdisciplinary context. It is often the case when biblical scholars join scholars from different disciplines who have gathered together to discuss a subject to which the Bible seems relevant, that the biblical scholar becomes at best a resource and at worst a dampener of enthusiasm. He or she is not an equal player in the discussion, but the one who can confirm whether biblical Hebrew supports such and such a reading, or whether a particular notion could possibly have existed in ancient Israel. In contrast to this, here in reception exegesis is a model for two-way interdisciplinary interaction in which biblical scholars do not merely give but also receive (another kind of reception history!).

Interpretation and Context

Sensitivity to the ancient contexts of biblical texts (or at least what scholars hypothesized those contexts to be) has been a defining feature of the historical-critical approach. What was typically not considered was the context of the interpreter, except in so far as detachment from that context was an ideal to be cherished and defended. Today we recognize that we are all located, culturally and politically (as noted above, this insight owes much to the work of Gadamer). Our backgrounds inevitably influence not only how we handle materials from the reception of Lamentations, but also what we select for treatment out of the vast body of material that could be highlighted. Moreover, we recognize that, of course, those who read the text before us were likewise specifically located. It was, for example, the traumatic experience of the fall of Jerusalem to the Romans in 70 CE and its aftermath that both rendered Lamentations newly relevant to many at that time and also shaped its reception in works such as the *Jewish War* of Josephus (Lam 2:22) and the Targum (Lam 5:8, 10). Again, it is no surprise that readers of Lamentations in the twentieth century should have made so much of the psychological potential of reading the book (Lam 3:17–18). And another rather specific modern example of how exegesis can be influenced by context may be seen in the way Tod Linafelt's immersion in Shoah literature sensitizes him to the need sometimes to resist rationalization and hope (Lam 2:19; 5:22).

The Structure and Method of This Commentary

The genre of reception history is relatively new and remains fluid. A glance at other volumes in this series reveals that a reception history of a biblical book can range from a volume that aspires to a comprehensive survey of the works and sources that allude to the book in question, through a narrative of reception or an anthology-like collection of verbal, musical and visual references to the biblical text, or a verse-by-verse presentation of allusions to and uses of the text, to a detailed review of how a small number of landmark interpreters handled the text in question. Our volume is based on a verse-by-verse or, better, unit-by-unit treatment of significant uses of the book of Lamentations. In each case we begin by citing the verse or unit at hand, offering our own English translation that has affinities with the translations of the New Revised Standard Version and the New Jewish Publication Society Version. One might, of course, argue that we should have used as our base text the King James Version, probably the most familiar English translation for many readers. But against that the point can be made that for most modern ears the King James Version calls too much attention to itself; central as the biblical text must remain in a reception history, the translation cannot be allowed to steal the show from its receivers!

Next we turn to a specific example of the interpretation or use of this unit, providing a brief note of historical and cultural context, along with biographical information about the interpreter. Inevitably, there is an extent to which our choices reflect our personal experience and interests, but also, as might be expected in a project like this, we have come across some of our more interesting examples by chance! We then explore the particular use of the text at hand, with special attention to the light it sheds, if any, on the text itself and, where appropriate, on issues of interpretation more generally. Time and time again we have found that musical, artistic, literary and other interpretations of Lamentations – even those whose aim is far from exegesis as traditionally understood – have much to teach us about the biblical text. In many cases, we return to the original verse at the end of our discussion of the receiving text or other medium. With respect to structure, then, our volume owes something to the organizational principles of midrash, a traditional Jewish form of exegesis in which the primary biblical verse is 'opened' or unlocked by means of an apparent digression built on a secondary verse or unit from elsewhere in the Bible, before returning to the base text, which is now revealed in a new light. In our case, what opens or unlocks the text of Lamentations is not usually another verse from elsewhere in the Bible, but rather an interpretative lens selected from the book's reception history. So for example, our treatment of Lam 1:1, 'How lonely sits the city that once was full of people', includes consideration of an essay by David Shatz on Jewish responses to the international catastrophe of 9/11, before returning to reflect on how best to translate and interpret the very first word of the biblical book, *eicha*, usually but inadequately rendered, 'How'. Or again, we open our discussion of Lams 3:1, 'I am the man who has seen affliction', with the early modern mystical poem 'The Dark Night of the Soul' by St John of the Cross. In the poet's hands the afflicted man of Lam

3:1 becomes the anguished soul, on its journey to its union with God. We turn from the Spanish mystic back to the Judahite poet with sensitivities newly attuned to the struggles of 'the man who has seen affliction'.

It should be clear by now that this volume is far from an exhaustive survey of the reception history of Lamentations. Rather, we present selected characteristic examples of how Lamentations has influenced and inspired generations of writers, thinkers, musicians and visual artists. In some cases our chosen interpreters are addressing explicitly a specific verse, while in others we have chosen to focus on one verse out of a number of possible verses that are addressed by the selected interpretative lens. For example, the second-century CE christological interpretation by Justin Martyr explicitly addresses Lam 4:20, 'The breath of our life, the LORD's anointed, was taken in their pits'. On the other hand, we have chosen to discuss Chagall's lithograph *The Capture of Jerusalem* in relation to Lam 3:41–2, 'Let us lift up our hearts and our hands to God in heaven', but these are by no means the only verses to which this image could relate. We have chosen this approach to reception history, including the 'reception exegesis' element, rather than an approach involving a comprehensive survey or a detailed analysis of parade interpreters, because we think it makes the best use of our particular skills and commitments, and because we hope it will interest our readers. As members of faith communities for whom Lamentations is a sacred text, we care about how the text has been used in church, synagogue and beyond. Alongside this, as trained biblical exegetes, we want to illuminate the ancient text. We hope in this volume to convey the wealth of inspiring uses of this short biblical book through the centuries, while at the same time standing on the shoulders of these later interpreters to see afresh the ancient text.

The Authors of This Commentary

Diana Lipton and Paul Joyce had their first extended conversation on a train ride from Amsterdam to Leiden, where they were both presenting papers on different aspects of Ezekiel at the 2004 Congress of the International Organization for the Study of the Old Testament. They had met once previously, when Paul delivered a paper on the book of Lamentations to the Old Testament Seminar at Cambridge, where Diana was teaching at the time. During the course of the train ride, Diana spoke to Paul about how much his Cambridge paper had interested and inspired her, but she told him that she herself would never want to work on Lamentations. From her perspective, it raised too many difficult questions about the Jerusalem Temple, its destruction, and the appropriate role of pleas for its restoration within Jewish liturgy.

Fortunately, Paul forgot about Diana's rash claim; a few years later he invited her to join him as a co-author for the present commentary. Diana had not forgotten, but in the meantime her views – intellectual and religious – were in flux, and she saw the project as a welcome challenge.

It is fairly easy to make the case that biographical information about the author has no role to play in a standard scholarly commentary on a biblical book. For example, we do not need to know much beyond professional qualifications when we read Adele Berlin's Old Testament Library commentary on the book of Lamentations (2002). When it comes to the authors of reception histories, however, it is harder to justify a strict separation between private and public, religious and academic. Even the choice of perspectives and 'lenses' is likely to reflect personal interests and life experience outside the realm of academic biblical studies. To be sure, any prospective reception-history author with access to Google and a library catalogue can generate a list of relevant themes and sources. But decisions about what to include, and how to present it, are likely to be influenced by what is already familiar to reception-history authors from the worlds of art, music, literature, liturgy and so forth, and by the interests and commitments that are important to them. A little biographical information about Paul Joyce and Diana Lipton thus seems to be in order, so that readers of the present commentary can better gauge their choice of material and the perspective from which it has been presented.

Paul Joyce read Theology at Oxford University, and then wrote a doctoral thesis on Ezekiel, attracted by that prophet's hope of the gift of a new heart and a new spirit. Although he is a Roman Catholic, his first job was at Ripon College Cuddesdon, a theological college of the Church of England, and he is married to Alison Joyce, an Anglican priest. From his time at Cuddesdon date his interests in feminist criticism and in psychology (the latter both intellectually and also through group work and psychoanalysis). His love of the book of Lamentations goes back to that time too. He subsequently moved to teach at the University of Birmingham and that multicultural city has been his home for over twenty years – picking up a fascination with cultures and religions nurtured during a childhood in Singapore. Reading the Bible in a multi-faith context is one of his particular interests. From Birmingham he has commuted to posts at Oxford and subsequently at King's College London. Being father to daughters Sinéad and Olivia is a central part of his life. From childhood to the present day, music, especially rock, has been for him an important source of inspiration and energy. Although an active Catholic, indeed a eucharistic minister, he is conscious of being a 'cradle Catholic' from an Irish background, who owes much intellectually and culturally to other traditions, not least to liberal Protestantism. He often finds himself in some tension with elements of his Catholic heritage but knows that he will never leave it.

Diana Lipton read English Literature at Oxford University, and spent a few years as an investment banker and then a full-time mother before undertaking a PhD at Cambridge University on dreams in the book of Genesis. She taught Hebrew Bible at Cambridge as a Fellow of Newnham College, one of the university's three remaining all-women colleges, and at Leo Baeck College, a non-Orthodox rabbinical seminary, and later went to King's College London as Lecturer then Reader in Hebrew Bible and Jewish Studies. Diana's first husband, Peter Lipton *z.l.*, a Philosopher of Science at Cambridge, originally from New York City, passed away in 2007. Jacob, the older of their two sons, is currently studying at Harvard Law School, after a degree in Classics and two years spent working for the Foreign Minister of Sierra Leone in Freetown. Jonah, their younger son, studied Archaeology and Anthropology (coincidentally at the Oxford college where Paul Joyce was a Fellow), and is about to commence a PhD on Sierra Leone in the Department of Anthropology at the London School of Economics. Jonah is a passionate musician, specializing in jazz, hip-hop and classic rock and roll. Diana's interest in music, art, museums and other cultures has been greatly enriched by Jacob and Jonah, as has almost every other aspect of her life. Because of her broader academic interests, an active Jewish home life, and years of work in the Jewish community, including many years on the 'bimah' (leading services) in a Reform synagogue, Diana has read widely in areas of Jewish Studies beyond Hebrew Bible and thinks a lot about questions of religious practice and Jewish culture. Since 2011, Diana has lived in Jerusalem with her second husband, Chaim Milikowsky, a professor of Talmud at Bar Ilan University. She attends a tiny Moroccan synagogue in the Baka district of Jerusalem, and sees the Temple Mount several times a week as she goes about her business in the world's most complicated city.

It would be easy to infer from the information we have just provided about ourselves that we have divided this book according to our respective – and often quite different – areas of knowledge, expertise and interest. On the contrary, however, we made a point of doing otherwise. Although Paul is male and Christian and Diana female and Jewish, we tried to ensure that Paul was as likely as Diana to write about gender and Jewish texts, and that Diana was as likely as Paul to write about Christian theology. And in those cases where we did follow our prior interests, and also more generally, we developed a process of writing and reading, commenting upon and responding to one another's draft work, that has – we hope – truly blurred the boundaries that we were committed to crossing. It is fair to say that we have only one major regret about this volume, a regret felt equally by both authors: we were unable to find a single clear reference to the book of Lamentations in the entire canon of Bob Dylan.

References

Alter, R. 1985. *The Art of Biblical Poetry* (New York: Basic Books).

Berlin, A. 2002. *Lamentations* (OTL; Louisville, KY, and London: Westminster John Knox).

Boer, R. 2011. 'Against "Reception History"', contribution to 'In My View', on *The Bible and Interpretation* (posted May 2011), at http://www.bibleinterp.com/opeds/boe358008.shtml.

Brueggemann, W. 1986. 'The Costly Loss of Lament', *JSOT* 36: 57–71.

Coggins, R. J. and J. L. Houlden (eds). 1990. *A Dictionary of Biblical Interpretation* (London: SCM Press and Philadelphia, PA: Trinity Press International).

Dobbs-Allsopp, F. W. 1993. *Weep, O Daughter of Zion: A Study of the City-Lament Genre in the Hebrew Bible* (Biblica et Orientalia, 44; Rome: Editrice Pontificio Instituto Biblico).

Exum, J. C. 2012. 'Toward a Genuine Dialogue between the Bible and Art', in *Congress Volume: Helsinki. 2010* (ed. M. Nissinen; VTSup, 148; Leiden: Brill) 473–503.

Gadamer, H.-G. 2004. *Truth and Method* (London: Continuum; New York: Crossroad; 2nd rev. edn). [German original, 1960]

Harasta, E. and B. Brock (eds.). 2009. *Evoking Lament: A Theological Discussion* (New York and London: T. & T. Clark).

Hillers, D. R. 1992. *Lamentations* (Anchor Bible, 7a; Garden City, NY: Doubleday: 2nd edn).

Holub, R. C. 2003. *Reception Theory: A Critical Introduction* (London: Routledge; 2nd edn).

Jauss, H. R. 1982. *Toward an Aesthetic of Reception* (Theory and History of Literature, 2; Brighton: Harvester; Minneapolis: University of Minnesota Press).

Lee, N. C. 2002. *The Singers of Lamentations: Cities under Siege, from Ur to Jerusalem to Sarajevo* … (Biblical Interpretation Series, 60; Leiden: Brill).

Lee, N. C. and C. Mandolfo (eds). 2008. *Lamentations in Ancient and Contemporary Cultural Contexts* (SBL Symposium Series, 43; Atlanta, GA: SBL).

Lieb, M., E. Mason and J. Roberts (eds). 2011. *The Oxford Handbook of the Reception History of the Bible* (Oxford: Oxford University Press).

Linafelt, T. 2000a. *Surviving Lamentations: Catastrophe, Lament, and Protest in the Afterlife of a Biblical Book* (Chicago and London: University of Chicago Press).

Mandolfo, C. R. 2007. *Daughter Zion Talks Back to the Prophets: A Dialogic Theology of the Book of Lamentations* (Semeia Studies, 58; Atlanta, GA: SBL).

Mein, A. and P. M. Joyce (eds). 2011. *After Ezekiel: Essays on the Reception of a Difficult Prophet* (LHBOTS, 535; New York and London: T. & T. Clark/Continuum).

Middlemas, J. 2005. *The Troubles of Templeless Judah* (Oxford Theological Monographs; Oxford: Oxford University Press).

Morgan, R., with J. Barton. 1988. *Biblical Interpretation* (Oxford Bible Series; Oxford: Oxford University Press).

O'Connor, K. M. 2002. *Lamentations and the Tears of the World* (Maryknoll, NY: Orbis).

Parris, D. P. 2009. *Reception Theory and Biblical Hermeneutics* (Princeton Theological Monograph Series, 107. Eugene, OR: Pickwick).

Parry, R. A. 2010. *Lamentations* (Two Horizons Old Testament Commentary; Grand Rapids, MI, and Cambridge: Eerdmans).

Parry, R. A. and H. A. Thomas (eds). 2011. *Great Is Thy Faithfulness? Reading Lamentations as Sacred Scripture* (Eugene, OR: Pickwick).

Provan, I. W. 1991. *Lamentations* (NCB; London: Marshall Pickering; Grand Rapids, MI: Eerdmans).

Pyper, H. S. 2001. 'Reading Lamentations', JSOT 95: 55–69.

Roberts, J. 2011. 'Introduction', in Lieb, Mason and Roberts 2011: 1–8.

Rowland, C. C. and I. Boxall. 2013. 'Reception Criticism/Theory', in *The Oxford Encyclopedia of Biblical Interpretation*, vol. 2 (ed. S. McKenzie; New York and Oxford: Oxford University Press).

Salters, R. B. 2010. *Lamentations* (ICC; London and New York: Continuum).

Sawyer, J. F. A. 2009. *A Concise Dictionary of the Bible and Its Reception* (Louisville, KY: Westminster John Knox).

Sawyer, J. F. A. 2011. 'Ezekiel in the History of Christianity', in Mein and Joyce (2011) 1–9.

Schüssler Fiorenza, E. 1988. 'The Ethics of Biblical Interpretation: Decentering Biblical Scholarship', *JBL* 107: 3–17.

Sherwood, Y. 2000. *A Biblical Text and Its Afterlives: The Survival of Jonah in Western Culture* (Cambridge: Cambridge University Press).

Thomas, H. A. 2011b. 'Lamentations in Rembrandt van Rijn: "Jeremiah Lamenting the Destruction of Jerusalem"', in Parry and Thomas 2011: 154–60.

Thomas, H. A. 2013. *Poetry and Theology in Lamentations: The Aesthetics of an Open Text* (Sheffield: Sheffield Phoenix Press).

Westermann, C. 1994. *Lamentations: Issues and Interpretation* (Minneapolis, MN: Augsburg Fortress; Edinburgh: T. & T. Clark).

Young, F. M. 1993. 'Allegory and the Ethics of Reading', in *The Open Text: New Directions for Biblical Studies?* (ed. F. B. Watson; London: SCM Press) 103–20.

¹:¹ How lonely sits the city
that once was full of people!
She has become like a widow
who was once great among the nations.
The princess among the provinces
has become a vassal.

Gendered Lament

This chapter, like most in the book, is an extended acrostic based on the twenty-two letters of the *alef-bet* (Hebrew alphabet). Chapters 1, 2 and 4 have twenty-two verses, one for each letter of the *alef-bet*; the first word of the first verse begins with *alef*, the first letter of the *alef-bet*, the first word of the second verse begins with *bet*, the second letter, and so forth. Chapter 3, with sixty-six verses, is more elaborate; in that case the first three verses begin with *alef*, the second three

Lamentations Through the Centuries, First Edition. Paul M. Joyce and Diana Lipton.
© 2013 Paul M. Joyce and Diana Lipton. Published 2020 by John Wiley & Sons Ltd.

with *bet*, and so forth. The personification of Zion as a woman characterizes the first two chapters of the book. It is a feature facilitated by the fact that *ir*[1] (the Hebrew word for city) is feminine, and is a motif shared with some other biblical books (cf. Sawyer 1989 on Isaiah). Parallels to the presentation of Jerusalem as a widowed city are to be found in other ancient Near Eastern literature (Cohen 1973), and there are other affinities with lament material in the ancient world, especially in Mesopotamia (Dobbs-Allsopp 1993).

The opening verse of the book of Lamentations powerfully brings together collective catastrophe in history ('How lonely sits the city that once was full of people!') with the deepest and most personal of individual human losses ('like a widow'). In this combination we find a key to the power of this small book to speak to numerous different human situations and conditions. It is commonplace to read this first chapter, and the next, as an empathetic account in which the narrator stands in solidarity with the bereaved widow. Such a stance is found as early as the Christian Fathers. In his *Funeral Oration on Meletius* Gregory of Nyssa (who died as Bishop of Antioch), (born Neocaesarea, Cappadocia, Turkey, *c.*335; died Nyssa, Turkey, *c.*395) draws on the first verses of Lamentations for pastoral purposes: 'You have heard certain mournful and lamenting words of Jeremiah, with which he bewailed Jerusalem as a deserted city, and how among other expressions of passionate grief he added this, "The ways of Zion do mourn" [Lam 1:4]. These words were uttered then, but now they have been realized. For when the news of our calamity shall have been spread abroad, then will the ways be full of mourning crowds' (Wenthe 2009: 276).

Gregory encourages his grieving audience to identify with tragic Jerusalem. But for many readers in modern times, even when identification with Zion persists, the language used in Lamentations has become seriously problematic. In 'Hiding Behind the Naked Women in Lamentations: a Recriminative Response', (1999), Deryn Guest presents a powerful and extensive exploration of the metaphor of Zion as a woman, informed by the exposure of the 'pornoprophetic' nature of much biblical literature by feminist critics such as Exum (1995) and Weems (1995). Guest pieces together ('re-members') the picture of Zion, isolated and without comfort (Lam 1:2, 16, 17, 21), exposed to humiliating nakedness (Lam 1:8), and robbed of her former dignity (Lam 2:15). Like many other interpreters, Guest finds reference to rape, not only in Lam 5:11 but also in this opening passage, in Lam 1:10: 'The foe has laid hands on all her precious things; she has even seen the nations invade her sanctuary' (see further on Lam 1:10, and also on Lam 1:8–9, 15–16; 2:21–2; 4:13–15). Zion is

---

[1] We have chosen to keep Hebrew words to a minimum in this volume and, where they are required, to transliterate them in the manner that we think makes them most accessible to non-Hebrew readers (and thus not according to scholarly conventions).

abused, betrayed and bereaved, and it is God who is the agent of the horrors that befall her (v. 5, 'the LORD has made her suffer for her many transgressions'). What is more, Zion blames herself (e.g. Lam 1:20, 'I have been very rebellious'). In short, she suffers utter humiliation at the hands of an avenging deity and provides the focal point for the guilt and shame of Israel. Guest argues that even if this metaphor was intended as a call to repentance for the community as a whole, led as it was by men, the female figure provides an easy scapegoat behind which the male community may hide. Another case in which the metaphorical nature of such language about women is at risk of becoming obscured is Ezekiel 23, a text broadly contemporary to Lamentations. In Ezek 23:48 the prophet (or perhaps a redactor not well attuned to the metaphor) declares: 'Thus will I put an end to lewdness in the land, so that all women may take warning and not commit lewdness as you have done' (cf. Moughtin-Mumby 2008: 163).

'The image of Zion/Woman found in Lamentations should be resisted', Guest contends, 'because it endorses a stereotypical view of women and sanctions a series of abusing punishments' (422). Among the stereotypes compounded is that women attract the abuse against them; the opening chapter 'provides an exposition on the just deserts of wilful provocation' (423). Guest also exposes the complicity of male commentators with the book's rhetorical thrust. Biblical studies have often, she says, been so preoccupied with questions of genre and with ancient Near Eastern parallels that one 'receives the impression that personification is merely a figurative device; it does not relate to any *real* female physical distress, and therefore there is no sense of its offensive nature' (421). Such studies 'erase, mask or simply do not consider the social realities from which the image derives', claims Guest (426). In such ways, the blame encoded in the text is reinforced in exegesis, with 'a shared value system between writer and reader' that is 'offensive and damaging' (445).

Whereas reception history is often a story of readers finding new meanings in old texts, we also encounter cases, as here, in which original meanings often prove uncongenial or even unacceptable in fresh contexts, as new circumstances and new sensibilities challenge continuity with the values of the ancient text. At this point, for some, the status of the text comes into question. Guest herself asks what, in the light of all this, can be done with Lamentations and she concludes that, for her at least, it cannot have authority as Scripture: 'I personally opt to stand with those who make a complete stand against the text *per se* and would advocate the removal of such texts from the biblical canon' (439). But censoring the Bible so that a smaller canon is retained is not an option that all readers will favor. Some will wish to leave aside the notion of scriptural authority altogether – if the text is valued at all, it is as a classic text rather than as religious Scripture. But for most of those who retain a relationship with the Bible as Scripture, whether Jewish or Christian, it is important that the whole canon designated within a particular tradition is retained and wrestled with, even if, as in the present case, some features of the text are so troubling that continuity with scriptural tradition comes at times close to breaking point.

Naming Necessity

According to Jewish tradition, the books of the Hebrew Bible are typically named after a book's reputed author, such as Ezekiel, after a central character, such as Ruth, or after the first significant word of the book; the book of Genesis, for example, is known in Jewish tradition as *Bereishit* ('In the beginning'). The practice of naming a biblical book after its first significant word can present a problem when it comes to translating the Hebrew name into English. The book of Lamentations is an excellent example. 'Lamentations' is a translation of the Greek *Threni*, which means 'Laments' and well describes the content of the book, which is indeed a series of laments. On the other hand, the first Hebrew word of the book, *eicha*,[2] is almost untranslatable (though NJPS does well with 'Alas!'). Robbed of its context, as is almost bound to be the case in a one-word title, the literal translation, 'How', does not begin to give a sense of what the book is all about.

One solution to the problem of naming *Eicha* in English emerges from a contribution by David Shatz to *Contending with Catastrophe: Jewish Perspectives on September 11th* (Broyde 2011), a collection of essays covering Jewish legal, ethical and theological responses to the events of September 2001. Towards the end of his broadly philosophical essay, '"From the Depths I Have Called You": Jewish Reflections on September 11th and Contemporary Terrorism' (Broyde 2011: 197–233), Shatz contrasts a point of view expressed by the medieval Jewish philosopher Rabbi Moses ben Nahman (born Spain, 1194; died Land of Israel, 1270), known as Nahmanides or Ramban, with a perspective held by the modern Jewish thinker, Rav Joseph Soloveitchik (born Pruzhany, Belarus, 1903; died Boston, Massachusetts, 1993). According to Ramban, thinking about the problem of evil is justifiable because it affords peace of mind. Soloveitchik, on the other hand, is concerned that we should by no means seek to come to terms with evil, as Ramban's quest for peace of mind seems to entail. For this reason, Soloveitchik would resist the impulse to ask why a catastrophe occurred lest his question generate understanding and with it an acceptance of the unacceptable. Yet Shatz claims that, nonetheless, the question 'Why?' has a legitimate use for

---

[2]   In transliterated Hebrew 'ch' is pronounced as in 'loch'.

Soloveitchik. 'There are times', Shatz suggests, 'that the question "Why?" is not a demand for an explanation; it is, rather, an expression of woe over the tragedy, a cry that betokens empathy and love, not theological rumination. Uttered in this spirit, "why?" is of a piece with *hesed* [loving-kindness], with benevolent action. It affirms one's grasp of the depths of the evil, which is a prerequisite to meaningful, ethical action. The prototype of this "why?" is the biblical lament "*Eicha* (how)"' (224). Shatz contends that the author of Lamentations is not really expecting an answer to his question. Instead, he suggests:

> The question is an exclamation, a '*krechts*', a wail, rather than a query. An answer would not even be an appropriate response, for *Eicha* is really an attempt to absorb the depth and scope of one's loss. One year after the September 11th attack, we still ask 'why?' and 'how?' But it is a 'why?' and 'how?' that do not await an answer. It is a 'why?' and 'how?' that makes us reach deeply into ourselves, into reserves of generosity and care we never knew we had, a 'why?' and 'how?' that drives us to action, to sympathy with the victims' families, to multifarious and wide-ranging acts of kindness, to concern for victims of evils anywhere and everywhere (224).

Shatz's 'Why and How?' pair, especially if we hear it in our mind's ear as a *krechts* (a Yiddish term meaning 'wail'), has much to recommend it as an English translation of the Hebrew title for the book of Lamentations. Like the book as a whole, 'Why and How?' evokes questions that may or may not have answers. It suggests a desire to understand that is more psychological-theological than politico-historical. And it conveys a subtle combination of responsibility taken and responsibility attributed. It is a powerful tribute to the author of Lamentations – though at the same time a tragic comment on the state of the world – that, as Shatz observed, his 'Why and How?' question about the fall of Jerusalem remained as relevant on 11 September 2001 as when he wrote it.

Alef-Bet City

The book of Lamentations has attracted the attention of many composers. One explanation for their interest is the demand for liturgical settings of Lamentations (on which more later), but another is that, like philosophers and theologians, composers are drawn to material that can help them to address present-day catastrophes, such as the events of 9/11 or the continuing turmoil in the Middle East. In this latter category is Andrew Lovett, an English composer of contemporary classical music now working and teaching at Princeton University. *Lonely Sits the City*, Lovett's one-act opera based on Lamentations, is a powerful exploration of the effects and aftermath of invasion.

It was premiered in Cambridge in 2009 and since then has been performed elsewhere in England and in America. Although several voices ('the prophet' and a chorus) may be heard off-stage, a lone female singer is the only on-stage presence, and the majority of words in the piece are hers. On several occasions throughout this searing opera, the book's opening Hebrew word, *eicha*, is repeated over and over by the female soloist or by members of the female chorus. Their voices vary in tone and volume, but they invariably demand an answer. On four of these occasions, the repetition of the word *eicha* is followed immediately or soon after by a recitation, this time by the female soloist or by the prophet, of the Hebrew alphabet, the *alef-bet*. If *eicha* is the question – Why and How? – then it would seem that the *alef-bet* is an answer.

This represents an ingenious solution on Lovett's part to a problem that faces all composers who set the book of Lamentations to music. How can its acrostics be represented in music? As we have seen, four of the five chapters are extended acrostics based on the twenty-two letters of the *alef-bet*. Many musical settings of Lamentations follow the acrostic form quite rigidly, and indeed make it more prominent than it is in most translations from Hebrew into another language. Typically, musical settings have the singer chant the letter in Hebrew at the beginning of each verse – a sort of musical bullet point.[3] Lovett, struggling, perhaps, to find a way to preserve the acrostic's meaning without becoming a slave to its form, chose to separate the Hebrew letters from their respective verses and to use them instead as … as what? The singer who performed in the opera's premiere interpreted the *alef-bet* hieroglyphically, underlining with prayer-like hand motions the sounds of the letters as she sang them: *alef, bet, gimel, dalet* … (A, B, C, D.) Her interpretation recalls the popular Jewish tale of the poor shepherd boy who comes to the synagogue on Yom Kippur, the Day of Atonement, the holiest day of the Jewish year, but is unable to pray because he had not learned how to read. Instead, he recites the *alef-bet*, and, naturally, God loves the simple shepherd boy's prayer best of all.[4]

Alternatively, the *alef-bet* can function as a sort of mantra, an exercise in discipline. After the agony of the question – *eicha*: why? how? – comes a response that gathers consolation and self-control in its wake: *alef, bet, gimel,*

[3] See our discussions of Tallis (at Lam 1:2), Palestrina (Lam 1:6), Couperin (Lam 1:10), and Frescobaldi (Lam 1:12).

[4] It also recalls a striking episode in the midrashic commentary *Lamentations Rabbah*'s *petihta* or proem 24 (see below on Lam 1:3 and on Lam 2:18), in which God summons the twenty-two letters of the *alef-bet* to testify against Israel at the time of the destruction of the first Temple. One by one Abraham convinces each letter not to testify, mentioning its unique significance in the Torah and for the Jewish people, so that *alef* is the head of all the letters, *bet* is the first letter of the Torah, the five books of Moses, and so forth. As each letter is reminded of its special role, it chooses not to testify against Israel.

dalet ... Yet again, the *alef-bet* can represent totality, the sum of things, world order, where to recite it is to recreate it.[5] Somewhere in between all these is an interpretation suggested by Virginia Woolf's portrayal in *To the Lighthouse* of Mr Ramsay, Oxford analytic philosopher par excellence, contemplating the universe and his own mind:

> It was a splendid mind. For if thought is like the keyboard of a piano, divided into so many notes, or like the alphabet is ranged in twenty-six letters all in order, then his splendid mind had [grasped] one by one, firmly and accurately, until it had reached, say, the letter Q. He reached Q. Very few people in the whole of England ever reach Q. Here, stopping for one moment by the stone urn which held the geraniums, he saw, but now far, far away, like children picking up shells, divinely innocent and occupied with little trifles at their feet and somehow entirely defenceless against a doom which he perceived, his wife and son, together, in the window. They needed his protection; he gave it them. But after Q? What comes next? After Q there are a number of letters the last of which is scarcely visible to mortal eyes, but glimmers red in the distance. Z is only reached once by one man in a generation. Still, if he could reach R it would be something. Here at least was Q. He dug his heels in at Q. Q he was sure of. Q he could demonstrate. If Q then is Q – R – . Here he knocked his pipe out, with two or three resonant taps on the handle of the urn, and proceeded. 'Then R ...' He braced himself. He clenched himself.

Perhaps this is what the poet of Lamentations, as rendered in words and music by Andrew Lovett, had in mind when he chose to use the acrostic form: disorder kept at bay by logic.

[1:2] *She weeps bitterly in the night,*
with tears on her cheeks;
there is no one to comfort her
among all her friends;
all her allies have betrayed her,
they have become her enemies.

Music and Church Politics

The book of Lamentations has played a key role in liturgy, both Jewish and Christian, through the centuries. It has a central place in the services of Tisha

---

[5]   Some have thought that the elaborate acrostic feature of Lamentations reflects a long development and prolonged polishing (cf. Kaiser 1992). However, as likely, and consistent with the above, is that 'this feature is evidence of the drive to establish order in a time of traumatic loss, and so is quite compatible with composition during the immediate aftermath of a great catastrophe' (Joyce 2001: 528–9).

B'Av, the ninth day of the Hebrew calendar month of Av, the annual Jewish fast day commemorating the destruction of the first and second Temples and subsequent catastrophes such as the expulsion of Jews from Spain in 1492 (see, for example, on Lam 4:13–15). In Jewish tradition, biblical texts other than Psalms are not usually set to music, but are chanted in a rhythmical way according to notations that first appeared on biblical manuscripts in the eighth or ninth century CE but are believed to go back to Temple times. In the Christian context, on the other hand, from the late Middle Ages onwards, and especially in the Renaissance era, the book of Lamentations was set to music for choirs to sing during Holy Week, the days leading up to Easter. Literally scores of such settings have been written over the centuries – it is truly remarkable that such a small biblical book attracted so many composers, from Allegri to Zelenka. Although an established program developed, covering the book as a whole, the majority of the settings are of Chapter 1, and that predominance is exacerbated by the fact that in some cases only material from the first chapter survived from a longer work.

Thomas Tallis (born *c.*1505; died Greenwich, London, 1585) flourished as a church musician in England during the turbulent sixteenth century. He occupies a prominent place in the history of English church music, and is considered among the best of its earlier composers. After working at Dover Priory he moved to Waltham Abbey, but his appointment there ceased upon the dissolution of the monasteries. Next he served at Canterbury Cathedral, until 1543 when he was appointed by Henry VIII as Gentleman of the Chapel Royal, in which role he spent the rest of his career. He composed and performed for Henry VIII (until the king's death in 1547), Edward VI (1547–53), Queen Mary (1553–58), and Queen Elizabeth I (1558 until his death in 1585). The vicissitudes of history during the century influenced noticeably the style of the music written: in Protestant times music became less florid and liturgical polyphony less common, whereas under the Catholic Mary Tudor the compositional style reverted to the more elaborate writing prevalent early in the century. Tallis managed to navigate his way through these and later tempestuous times in a way that reflects the changing musical conventions and yet also articulates his own evolving vision and style.

He certainly had his ups and downs. In 1575, Queen Elizabeth granted a twenty-one-year monopoly giving exclusive rights to print music in England, in any language, to Tallis and his much-younger pupil William Byrd (born *c.*1540; died Essex, 1623), who also set Lamentations to music. But in spite of this great advantage, they soon got into serious financial difficulty through a grandiose and ill-judged joint publication known as '*Cantiones Sacrae*' and by 1577 they had to petition Queen Elizabeth for help. But throughout his service to successive monarchs as organist and composer, Tallis avoided the religious controversies that raged around him, in some ways like the subject of the eighteenth-century satirical song 'The Vicar of Bray' (which may originally have referred to this same Tudor period). Paul Doe argues that the tradition of regarding musicians as anonymous craftsmen explains in part how someone in Tallis's position could continue to serve quietly under any religious or political conditions (Doe 1968). Tallis has been variously claimed by scholars to have been a Protestant, a Catholic, or a religious pragmatist; be that as it may, what is clear is that he commanded respect throughout the bewildering sequence of opposing religious movements. It has been suggested that Tallis's music sometimes manifests characteristics of the turmoil, as in the way it oscillates between major and minor modes. And yet he is a resolute survivor, not unlike Jeremiah, the traditional author of Lamentations, who lived through the buoyant days of Josiah, the tragedy of the Babylonian conquest of Jerusalem, and the refuge of Egyptian diaspora.

Tallis's settings of Lamentations derive from the Elizabethan years, that is, late in his career. There are two sets, scored for five voices, the first covering Lam 1:1–2 and the second Lam 1:3–5. The two happen to use successive verses, but the pieces are in fact independent, set in different modes. It is likely that they were intended as motets for general use during Holy Week rather than for use as part of the Liturgy of the Hours (the official set of daily prayers recited at set hours). Some see the use of the words of the Latin Vulgate, in a Protestant period in which the vernacular was used increasingly, as a symptom of continuing Catholic sympathies on Tallis's part, an expression of Catholic nostalgia. Indeed, Doe speculates that 'they were not conceived as church music at all, but rather for private recreational singing by loyal Catholics' (Doe 1968: 39). Both sets end with the concluding refrain: 'Ierusalem, Ierusalem, convertere ad Dominum Deum tuum' ('Jerusalem, Jerusalem, return unto the Lord thy God'). These additional words are a common feature of the Lamentations musical tradition. They are not from Lamentations, but freely adapted from Hos 14:1 (Hebrew, v. 2): 'Return, O Israel, to the LORD your God, for you have stumbled because of your iniquity' (NRSV). Peter Phillips suggests that for Tallis they may well have had symbolic meaning, if he was indeed a Catholic in a Protestant country, praying for a national return to Roman allegiance. Yet Tallis is hard to pin down. Jeremy Summerly finds the 'influence of Reformation ideology' and suggests that Tallis's treatment of the words 'plorans ploravit in nocte' (Lam 1:2, 'She weeps bitterly in the night') reveal humanistic influence in their melismatic and expansive, emotive style. In interpretation Tallis in fact defies easy categorization, and this elusiveness may hold a clue to how he endured so successfully through so many decades of the sixteenth century.

¹:³ Judah has gone into exile with suffering
and hard servitude;
she settled among the nations,
and found no rest;
all her pursuers have overtaken her
in her dire straits.

Exegetical Conversations

While the long-held view that Jeremiah was the author of Lamentations has generally been abandoned in the academic world, the majority of scholars still see the book as coming from around the same time as the biblical prophet with whom it has been so closely associated, and as shaped by events that he too addresses – the Babylonian conquest of Judah and its aftermath in the sixth century BCE. But exactly how each verse or unit of Lamentations stands in relation to those events is inevitably a matter of debate. For example, Rudolph (1962) makes a case for treating Chapter 1 as having been written shortly after the first capture of Jerusalem in 597 BCE, and not, as with Chapter 2, after the destruction of the Temple in *c.*587 BCE. The subject of the first line of Lam 1:3 is Judah, but the precise meaning of the line is far from clear. With great care, Robin Salters attempts to bring light from the history of exegesis to aid the task of interpretation here (Salters 1986; cf. Salters 1999). The history of interpretation is a rich quarry of insights into possibilities with regard to the meaning of the text. Not to be overlooked here is the importance of translators: though neither Jerome nor Luther produced commentaries on Lamentations, the translations for which they were responsible are themselves immensely revealing of the options each took in interpretation. The culmination of Salters's work, the magisterial International Critical Commentary *Lamentations* (2010) provides a model of rigorous exegesis, conducted in close conversation with his fellow interpreters down the ages, whether in Hebrew, Aramaic, Syriac, Greek, Latin, German or English. What makes his approach especially effective is in part the contextual continuity mentioned above. Even if Lamentations has been separated from its traditional author, there has been no paradigm shift with regard to its traditional historical context. In cases such as the book of Deuteronomy, where scholarly opinions about the book's origins and setting have changed beyond recognition in modern times, the earlier history of interpretation is arguably less valuable for exegesis. In the case of Lamentations, the underlying assumptions have remained more stable, enabling a more productive dialogue between interpreters past and present.

Exegetes have tended to read the first words of Lam 1:3, *galeta yehuda*, as referring specifically to the Babylonian captivity, perhaps because the motif of a forcible and total deportation has been dominant in tradition. Thus, for example, the Jerusalem Bible reads 'Judah is exiled', as though the verb were passive. The Greek Septuagint (LXX), which gives a passive sense to the verb, may be the first witness to this interpretation, and its rendering was among factors that influenced some later readers to interpret in terms of the Babylonian captivity. Luther's 'Juda ist gefangen' represents an example of this tendency (and in this line of interpretation we should also note *Lamentations Rabbah* [*Rabbati*], a compilation of midrashic interpretations of the biblical book emanating from fifth–seventh century CE Palestine). On the other hand, Jerome's Vulgate rendering is 'Migravit Juda …'. Salters argues that this probably meant that Judah had migrated voluntarily in the hope of escaping to better situations in the neighboring territories, and moreover he contends that this is the most appropriate interpretation of the active Hebrew verb. His own rendering, for which he cites the support of both the medieval French Jewish commentator Rashi and the sixteenth-century French Reformer Calvin, happens to coincide with the translation given above, 'Judah has gone into exile' (Salters 2010: 42). The reference is to the Judahites who scattered to various destinations, in flight from the intolerable conditions in their occupied homeland, as reflected in Salters' further translation, 'from affliction and harsh service'. This insight nuances our reading of the verse and our understanding of the book as a whole. In this as in most other humanitarian crises, dispersion was not only a matter of forced deportation but also an issue of personal choice – some people in dire social and economic circumstances chose to flee.

[1:4] *The roads of Zion mourn,*
empty of festival pilgrims;
all her gates are desolate,
her priests groan;
her young girls grieve,
and her lot is bitter.

Lamentations in the Dead Sea Scrolls

When a Dead Sea Scroll fragmentary text with five parts (hereafter Qumran fragment) containing striking parallels to the book of Lamentations was discovered in Cave 4 at Qumran, it was quickly identified as having been at the very least influenced by the text of Lamentations preserved in the Bible (hereafter 'Biblical Lamentations'). The Qumran fragment was thus labeled '4QLamentations'. It is not surprising that scholars assumed at first that the author(s) of the Qumran fragment must have imitated, or at least been aware of, 'Biblical Lamentations'. Members of the academy and of faith communities alike had long been accustomed to placing the Bible at the very center of its own universe. It was not easy to come to terms with the idea that, at more or less the same time and in the very same place, similar texts were being written by authors unfamiliar with the writings so well known to us from the Bible. The sense of the Bible's importance, not to mention its uniqueness, is seriously compromised if we speculate that there were once many laments just like the book of Lamentations (or many love poems just like the Song of Songs), and further that 'our' Lamentations may have been no more significant than the rest at the time when they were written. Nevertheless, scholars soon began to reconsider their identification of the Qumran fragment as an imitation of, or influenced by, 'Biblical Lamentations'. More likely, they suggested, the Qumran fragment was simply another example of the lament genre, well attested, as we know, in other ancient Near Eastern cultures (Cohen 1988). The Qumran fragment was renamed '4QApocryphal Lamentations', a designation that places it firmly in the category of literature that emerged in the same world as the Bible and, in other circumstances, might even have found its way into the biblical canon.

In 'Gender and Lamentations: 4Q179 and the Canonization of the book of Lamentations' (Ilan 2008), Tal Ilan, a professor of Jewish Studies at Berlin's Freie Universität, returns part-way to the first scholarly identification of the Qumran fragment. She points out that the fragment – by now known formally as 4Q179 – really is too similar to the biblical text to be just an unrelated ancient Israelite lament, and that the original scholarly label for it, 4QLamentations, may be less misleading than once thought. She departs from the earliest scholarly tradition, however, in seeing the Qumran fragment not as a text influenced by 'Biblical Lamentations', but rather as another version of it that was in circulation before it reached its final form. The notion that there once existed multiple versions of a given biblical book, each with its own variations, presents theological difficulties of its own, of course, and some readers would find this even more challenging than the idea of a lament written at the same time as Lamentations whose author was unaware of the existence of 'Biblical Lamentations'. In academic terms, however, Ilan's theory has much to recommend it.

From the starting point that the Qumran fragment represents a parallel version, Ilan attends to differences between the fragment and 'Biblical Lamentations'. Her thematic focus is gender, and she shows by means of a verse-by-verse comparison that the Qumran fragment has considerably more feminine forms than the verses that are its closest parallels in 'Biblical

Lamentations'. Her claim is readily supported by means of a comparison between the Qumran fragment and Lam 1:1–5:

4Q179 Fragment 2

1.
2.
3.] in your tent[
4. How did sit]alone the city [Jerusa]lem
5. among the nati]ons, princess of all real[ms] is desolate like a [ ] and all her daughters
6. like a wo]man naked, like one suffering, and like one abandoned [by her husband]. All her places
7. like] a barren and impoverished woman. All [her] road[s]like a woman of bitterness
8.] and all her daughters are like mourners over [their] hu[sbands]; her [ ]are like those bereaved
9.]of their only ones. She weeps constantly and [ ] on her cheek over her children.[6]

Needless to say, there is already an unusually strong emphasis upon the feminine in Lamentations 1, with its focus on the widowed daughter of Zion. Yet Ilan shows that the feminine emphasis is stronger still in the Qumran fragment. In Lam 1:4, for example, the term 'desolate' (*sh-m-m*) occurs in the masculine form in relation to the 'gates' of Jerusalem (and later with respect to Jerusalem's male 'children' in Lam 1:16). By contrast, 4Q179 applies the term 'desolate' in the feminine form to the grieving woman. Similarly, while 'Biblical Lamentations' states only that the woman's lot is 'bitter' (Lam 1:4), 4Q179 speaks more emphatically of a 'woman of bitterness'. At the same time, Ilan sees the portrayal of women as far more nuanced in 4Q179 than in 'Biblical Lamentations'. The feminine images of Jerusalem in 'Biblical Lamentations' are all, in different ways, Ilan argues, extreme: she is a 'widow' (Lam 1:1) whose husband cannot, by definition, return to her; her daughters are young girls (Lam 1:4, 15, 18), most likely virgins; and she is an unclean (Lam 1:8, 17), like a menstruating woman. By contrast, 4Q179 offers what Ilan characterizes as the less extreme 'desolate' (*sh-m-m*), 'abandoned' (*a-z-v*) and 'infertile' (*a-q-r*); this woman's husband is not dead but has merely abandoned her and could return, and though barren now, she could become fertile. To be sure, all these terms – from the Qumran fragment and from 'Biblical Lamentations' – entail

---

[6] Ilan's translation. The numbers represent the lines of the fragment, and do not relate to the verse numbers of the biblical text.

value judgments in the context of the ancient world, where widowhood, barrenness and abandonment were seen as punishments, and virginity was equated with innocence. Nevertheless, Ilan's overarching argument is persuasive: in comparison with closely related material that existed at around the same time, the author of 'Biblical Lamentations' chose 'to diminish the role of women, and at the same time make more extreme the character of the female'. Regardless of the view one takes about the relationship between the Qumran fragment and 'Biblical Lamentations', Ilan's observations about the differences between them illuminate them both with respect to the important subject of gender.

1:5 Her foes have become the masters,
her enemies are at ease,
because the LORD has made her suffer
for her many transgressions;
her infants have gone into captivity,
before the foe.

Lamenting Intertextually

Alongside the many new interpretations that have bloomed in biblical studies over recent decades, many new methods of interpretation have blossomed. One of these (really a cluster of methods) is the literary approach. It is indebted to diverse influences, from traditional Jewish reading through to secular literary theory. In relation to Lamentations, contributions to a literary appreciation of the text range from a valuable essay by Francis Landy in Alter and Kermode's *Literary Guide to the Bible* (Landy 1987), which is relatively conservative in that it confines itself largely to observations about imagery and style, through to the more radical work of Jannie Hunter (Hunter 1996), which draws upon the insights of poststructuralism and deconstruction, focusing in particular on Lam 1:1–11.

In *Faces of a Lamenting City*, Hunter gives special attention to the possible implications of radical literary theory for reading Lamentations. The central concept Hunter emphasizes is that of intertextuality. (For a valuable recent overview of intertextuality in Hebrew Bible research, see Miller 2011.) Although the term 'intertextuality' is sometimes used in a diluted sense to include questions of literary dependence, strictly speaking it is to be understood in the context of poststructuralist thought and relies on a purely synchronic analysis of texts. The focus is solely on the reader and the connections that he or she draws between two or more texts. A text has meaning only when read in conjunction with other texts, and it is irrelevant whether or not these texts were intentionally alluded to by the author, or even available to the author. A text can have multiple meanings as new intertexts are read and as new readers read them.

Hunter argues that intertextuality tends to 'disseminate' or 'destabilize' meaning, since 'no single text uses words in exactly the same sense and meaning' (Hunter 1996: 32). When one takes account of other 'disseminating' factors, such as the interpreter's own projections onto the text, it becomes clear that any search for definitive meaning is doomed to failure. In such ways, Hunter concedes much to the insights of poststructuralism and deconstruction. How then can the interpreter operate? Two features of Hunter's strategy may be highlighted here. First is his insistence that every text has what he calls its 'individuality'; that is, an element of originality and particularity is always present. Meaning is still elusive, but 'a text features individuality as much as it features intertextual references' (38). And so, Hunter argues, 'Meaning does exist, even if it is for an interpretive moment' (37). Second, Hunter brings to his theoretical discussion the practical observation that (in spite of all his acknowledgement of indeterminacy) 'interpretations are normally communicated to other people, who are thought to understand the interpretations' (37).

Hunter tests out his approach on the first eleven verses of Lamentations, which he sees as establishing the 'idea world' of the rest of the book. As well as being foundational for the later sections, Lam 1:1–11 are of course also illuminated by all that follows, since everything is intertextual and bi-directional from the beginning. Hunter reads these verses in association with a range of texts from the Hebrew Bible (mostly the prophetic books) and the ancient Near East, as well as (crucially) in relation to the rest of the book of Lamentations. For example, he finds the themes and language of Lam 1:5 picked up numerous times in the remainder of the book, both within the second half of Chapter 1 (vv. 12–15, 18, 21) and also in all the other chapters (e.g. Lam 4:6, 11, 13, 16). He develops his discussion primarily in terms of these intertextual relationships within Lamentations itself (111–20). The texts from elsewhere in the Bible that he draws in include Isa 13:13; Ezek 33:25; Mic 2:3; and Zeph 1:14. The reference to 'children' in the last line of Lam 1:5 (the Hebrew word used is *olal*, translated 'infant' above) is discussed by Hunter in the light of intertexts elsewhere (including Lam 1:18), which reveal the possibility that it might here be a comprehensive metaphor for the people of Jerusalem (the meaning favored by Van Selms [1974: 112]). And yet, in spite of this 'disseminating' factor in interpretation, Hunter endeavors to articulate his understanding of the 'individuality' of this verse, concluding rather that the verse indicates the extent of the exile by emphasizing that it included even children (Hunter 1996: 112–13).

1:6 From daughter Zion has departed
all her majesty.
Her princes have become like stags
that found no pasture;
they fled without strength
before the pursuer.

Holy Week Polyphony

The Christian choral traditions of Italy are a particularly rich source of musical settings of Lamentations. Among the most distinguished composers was Giovanni Pierluigi da Palestrina (born Palestrina, near Rome, *c*.1525; died Rome, 1594). The name of Palestrina is synonymous with the Counter-Reformation, the Latin Mass, and the refinement of the Roman Catholic liturgy. He is the best-known sixteenth-century representative of the Roman school of musical composition. He spent most of his career in the city of Rome, much of it at St Peter's, where he became Maestro di Cappella of the papal choir in 1551. The young Palestrina was much influenced by the northern European style of polyphony, but he developed a distinctive style of his own and had a lasting influence on the development of church music, his work often seen as the culmination of Renaissance polyphony. Palestrina has a reputation for being the 'saviour of church music' during the reforms of the Council of Trent (1545–63), when some, fearing the incursions of secularism, wished to abandon contrapuntal music (polyphony) and revert to exclusive use of Gregorian chant, the directly homophonic nature of which was thought more conducive to making text intelligible, in keeping with the emphasis of the Counter-Reformation. His victory is celebrated in the opera *Palestrina* by Hans Pfitzner (first performed in 1917), in which Palestrina's composition of the polyphonic and yet accessible *Missa Papae Marcelli* saves the day. There are elements of apocryphal legend about this story, but it does symbolize the stature of Palestrina and his role in establishing the long-term place of polyphony in Roman liturgy. Conservative music of the Roman school continued for a long time to be written in his style (which in the seventeenth century came to be known as the 'prima pratica'). Palestrina's music is still regularly performed and recorded, and drawn upon for models in the study of counterpoint.

Palestrina's settings of Lamentations (from 1564 onwards) are judged to be among his most mature works and, along with works of other composers, they replaced the settings of Carpentras in the papal chapel from 1587. He set Lamentations to music no fewer than five times; one set was published in 1588, the other four are in manuscript only. The occasion for performance of the settings was the service of 'Tenebrae' (Latin for 'shadows'), a service of lessons accompanied by the gradual extinguishing of lights, held on successive evenings of Holy Week, the week leading up to Easter. The Council of Trent (1545–63) established the readings to be used and Palestrina naturally follows this sequence in his settings, albeit somewhat abbreviated. Palestrina features three sequences of three lessons: Lam 1:1–2; 1:6–8a; 1:10–12 (Maundy Thursday); Lam 2:8–10; 2:12–14; 3:1 (Good Friday); and Lam 3:22–25; 4:1–3; 5:1–5 (Holy Saturday).

Like many other composers, Palestrina sets to music the announcements that precede the settings proper. The first lesson on Thursday begins with 'Incipit Lamentatio Ieremiae Prophetae' ('The Lamentation of Jeremiah the Prophet begins'), while the first lesson on both Friday and Saturday begins with 'De Lamentatione Ieremiae Prophetae' ('From the Lamentation of Jeremiah the Prophet'); and the third lesson on Saturday (setting Lam 5:1–5) begins with 'Incipit oratio Jeremiae Prophetae' ('The Prayer of Jeremiah the Prophet begins'). Following established tradition, Palestrina reflects musically the acrostic element of Lamentations, setting the name of the appropriate Hebrew letter (in the case of the present verse, the sixth letter, *waw* or *vav*) before the corresponding verse, cited in the Latin of the Vulgate. Palestrina's settings of the Hebrew letters are melodically and rhythmically ornate and beautifully melismatic. They have been likened to the illuminated initials in a medieval manuscript (Massenkeil 1980: 411). Musician Bruno Turner has observed that: 'Palestrina seems to have written them as little private sound worlds in which the listener may be swept up in the contemplation of the Passion'.

Palestrina's musical setting of the verses themselves, on the other hand, is unusually restrained. Lamentations 1:6, with its image of daughter Zion relinquishing her majesty, her princes left like stags without pasture, is undeniably poignant and moving, and yet the musical setting, while lush, sounds decidedly austere in its restraint. It has been speculated that Palestrina's seemingly dispassionate approach to expressive or emotive texts could have resulted from his having to work too much to order, or perhaps from a deliberate decision that any intensity of expression was unbecoming in church music. Be this as it may, Palestrina produced in the verse settings a smoother type of polyphony than had previously been known, and this is now considered to be characteristic of late Renaissance music. Each unit of the setting ends with the standard concluding refrain: 'Ierusalem, Ierusalem, convertere ad Dominum Deum tuum' ('Jerusalem, Jerusalem, return unto the Lord thy God'; see on Lam 1:2). In these endings Palestrina appears to contrive a hint of optimism, especially in the very last, on Holy Saturday, when he seems to anticipate Easter, not least through the introduction of a pair of falsetto parts. Majesty may have departed from daughter Zion (Lam 1:6), but the 'Jerusalem, Jerusalem' refrain at the end of each of the units raises the hope that repentance may yet usher in a new future, in a way evocative of the penultimate verse of the book of Lamentations itself (on which see the commentary on Lam 5:21).

1:7 Jerusalem remembers,
  in the days of her affliction and sorrow,
all the precious things
  that she had in days of old.
When her people fell into the hand of the foe,
  and there was no one to help her,
the foe looked on mocking
  over her downfall.

[*1:11 All her people groan*
  as they search for bread;
they traded their treasures for food
  to preserve their lives.
Look, O LORD, and see
  how worthless I have become.]

Mourning Jerusalem in Tel Aviv

The Israeli novelist and playwright Aharon Megged was born in Poland in 1920, and six years later left with his parents for what was then Mandate Palestine. As a young man, he was active in a pioneer youth movement and later joined a kibbutz on the coast near Haifa. He was a founder and later editor of a weekly literary magazine, and worked as a literary editor for daily newspapers. Unlike many of his contemporaries, Megged resisted the urge to contribute to a new, modern, secular Israeli culture that was divorced from Jewish tradition. Instead, he aspired in his work to a Jewish-Israeli fusion, engaging intensely with Jewish sources, not least the Bible, in even the most secular of Israeli contexts. Megged's novel *The Living on the Dead*, first published in 1965 in Hebrew and translated into English by Misha Louvish (Megged 2005), is the story of Jonas, an acclaimed biographer whose trials and travails include a lawsuit brought against him for his inability – part psychological, part professional, and part political – to deliver his latest commission, a biography of an Israeli pioneer and national hero called Abrasha Davidov.

Jonas's distractions from his work include a group of friends and lovers who meet regularly at The Cellar, a bohemian Tel Aviv café. Discovering to their surprise that their refuge of choice is closed for Tisha B'Av, the fast day 'when the pious mourn the destruction of the Temple', Jonas and his friends reconvene in the home of Nakdimon, a poet. 'Warmed with whisky' (the twenty-four-hour Tisha B'Av total fast notwithstanding), Nakdimon entertains the group with a recital of his own works before announcing that he is going out in search of 'some virgins girded in sackcloth for the midnight threnody'. Meanwhile, the other friends arrange their own commemoration of the destruction of the Temple. One of them, Elirez, 'looked for a Bible in the bookcase, opened it at Lamentations, and began chanting to the synagogue melody, adding trills and rhymes to every verse. At his command, we sat on the floor and chanted the responses, swaying from side to side: "Comfort, O Lord our God, the mourners of Zion, and the mourners of Jerusalem, and the city that is in mourning and laid waste ..." And we all accompanied him with weeping and wailing, with heartbroken sighs and moans, until the tears came into our eyes.' Their mock-solemnity is short-lived: 'Suddenly, the walls were breached and the room was invaded with howls and shrieks of laughter by four girls ...'. This is surely an allusion to the Temple walls, and Megged must have in mind verses such as Lam 1:10, 'She has even seen the nations invade her sanctuary, those whom you forbade to enter your congregation', and Lam 2:7, 'He has delivered into the hand of the enemy the walls of her citadels; they raised a cry in the house of the LORD as on a festival day'.

Beyond this, it is unclear how far he refers explicitly to Lamentations in his description of the Tisha B'Av party, but accidentally or otherwise he highlights a theme that runs throughout the biblical book, and is especially concentrated in the first chapter: sight and seeing. Our attention to this theme is drawn when Elirez 'looks for a Bible in the bookcase; It is telling both that this non-religious Jew expects to see a Bible in the home of his non-religious friend, and that he knows the 'synagogue melody', presumably from his childhood. These are secular Jews who have maintained a connection, however problematic, to their tradition, but they are nevertheless religious outsiders. This is underlined by what seems to be a parallel between the original enemy who 'looked on mocking' in Lam 1:7 (above) and the Tel Aviv mockers, who are, paradoxically, none other than the spiritual heirs of the original victims. To be sure, they are at least engaged; Elirez's comic performance of the book of Lamentations brings tears to the eyes of his audience. But their tears are tears of laughter, not the tears of lament mentioned over and over again by the biblical author (see e.g. Lam 1:2, 16; 2:11).

The arrival of the four girls at Nakdimon's apartment quickly changes the mood. In a literal reversal of Lam 5:15, instead of mourning (albeit in jest), there is dancing. The carpet is rolled aside and before long one of the dancers has 'put out the lights, leaving only a single red watchful eye, and laughter broke out from time to time in the glimmering half-light'. By midnight, a couple is quarrelling and the others hear a woman's angry parting words in the hallway: 'You can make eyes at anyone you like, I don't care. Just don't come home, that's all I ask!' 'Shall I describe', the narrator's voice asks his readers provocatively, 'what went on later in the three rooms of the house …? No, I will not describe it. Nor will I say anything about Hagit, that slender green-eyed girl … who from that night onward started to frequent my room.' The woman's suggestion that her partner can 'make eyes' at anyone he likes provided she does not have to witness his infidelity recalls the sexually inappropriate behavior (revealed nakedness) that, in Jerusalem's case, was there for all to see: 'Jerusalem sinned greatly … all who honored her despise her, for they have seen her nakedness …' (Lam 1:8). And the lamp that remained when the lights were extinguished, the 'single red watchful eye', recalls God, who looked down as Zion was degraded, and whom she now begs to look at her suffering: 'she sank appallingly, with none to comfort her. O LORD, look at my affliction' (Lam 1:9), and 'Look, O LORD, and see how worthless I have become' (Lam 1:11). And what of Jonas's mysterious green-eyed girlfriend Hagit, whose name is related to the Hebrew term for festival, who began to frequent his room on that upside-down festival night? To be sure, Megged's reference to her eyes brings the prevailing imagery to a focal point – green is the most striking eye color, at least in description; but more than that, since jealousy has already raised its head explicitly in the guise of the quarrelling couple, and given that green eyes are identified with jealousy in many cultures including modern Israel, perhaps Hagit's green eyes may even recall the Lord's fierce anger (Lam 1:12), occasioned, as we learn from sources such as Num 25:11 and Ezek 5:13, by his jealousy.

1:8 Jerusalem sinned greatly,
so she has become a mockery;
all who honored her despise her,
for they have seen her nakedness;
she herself groans,
and shrinks back.

1:9 Her uncleanness was in her skirts;
she gave no thought to her future;
she sank appallingly,
with none to comfort her.
'O LORD, look at my affliction,
for the enemy has triumphed!'

The Reluctant Propagandist?

Following a lead from Naomi Seidman (see also on Lam 4:13–15), Hugh Pyper explores the complicity of the writer of Lamentations in the humbling and humiliation of Zion, through an intertextual comparison with the brief novella *Five Letters from an Eastern Empire* (1995), by the Scottish writer and artist Alasdair Gray (born Glasgow, 1934). Seidman writes, with reference to Lam 1:8–9:

> Whatever the Babylonians did to turn Jerusalem the city to rubble, it is the Jewish poet, I can't help feeling, who rips the bride Jerusalem's jeweled veils from her forehead, stripping the embroidered robes to flash us a glimpse of her genitals, *ervatah*, translated by the squeamish or modest translator as 'her nakedness'. (Seidman 1994: 282)

Pyper concurs: 'it is the poet of Lamentations who has chosen to centre the book on this strange, abhorrent metaphor of Zion as the raped woman, or, even more loadedly, the raped mother. The text both bewails and yet dwells on the violation of the inner sanctuary, the most secret places, paradoxically exposing them to view in the ostensible act of expressing outrage' (Pyper 2001: 55–6). He discerns an ambivalence between compassion for Zion as a victim and yet justification of the punishment for her lasciviousness, reading this as a symptom of melancholia, in Freud's term, and so of an ambivalence that turns the survivor's anger against the dead victim. 'So,' writes Pyper of Lamentations, 'the book would become the sentence of death passed on those who had already died. The Jewish poet thus becomes the one who psychically, if not literally, condemns the dead to their fate' (63), for 'the city suffers the just punishment it deserves for the abandonment of its children, though that is a state brought about by the very events that befell it' (64).

In *Five Letters from an Eastern Empire* Alasdair Gray constructs a mythical empire and presents the letters of a young official poet, Bohu, to his parents. He is looking forward to the great poem that he is to write for the Emperor. When the poem is commissioned, however, Bohu is devastated to learn that the old capital, his home town where his beloved parents continued to live, has been totally destroyed on the orders of the Emperor. He is charged to compose a lament upon the loss of the city. In his grief and his anger, he writes a subtle but excoriating judgment on arbitrary tyranny, under the title *The Emperor's Injustice*. The authorities, however, have the last word, literally. The word *Injustice* is changed to *Justice*, and, thus altered, the poem is distributed throughout the empire on the very day on which the imperial army is ordered to destroy the old capital (in terms reminiscent of the condemnation of Zion to destruction in Lam 2:8; 4:11). That atrocity is in fact only now to be committed, with Bohu's poem harnessed for the propaganda purposes of the regime. Thus is Bohu implicated in the demise of the city he mourns, in a manner chillingly comparable to the way Pyper shows the poet of Lamentations to be complicit in the degradation of Zion.

Returning to Lam 1:8–9, the experience of reading these verses is now all the more disturbing: Jerusalem may have sinned grievously; the enemy has certainly triumphed; the poet has been shown to be complicit in compounding Zion's humiliation. But more – as readers we too are now implicated; we too have seen her nakedness, and witnessed the uncleanness in her skirts; and we find ourselves among those who have failed to comfort her.

1:10 The foe has laid hands
on all her precious things;
she has even seen the nations
invade her sanctuary,
those whom you forbade
to enter your congregation.

[*1:14 My transgressions were bound into a yoke;*
lashed tight by his hand;
they weigh on my neck,
sapping my strength;
the Lord handed me over
to those whom I cannot withstand.]

Lamentations at the Races

Among the most beautiful of the musical settings of Lamentations for the Christian Holy Week services of 'Tenebrae' ('shadows') are the *Trois Leçons de Ténèbres*, composed by François Couperin (born Paris, 1668; died Paris, 1733). This one surviving setting of his follows precisely and fully, albeit only for the first day of the sequence, the program of readings established by the Council of Trent (1545–63), namely Lam 1:1–5, 6–9 and 10–14. Soon after composing this setting in about 1714, Couperin became the official organist and composer to the French royal court. He was working in the by-then well-established tradition of setting Lamentations to music, premised on the religious connection Christians had long made between the sufferings of personified Zion and those of Jesus. Couperin's music conveys a genuine note of poignancy fitting to the text, and it is also faithful to the acrostic element (see on Lam 1:1, 6, 12). However, there are also some jarring disjunctions. The ethereal and lyrical fullness of Couperin's setting seldom reflects the meaning of the Latin words rendered, and there is no apparent differentiation between verses depending on their content. Many commentators and interpreters (e.g. Berlin, 2002: 55; Mintz, 1984: 25) find in Lam 1:10 an allusion to rape. The Hebrew of the verse refers to 'hand' in the singular (as in the KJV, 'The adversary hath spread out his hand'). 'Hand' can be taken as a euphemism for the penis, with 'her precious things' and 'her sanctuary' correspondingly read as euphemistic allusions to the female body. Even if Lam 1:10 deals not with an actual sexual crime but with military invasion cast in sexual language, violence is by no means reflected in Couperin's setting. The language of Lam 1:14 raises some text-critical difficulties, but it is clear that the verse refers to imperial oppression, and arguably to torture, and yet Couperin's harmonious musical setting is far removed from such brutal realities.

This disjunction is still more stark, and indeed problematic, when viewed against the background of the social setting of many of the performances of Couperin's *Ténèbres*. He composed his setting for the nuns of the Franciscan Abbey of Longchamps, founded by St Isabelle of France in 1256 in the Bois de Boulogne, to the west of Paris, near the site of the modern Longchamps racecourse. But it became fashionable for the Parisian elite to go out to Longchamps to hear the female star singers of the Opéra perform the *Ténèbres*. Some of the favorite performers of the day used the liturgy at Longchamps to display their skills, to the delight of a sophisticated but often-frivolous high-society public, generally more interested in diversion than in prayer and repentance. Even the scheduling of the service times at Longchamps was adjusted for the convenience of the fashionable set.

All this can, it is true, be set in the context of a longer-term French trend whereby Lamentations had a broader role in society than in most countries. For example, settings were performed in the courtly presentations of Louis XIV. The public profile of Lamentations in France is reflected also in literature, as in the reference to the musical setting of the Italian Niccolò Jommelli (born near Naples, 1714; died Naples, 1774) in the dialogue *Le Neveu de Rameau* by Denis Diderot (born Langres, 1713; died Paris, 1784): 'As he was singing snatches from Lamentations by Jommelli, he brought out the most beautiful parts of each piece with precision, truth, and an incredible warmth. That beautiful recitative in which the prophet describes the desolation of Jerusalem he bathed in a flood of tears which brought tears to everyone's eyes' (Massenkeil 1980: 412).

Nonetheless, the use of ancient Jewish poetry about the grimmest of human experiences on occasions of frivolous entertainment such as some of the performances at Longchamps takes us so far from the origins of the text that an ethical issue is raised. Is it appropriate that a text referring to oppression and invasion, indeed likely to rape and torture, has been removed so far from the shocking sufferings of Zion? Is it right that words that cost ancient Jerusalemites so much should end up as an entertaining diversion? Lest this be thought of as a question merely about the past: should we today feel fully at ease listening to our compact discs of Lamentations for aesthetic pleasure? Consider the musical use of another text from the exilic age: is it entirely unproblematic to enjoy Boney M's 1978 disco hit, 'Rivers of Babylon', with its carefully edited portions of Psalm 137 (needless to say, excluding v. 9 with its reference to dashing babies against rocks)? This particular case might appear less problematic when one discovers the song's Rastafarian history, wherein a real analogy can be drawn between the oppression of Judah under Babylon and that of Afro-Caribbeans in the wake of the slave trade. But even then, is it right that the hard-won words of particular sufferers should be co-opted by other sufferers? This last question is arguably given added force by the claim to the uniqueness of Zion's sufferings: 'Look and see if there is any agony like my agony' (Lam 1:12; cf. 2:13). In the case of the musical settings of Lamentations, there is the specific question of Zion's suffering being co-opted by Christians for reflection on Jesus' passion. Yet another text from the exilic age comes to mind: the so-called 'Suffering Servant' material of Isaiah 40–55, traditionally read by Christians of the sufferings of Jesus in a way that generally fails to acknowledge that the words were, so to speak, written in the blood of the exiles. As with the Lamentations case, this raises the fundamental theological question about the appropriation of the Jewish scriptures by the Church. In one sense it may seem entirely reasonable that the scriptures that formed Jesus and Paul should be treasured and made accessible by their followers. But the supersessionist manner in which Christian identity has so often been articulated (asserting the superiority of Christianity as a religion that has replaced Judaism) complicates considerably the phenomena of decontextualization and re-use.

1:12 May it never befall you,
all you who pass along the road,
Look and see
if there is any agony like my agony,
which was dealt out to me,
which the LORD inflicted
on the day of his fierce anger.

Mourning Jerusalem in Rome

Lamentations as a text for musical settings remained popular throughout the early modern period, inspiring many complex liturgical pieces that reflect the Christian religious environments and occasions for which most or all the compositions were intended. These musical settings are usually choral, or else evoke plainsong. Clearly, the composers' choice of text was significant, and yet, as we have seen especially in the case of Couperin (see on Lam 1:10), the music seldom so much as hints at the meaning of the words it renders, which were in any case in Latin, and thus doubly susceptible to death by measured devotion. In almost all cases, the music of settings of Lamentations from this time hovers harmoniously above the language of the text, failing to distinguish the most violent curses from the most poignant laments, the most aggressive military scenes from the most touching domestic visions, the triumphal from the tragic. In these circumstances the music can serve to evoke a general impression of Lamentations as a whole, but it cannot act as an interpretative guide to the content of individual verses or their specific words and images.

A small number of composers who set Lamentations stand out for being different with respect to the relationship between words and music. One is the Spanish Tomás Luis de Victoria (born Sanchidrían, Ávila, 1548; died Madrid, 1611), considered the greatest of Spanish Renaissance composers. According to F. Jane Schopf, Victoria reacted against the norm of producing stylized settings of Lamentations that did not aim to reflect the texts, utilizing instead the most modern aspects of ecclesiastical compositional style to respond to the text in a very personal, dramatic way, illustrating in sound the essence of the words (Schopf 2011: 147–8). Another is Victoria's slightly later Italian contemporary Girolamo Frescobaldi (born Ferrara, Italy, 1583; died Rome, 1643). Frescobaldi was a keyboard musician, a long-serving organist at St Peter's in Rome, a contemporary of Claudio Monteverdi (born Cremona, Italy, 1567; died Venice, 1643); and a musical influence on J. S. Bach, among other composers. He was working at the time and in the place of the birth of opera. Yet unlike his better-known contemporary Monteverdi, Frescobaldi has not been associated in the history of music with the emergence of this new musical genre. This is surprising. His setting of Lamentations for solo voice strongly anticipates opera, and certainly has more in common with it than with the more conventional liturgical compositions produced by most of his contemporaries. Frescobaldi's Lamentations is lyrical, emotional, almost erotic, playing the female voice as an instrument, and engaging biblical poetry as if it were a living language with something to say. In particular, it gives life to ancient characters and reveals their individual voices, very much in the tradition of opera as it would develop.

Like many of his peers, Frescobaldi prefaced each verse of Lamentations with an ornamented rendition of its first Hebrew letter. This is at once a faithful reflection of the acrostic form of the biblical text (see our discussion of Lam 1:1 and 1:6), and similar to the reassuring structure that underpins many other liturgical settings. But then Frescobaldi seems to break loose, both from the constraints of the form, and from the limitations of convention. He elaborates the Hebrew letter *lamed* that begins Lam 1:12 in about twenty trilling syllables. From this vocally complex opening, the lone female voice singing the Latin of the verse itself emerges organically, emoting raw anguish. The articulation of collective suffering by an individual voice – especially a female voice – is a crucial component of the art of the book of Lamentations. Frescobaldi's setting of Lam 1:12, with its pungent color, used for expression not aesthetics, and the uneven tempo, antithetical to liturgy, that distinguished his keyboard music, showcases here the speaker's insistent claim to suffer uniquely: 'Look and see if there is any agony like my agony …'. Most excruciatingly, Frescobaldi reveals the speaker's pain at being God's victim: 'which was dealt out to me, which the LORD inflicted on the day of his fierce anger'. In a manner so different from many other musical settings of the time, and even much later, this music clings like a lover to every nuance of the words it renders. Its composer's decision to accent two particular words in Lam 1:12 is theologically sublime. Hearing the slow-growing pain manifest in: 'if there is any agony like my agony' – even a listener without Latin understands precisely what must be signified by the exquisitely harmonious concentration on the words 'sui' and 'Dominus', that is, 'me' and 'LORD' – 'which was dealt out to *me*, which the LORD inflicted' (Lam 1:12). It is this, above all, that renders the pain unbearable: it came from God.

Yet some questions remain. To begin with, precisely who was the 'me' in Lam 1:12 as set to music by Frescobaldi? Was it Zion, the abandoned widow of the first chapter of the biblical book of Lamentations, or was it Christ, the suffering figure of Lamentations as transformed by its Christian context, the Tenebrae services of the Holy Week leading up to Easter? If Frescobaldi had in mind Christ, rather than Zion, can he be accused of aiding and abetting a religious-imperialist project of subverting the original meaning of the biblical book? Worse still, given the scarcity of women's voices in Jewish and Christian sacred texts, was he guilty of a gender-related crime as well as a theological one – silencing the female figure of daughter Zion for the benefit of the male figure of Christ? And, if so, was he a willing participant or an ignorant accomplice? That is, given his own Christian background, did Frescobaldi even know that these words were originally spoken by Zion, not Christ? Or should Lamentations be considered public property – open once it was canonized to any meaning that later interpreters wished to impose upon it – in which case Frescobaldi committed no crime at all? But what of us, the twenty-first-century audience of Frescobaldi's musical setting? If we hear it in the Christian religious context for which he wrote it, we will probably think in the first instance of Christ, as he probably did. But if we listen to it at home on our music systems, perhaps – depending on our own education and religious outlook – we will think in the first instance of daughter Zion, being thus true to the Hebrew Bible original, but false to Frescobaldi and his Christian context. These are some of the questions that emerge from the genre of reception history, difficult to answer, but important – and fascinating – to ask.

Sing-along Messiah

Lamentations 1:12 features also in one of the most widely known and most frequently performed of all choral works, Handel's oratorio *Messiah*. The great majority of Hebrew Bible texts in the work are from Isaiah and the Psalms, but there is one aria based on Lamentations. In the middle of Part 2 of the oratorio, a tenor sings, 'Behold, and see if there be any sorrow like unto His sorrow' (Lam 1:12). *Messiah* was composed in 1741 by the German-British baroque composer George Frideric Handel (born Halle, 1685; died London, 1759), with a libretto of scriptural texts compiled by Charles Jennens (born Leicestershire, 1700; died, Leicestershire, 1773). While sharing some features with Handel's other biblical oratorios (on which see Rooke 2012), the theological scope of this work is grander and more ambitious. Jennens's text is an extended reflection on Jesus as Messiah, moving from the prophetic predictions (according to Christian tradition) of Isaiah and others, through the Incarnation, Passion and Resurrection of Christ to his ultimate glorification in heaven. *Messiah* was first performed in Dublin on 13 April 1742, and was an immediate success, receiving its London premiere the following year.

It is interesting to note how Jennens made this Lamentations verse serve its purpose in this context through two strategies, textual emendation and intertextual juxtaposition. The libretto reads: 'Behold and see if there be any sorrow like unto His sorrow.' This is the King James Version, but the librettist emends the text to create a christological reference: he replaces the word 'my' with 'His', transposing from first to third person. As for the second strategy, intertextual juxtaposition, he sandwiches the Lamentations verse between a verse from Ps 69:20, 'Thy rebuke hath broken His heart: He is full of heaviness. He looked for some to have pity on Him, but there was no man, neither found He any to comfort Him' (this too transposed from first to third person) and a verse from Isa 53:8, 'He was cut off out of the land of the living: for the transgressions of Thy people was He stricken' (the latter not requiring change). The Isaiah verse in particular, coming from one of the so-called 'Suffering Servant' passages, serves to provide an interpretive comment on the Lamentations verse. It encourages a messianic reading of Lam 1:12 that would not suggest itself in another context, and more specifically brings an emphasis on the substitutionary death of the Messiah as understood in some Christian theology. A similar technique of interpretive juxtaposition is employed at the start of Part 3 of the oratorio, where the well-known aria, 'I know that my Redeemer liveth, and that He shall stand at the latter day upon the earth. And though worms destroy this body, yet in my flesh shall I see God' (Job 19:25-26), is followed by words from Paul's First Letter to the Corinthians that encourage a reading of the somewhat opaque Job text in terms of hope for resurrection: 'For now is Christ risen from the dead, the first fruits of them that sleep' (1 Cor 15:20).

In the course of the twentieth century Handel's *Messiah* became a remarkably popular piece in Britain and around the world, with performances both by professional choirs and amateur choral societies, and even 'sing-along' occasions with hundreds of members of the general public singing to raise money for charities or just for fun. Performances are especially popular during the Christmas holiday season, often involving members of other faiths and none. It may well be the case that in present-day Britain, it is when singing or hearing Handel's *Messiah* that a person is most likely to hear a verse from Lamentations.

[For Lam 1:13 see Lam 3:49–50]
[For Lam 1:14 see Lam 1:10]

1:15 The Lord *has rejected*
all my heroes in my midst;
he has proclaimed a time against me
to crush my young men;
the Lord has trodden as in a wine press
the virgin daughter Judah.

1:16 For these things I weep;
my eyes flow with tears;
for a comforter is far from me,
who might revive my spirit;
my children are desolate,
for the enemy has prevailed.

Unforgiveable?

In her essay 'Human Suffering and Divine Abuse of Power in Lamentations' (2003), the biblical scholar Johanna Stiebert reflects on forgiveness in the context of the work of South Africa's Truth and Reconciliation Commission. The Commission was a court-like restorative justice body set up in 1995 after the abolition of apartheid. Witnesses who were identified as victims of gross human rights violations were invited to give statements about their experiences, and some were selected for public hearings. Perpetrators of violence could also give testimony and could request amnesty from both civil and criminal prosecution. The Commission met, under the chairmanship of Archbishop Desmond Tutu, from 1996 to 1998. Questions of who can forgive whom and under what conditions (if any) were raised by the process. In her essay Stiebert expounds the connections between victims and perpetrators of violence in Lamentations on the one hand and in post-apartheid South Africa on the other. She interrogates the nature of forgiveness from a theological and contextual perspective, examining whether forgiveness ought to be conditional and if the God of Lamentations would be eligible for amnesty.

Stiebert argues that Lamentations depicts the deity as torturer-God. He sends fire into the bones of his victim, spreads a net for her feet and persecutes her, though she is stunned and faint (Lam 1:13). Reminiscent of a slave-master, God makes a yoke and plants it on his victim's neck before handing her over, sapped of strength, to others (Lam 1:14). Stiebert judges the words of Lam 1:15, 'the Lord has trodden as in a wine press the virgin daughter Judah', most affecting of all because here the contrast between Jerusalem's weakness and vulnerability and her abuser's power and gratuitous cruelty is so stark. Stiebert calls God 'the brute of Lamentations' (Stiebert 2003: 205), and refers to the book as 'a particularly virulent example of the divine abuse of power' (206). Against this overwhelming catalogue of cruelty, the appeals to the deity's 'faithfulness' (Lam 3:23), 'salvation' (Lam 3:26), 'compassion' and 'kindness' (Lam 3:32) are hard to take seriously. Given the wider context, they read like 'macabre sarcasm', says Stiebert (199). The deity as presented in Lamentations is not forgiving, not merciful and not repentant: 'Can and should he be forgiven?' she asks. The suffering of victim Jerusalem in the book has strong affinities with the accounts brought before the Human Rights Violations Committee of the Truth and Reconciliation Commission, while the brutality of the divine perpetrator has pronounced points of connection with the descriptions of amnesty seekers. Is there a category of 'unforgivable', and do God's offences recounted in Lamentations belong in this category? Stiebert's answer to both these questions is 'yes'. In the context of the Truth and Reconciliation Commission, forgiveness – or, more precisely, amnesty – is conditional: forgiveness and reconciliation are dependent upon 'justice'. Given the Commission's criteria, Israel's God would not be granted amnesty: nowhere is he repentant; indeed, throughout the book he is silent. The God of Lamentations, Stiebert concludes, does not deserve forgiveness.

An interesting question is raised here. How legitimate is it to isolate the presentation of the deity in one particular biblical book from the broader picture presented in the Bible as a whole? We have learned to distinguish the theological perspectives of different biblical writers (some would go so far as to distinguish between different perspectives combined within a book like Genesis). No one, including religious believers, need hesitate to acknowledge that human beings to some extent 'construct' the image of the deity of whom they speak. It is of value to note what specific biblical witnesses do and do not say about God. But then, having secured those insights, many will legitimately move on to speak of the God of the Bible in a broader context (which some, but not all, will relate to a transcendent reality). What is meant by the broader biblical context will vary, of course; so, for example, Christians have the New Testament (which they may or may not choose to draw into particular discussions), and different groups of Christians will attribute full scriptural authority to slightly varied lists of Old Testament books, depending on the canon of their particular tradition.

The God presented in Lamentations, and not least in these verses, is problematic indeed. When we read, at the end of Lam 1:16, 'for the enemy has prevailed', it is by no means clear that the reference is to the Babylonians. After all, in the previous verse it is 'the Lord' who 'has trodden as in a wine press the virgin daughter Judah' (cf. Lam 2:5, 'The Lord has become like an enemy; he has laid waste Israel …'). The Roman Catholic biblical scholar Ulrich Berges applies what he calls an 'ideological-critical' approach to discussion of the violence of God in the book of Lamentations, and sets his discussion in the context of the Old Testament as a whole (Berges 2005). He criticizes the ideology that God is free of any contradictions: the image of a 'soft' and always loving God is wishful thinking and even idolatry, he contends. In the Old Testament as a whole, in his view, the God of Israel's wrath and violence against his own people is counterbalanced by his tenderness. He argues that, although this notion seems to be absent in the book of Lamentations, Lam 3:31–3 show that God does not reject forever nor afflict 'out of his heart' (NRSV, 'willingly'). Berges contends that the biblical protest against the God of Israel, when he appears to act in contradiction to his own ethical standards, is rooted not in a cultural disapproval of a violent God but in the hope of experiencing his benevolence again.

1:17 Zion stretches out her hands,
but there is no one to comfort her;
the Lord has summoned against Jacob
his enemies all about him;
Jerusalem has become
among them a thing unclean.

Reformed and Humanist

Luther wrote no commentary on Lamentations, though his translation of the Bible into German represents an important contribution to interpretation (as noted at Lam 1:3). The other giant figure of the Reformation, John Calvin (born Noyon, France, 1509; died Geneva, 1564) did write a commentary on the book, which was first published in 1563. Truth to tell, it was not so much a formal commentary as notes written up by those attending the series of eighteen lectures on Lamentations that he gave in the Academy in Geneva between September 1562 and January 1563, towards the end of his life.

Calvin's commentary reflects his humanism. This is seen particularly in its attention to historical context and the intention of the author, assumed of course to be Jeremiah. He introduced his course with a discussion of these two issues. It is evident also in his striving to establish the plain sense of the text (in contrast to allegorical interpretation). He begins his discussion of each verse by giving a Latin translation from the Hebrew text, and offers some discussion of grammatical matters. He also comments on the overall form of the book, notably the acrostic feature, and interestingly – yet another reflection of humanism – refers more to classical authors than to other commentators on Lamentations. Somewhat surprisingly, but best understood in the humanist context, Calvin commends Jeremiah's readiness to complain and asserts that he even provides a model of protest against God: 'The Prophet then dictates for all the godly such complaints as they might, so to speak, pour forth confidently and freely into the bosom of God' (Calvin 1855: 400; cf. Wilcox 2011: 129).

Calvin presents a systematized theology of the book of Lamentations, starting with judgment, and moving on through exhortation to repentance and encouragement to hope, and on to prayer and appeal to God's mercy, all depending upon faith. Although it arguably misrepresents the book somewhat, a systematization such as Calvin's, which emphasizes Zion's responsibility for her fate and plays up the element of hope, is similar to the strategies whereby other interpreters, Christian and Jewish, apply the book to new circumstances and sustain its functioning as Scripture (see our discussion on Lam 2:3–5). Indeed, as Parry demonstrates (2010: 219–20), Calvin strongly highlights the parallel between Zion and the Church on this road from judgment through repentance to hope, as is clear in his exegesis of Lam 1:17:

> Now, if such a thing happened to the ancient church [i.e. Israel], let us not wonder if at this day also God should deal with us more severely than we wish. It is, indeed, a very bitter thing to see the church so afflicted as to have the ungodly exulting over its calamities, and that God's children should be as the refuse and filth of the world. But let us patiently bear such a condition; and when we are thus contemptuously treated by our enemies, let us know that God visits us with punishment, and that the wicked do nothing except through the providence of God, for it is his will to try our faith, and thus to show himself a righteous judge: for if we rightly consider in how many ways and how obstinately we have provoked his

wrath, we shall not wonder if we also be counted at this day an abomination and a curse. (Lecture 3, on Lam 1:11–18, in Calvin 1855: 325)

1:18 The Lord is in the right,
for I have rebelled against his word.
But hear, all you peoples,
and behold my agony:
my young women and young men
have gone into captivity!

[*2:6 He has devastated his booth like a garden,*
he has destroyed his tabernacle;
the Lord has abolished in Zion
festival and sabbath,
and in his fierce indignation has spurned
king and priest.]

Sacred and Profane?

Under the Roman Empire, in a practice sharing some features with the ancient Greek institution of ostracism (Forsdyke 2005), a person who committed the crime of oath-breaking was banned from society and all his rights as a citizen were revoked. He thus became a *homo sacer* (a person set apart, both 'sacred' and 'accursed'). In consequence, he could be killed by anyone with impunity but he could not be sacrificed in a ritual ceremony. Since the oath-breaker was already the property of the oath deity, he could no longer belong to human society, nor be consecrated to another deity; if the oath-breaker was killed, this was understood as the revenge of the god to whose power he had given himself. The Italian political philosopher Giorgio Agamben (born Rome, 1942) has explored the concept of the *homo sacer*, what he calls the 'bare life' figure, in relation to conceptions of sovereignty, especially in *Homo Sacer: Sovereign Power and Bare Life* (1998, Italian 1995). Sovereignty is conceived as the power that determines what is to be incorporated into the political body by means of the exclusion (or 'exception') of that which is to remain outside. It is the 'sovereign power' who controls inclusion and exclusion within the political landscape: the 'bare life' figure is located outside the juridical realms of religion and politics, and is defined by exclusion.

Drawing upon these ideas, biblical scholar Amy Meverden considers the figure of Daughter Zion in Lamentations as *homo sacer*, the 'bare life' figure: 'While many figures in the Hebrew Bible portray either the guilty or the abject qualities of the bare life figure (abject encompassing inability to be sacrificed, expendability without consequence, and exclusion), ... the construction of one who stands both guilty and abject, whose death fails to satiate any grievance through sacrifice, whose death warrants no recompense, and whose inclusion is not recognized by the sovereign power, exists in the exiled image of Daughter Zion' (Meverden 2011: 401).[7] In spelling out the parallels, Meverden cites Lam 1:18 ('The LORD is in the right, for I have rebelled against his word; ... behold my agony'), along with Lam 1:10–11 ('The foe has laid hands on all her precious things. ... Look, O LORD, and see how worthless I have become'); Lam 2:6–7 ('He has devastated his booth, ... he has destroyed his tabernacle. ... The Lord has scorned his altar, disowned his sanctuary'); and the two verses reporting that Judahite women were driven to eat their own children (Lam 2:20; 4:10). Though not cited by Meverden, Lam 1:14 is another verse illuminated by her adaptation of the concept of the 'bare life' figure: 'My transgressions were bound into a yoke; lashed tight by his hand; they weigh on my neck, sapping my strength; the Lord handed me over to those whom I cannot withstand.'

Who is the 'sovereign power' in the book of Lamentations? At the political level equivalent to Agamben's Roman Empire it is obviously the Babylonian conqueror, the agent of siege warfare, the deportation of the elite, and the plundering and destruction of the city and the Temple. However, the book of Lamentations directs its grievances instead to God: 'my agony ... which the LORD inflicted on the day of his fierce anger' (Lam 1:12); 'the Lord has trodden as in a wine press the virgin daughter Judah' (Lam 1:15); 'How the Lord in his anger humiliated daughter Zion!' (Lam 2:1); 'The Lord has become like an enemy; he has laid waste Israel' (Lam 2:5). Indeed, as Meverden puts it, 'the Deity is complicit with the Babylonian Empire, both serving the role of the sovereign power in dictating the fate of Daughter Zion as the bare life figure' (406).

This parallel with Roman concepts and practice sheds light on the austere and rigorous presentation of the deity in Lamentations. As the 'bare life' figure in ancient Rome was not an isolated phenomenon but rather an intentional manifestation of the 'sovereign power', demonstrating his absolute control over the political landscape, so as applied to Daughter Zion in Lamentations, the 'bare life' figure is not only a grim spelling out of the consequences of wrongdoing and apostasy (Lam 1:18, '... for I have rebelled against his word'), but a deliberate manifestation of God's power, making visible his principles of social and cosmic order (Lam 1:18, 'The LORD is in the right'). But Meverden's exploration of this theme in relation to Lamentations is also profound in its humane capacity to evoke empathy. She concludes, 'The cries of despair from Lamentations resonate with cries from the bare life figure in the Roman Empire, as well as with the cries of the bare life figure suffering from

---

[7]   Meverden has also explored reading the Levite's concubine of Judges 19 as 'bare life' figure.

displacement and abject treatment at the hands of the sovereign power in contemporary times' (406).

¹:¹⁹ I called out to my friends
but they deceived me;
my priests and elders
perished in the city
while seeking food
to keep themselves alive.

¹:²⁰ See, O LORD, how distressed I am;
my stomach churns,
my heart is wrung within me,
because I have been very rebellious.
In the street the sword bereaves;
in the house it is like death.

[*¹:²² Let all their wrongdoing come before you;*
and deal with them
as you have dealt with me
because of all my transgressions;
for my groans are many
and my heart is sick.]

Body Language

David Mumford's 'Emotional Distress in the Hebrew Bible. Somatic or Psychological?', published in the *British Journal of Psychiatry* (1992), contributes to a broader discussion of how different cultures articulate psychological states. Mumford builds on influential work by Julian Leff, including an article in which Leff argues that languages outside the Indo-European group have few specific words for depression and anxiety, and that these non-Western cultures present emotional distress somatically, that is, through the body (Leff 1973), and a book responding to calls for a more nuanced account, including the suggestion that bodily complaints can be symbolic (Leff 1988). Mumford aims to add a historical dimension to Leff's geographically diverse work on the somatic presentation of negative emotions, and his chosen source is the Hebrew Bible. The acknowledgements in his paper indicate his credentials for this work; alongside his psychological qualifications he has an MA in theology, and was able to consult his Hebrew teacher among others.

On Mumford's understanding, biblical statements about the body, especially its internal organs, are often intended to convey emotional, not physical, states.

To support this view, he provides an extensive list of biblical references to bodily pain whose significance seems to be psychological. Not surprisingly, given its themes and its poetic nature, the book of Lamentations is a rich mine of such references. Over and over again, it represents the body as at once the sign of physical suffering and the signifier of psychological causes and effects. Necks are heavy (Lam 1:14), eyes flow (Lam 1:16; 3:48, 49), stomachs churn (Lam 1:20; 2:11), heads are bowed (Lam 2:10), bile pours (Lam 2:11), infants faint (Lam 2:12, 19), tongues are parched (Lam 4:4), skin shrivels (Lam 4:8), and lives drain away (Lam 4:9). In Lam 1:20 a physical ailment, a churning stomach (Hebrew *meʿei*, 'innards' or 'guts') is preceded by an explicit statement of distress (Hebrew *tzar*, 'troubled'). Following Mumford, this conjunction indicates that the main interest of the verse is psychological, not physical. And yet the reference to a churning stomach immediately after a verse that describes the leaders who died while seeking food (v. 19 above) suggests a strong physical component; the speaker's stomach is churning because of famine in the besieged city. As Mumford suggests, bodily and psychological language often go hand in hand in the Hebrew Bible.

What is the import of the body language in Lam 1:20?[8] It may be possible to gain insight into this complex relationship between bodily pain and psychological suffering by fast-forwarding from ancient Israel to present-day Sierra Leone. Researchers in the Politics of Building Peace project at the Center for Conflict Studies, Philipps University Marburg, Germany, have been interviewing citizens of four post-conflict countries who lived through recent civil wars about their experience of war and their hopes for justice in its aftermath.[9] A sample of testimonials, all gathered from one particular village in Sierra Leone, suggests that the people affected by the civil war are reluctant either to describe in detail the atrocities that were committed or to identify the perpetrators. They show a marked lack of interest in punishment or other forms of legal recourse, and they make almost no reference to psychological trauma. Instead, they speak in general terms (almost certainly understatements!) about the crimes that were committed, and emphasize that the physical pain and illnesses they endured as a consequence are still with them:

> If I tell you that the war don't reach us, no it reached us! But for now we thank God. It's only for what we eat now and the medication is the problem. Because when the rebels reached this village, they were flogging us, they gave us heavy loads to carry, all those pains overcame our bodies. That's why we don't have well body, we're not healthy, until now. The time that the war was not here, people

---

[8]   Nancy Lee (see on Lam 4:5, 7, 8 in this volume) highlights affinities between Lam 1:20, 22 and Jer 4:19; 8:18.

[9]   www.uni-marburg.de/konfliktforschung/personal/buckley-zistel/dfg_tj

were physically healthy, sicknesses were not too much. But after this war now, to the present, there are so many sicknesses, so many problems, then also the kids are so many, they have to eat. The war is over but we are still suffering. (Extract from a 2011 interview conducted by Friederike Mieth).

For these modern-day survivors, as for those described in the book of Lamentations, the trauma of war is played out mainly in their bodies, not in their heads.

Mumford claims plausibly that, as far as the Bible is concerned, the heart (*lev*) is the most complex of the inner organs to analyze; it is mentioned more than seven hundred times, in a range of different contexts, and in relation to a wide range of different emotional and physical states. According to Lam 1:20, the speaker's heart is 'wrung' within him, possibly physically or psychologically, but certainly negatively. The Hebrew verb translated above as 'wrung' is *hapach*, literally 'turned',[10] prompting some interpreters to envisage repentance. Moving far away (too far, one might suggest) from the body language of the original Hebrew, NJPS offers: 'I know how wrong I was to disobey.' Yet NJPS is surely correct in sensing that guilt is implied: the next clause mentions the speaker's rebelliousness, as if offering an explanation for why his heart has turned; and this reading is consistent with references to the heart elsewhere in the book of Lamentations. Lamentations 1:20 contains the first of nine references in the book, as a whole, to the heart: Lam 1:20, 22; 2:18, 19; 3:21, 41, 65; 5:15, 17. In Lam 2:18 and 19 the heart is the locus of contrition, crying out to the LORD (v. 18) and being poured out like water in his presence on behalf of the city's starving infants (v. 19). The reference to the heart in Lam 3:21 is usually read idiomatically: 'this I call to mind' (similar to modern Hebrew's *sim lev*, 'pay attention'). Read literally, however, the verse speaks of something that is being restored to the heart: 'this I cause to return to my heart'. The verb is *shuv*, not *hapach* as in Lam 1:20, but both involve some kind of turn-about or about-turn.

Lamentations 1:22 involves another turn-around; it begs God to stop punishing Zion and turn his attention to its enemies, 'for my groans are many and my heart is sick'. In Lam 3:41, the heart is again a site of contrition, lifted by or along with the hands towards the heavens because the people have transgressed and God has not forgiven. Lamentations 3:65 calls for God to punish Israel's enemies according to their deeds, giving them 'anguish of heart', which plausibly entails guilt. Lamentations 5:15 describes a change of state: the people's hearts have ceased to be joyful, and their dancing has turned (*hapach* again) to mourning, while Lam 5:17 claims that the people's hearts are sick because of the desolation of Mount Zion (v. 18). This expression of hopelessness is

---

[10] See the discussion of Sodom in Lam 4:6.

followed immediately by the surprising (in the context) declaration of God's eternity: 'But you, O Lᴏʀᴅ, are enthroned for ever' (v. 19). Taken together as a group, the references to the heart in the book of Lamentations seem to signal a turning point, primarily the moment at which responsibility is accepted and the chance to move on is requested. Returning to Sierra Leone, we see the same phenomenon:

> To crown it all, I can say, it is a bad heart that brought about this war. Because if we love ourselves, we like ourselves, we don't have bad heart for ourselves, we will not agree for a bad thing to come to us. That is what I think. Just because we have different thinking for ourselves, self-interest, that only. Bad heart, only. (Extract from a 2011 interview conducted by Friederike Mieth)

For those affected by Sierra Leone's civil war, it seems, their suffering, whether physical or psychological, is mapped out on their bodies. Their hearts, however, are distinct from the rest of their bodies, and are reserved for guilt and self-blame: 'it is a bad heart that brought this war'. While Lamentations offers no comparable hint that the heart was the cause of Zion's suffering, it too, never-theless, links the heart with something approaching self-blame: 'my heart is wrung within me, because I have been very rebellious' (Lam 1:20). Mumford's historically diverse perspective on somatic suffering, supplemented by the geo-graphical diversity offered by comparisons with testimonials by residents of a village in Sierra Leone, sheds a new light on the significance of the heart in the book of Lamentations.

1:21 They heard how I was groaning,
with no one to comfort me.
All my foes heard of my plight and rejoiced
that you have done it.
Bring on the day that you announced,
and let them become like me.

Isaiah Reading Lamentations?

The book of Lamentations is almost always read against a specific historical background. Treves favored the second-century Maccabean crisis as a context (Treves 1963), and Morgenstern the early fifth century (Morgenstern 1956, 1957, 1960), but overwhelmingly the most common view is that these laments emerged from the aftermath of the fall of Jerusalem to the Babylonians in *c.*587 ʙᴄᴇ. This view survived as a consensus position (e.g. Hillers 1992), long after the traditional ascription to the prophet Jeremiah had been abandoned by almost everyone in the academic world.

This prompts the question whether Lamentations was known by the anonymous exilic poet to whom Chapters 40–55 of the Book of Isaiah are commonly attributed by scholars. The issue of the possible reception of Lamentations by the so-called 'Second Isaiah' has generated an extensive and lively scholarly literature (e.g. Willey 1997; Seitz 1998; O'Connor 1999; Sommer 1999; Linafelt 2000a: 62–79). Zion's predicament is spelled out poignantly in Lam 1:17 in terms of her lack of a comforter, 'Zion stretches out her hands, but there is no one to comfort her', and in very similar terms in three other verses: 'there is no one to comfort her among all her friends' (Lam 1:2); 'she sank appallingly, with none to comfort her' (Lam 1:9); 'To what can I liken you, that I may comfort you, O virgin daughter Zion?' (Lam 2:13). These verses refer to Zion in the third or second person. Lamentations 1:21 places a plea for comfort on the lips of personified Zion herself: 'They heard how I was groaning, with no one to comfort me' (Lam 1:21). All five verses employ the same Hebrew verb, *n-h-m*, to 'comfort'. Carleen Mandolfo, in the context of her 'dialogic theology' of the book of Lamentations, highlights the observation that God's silence in Lamentations leaves us with an unresolved tension (Mandolfo 2007: 103). Turning to Isaiah 40–55, on two occasions an apparent response to Zion's lack of a comforter is given: first in the opening verse of this section of the book, 'Comfort, O comfort my people, says your God' (Isa 40:1), and then later, 'For the LORD will comfort Zion; he will comfort all her waste places' (Isa 51:3). Both these Isaiah verses employ the same *n-h-m* root that is used in Lamentations.

Was Lamentations known and responded to by Second Isaiah? The issue of the comfort of Zion could have been suggested to Second Isaiah by the historical circumstances and theological questions of the people around him. On one occasion he himself poses the question in terms similar to Lam 1:17, 21, employing the same *n-h-m* root: 'These two things have befallen you – who will grieve with you? – devastation and destruction, famine and sword – who will comfort you?' (or 'how may I comfort you?') (Isa 51:19). This might suggest that Isaiah need not know Lamentations in order to answer this question in the way he does in Isa 40:1 and 51:3, but alternatively Isa 51:19 can itself be read as evidence of knowledge of Lamentations. The issue is potentially complicated by matters of geography. While the scholarly consensus has placed Lamentations in Judah, there has been less unanimity over the location of Second Isaiah. Whereas many scholars have favored a Babylonian provenance for Isaiah 40–55, there has been a growing trend to locate the chapters rather in Judah, and several of those who argue strongly for knowledge of Lamentations by Second Isaiah do so in the context of a Judahite context for the latter

(Tiemeyer 2007; 2011; Parry 2010: 163). Be this as it may, given evidence of communication between the two communities (cf. Gottwald 1962: 44–6), the knowledge of Lamentations by Second Isaiah is not dependent on both being in the same place. On balance, it seems likely that Second Isaiah does indeed reveal an awareness of the plea for 'comfort' in Lamentations and that he has provided a response.

There are other possible links between Lamentations and Isaiah. Patricia Tull Willey presents the thesis that 'Second Isaiah seems to have reemployed Daughter Zion from Lamentations 1–2' (Willey 1997: 218). Robin Parry goes so far as to argue that 'Texts from all five chapters of the lament are taken up and reused in the prophecy' (Parry 2010: 163). A tantalizing potential link is between the 'I am the man who has seen affliction' material of Lamentations 3 and the 'Suffering Servant' theme of Isaiah 40–55. Jill Middlemas proposes that Lamentations 3, if not actually written by Second Isaiah, represents an insertion in the middle of the book of a distinctively exiled perspective, contrasting with the remainder of the work (Middlemas 2006), whereas Willey argues, more plausibly, that Lamentations 3 provides the paradigm for the 'Servant' material (Willey 1997: 214–19), another case of reception of Lamentations. Finally, broadening the focus to the whole of the book of Isaiah, consider Isa 1:21: 'How the faithful city has become a whore! She that was full of justice, righteousness lodged in her – but now murderers!' This is very similar to Lam 1:1, even beginning with the same word, *eicha*, 'how': 'How lonely sits the city that once was full of people! She has become like a widow who was once great among the nations. The princess among the provinces has become a vassal.' Chapter 1 of Isaiah may well be a late prologue to the whole book of Isaiah (cf. Williamson 1994), and it is possible that Isa 1:21 reflects an awareness of Lam 1:1, arguably constituting another early case of the reception of Lamentations.

As indicated above, most scholars believe that Lamentations derived from the exilic age of the sixth century BCE. But can we ever be certain about the date of this book, and do we need to know? Iain Provan in his commentary (Provan 1991) argues that there is no clear indication in the book as to when it might be dated; and so he adopts what one might call a position of historical agnosticism, arguing moreover that it is not crucial which particular historical crisis the book has in mind. A different route to a similar stance is by a synchronic literary approach, in which the intertextual relationships with the book of Isaiah can be explored without even asking questions about the relative dating of texts (see on Lam 1:5). Lamentations has, in practice, often been read with little attention to matters of ancient history as, for example, in liturgical use (see on, e.g., Lam 1:6) or in psychological interpretation (see on Lam 3:17–18). The fact that it can be so read is a key factor in how it has served so many different ages so fruitfully (see further Joyce 1999).

References

Agamben, G. 1998. *Homo Sacer: Sovereign Power and Bare Life* (Stanford, CA: Stanford University Press). [Italian original, 1995.]

Berges, U. 2005. 'The Violence of God in the Book of Lamentations', in *One Text, A Thousand Methods: Studies in Memory of Sjef van Tilborg* (ed. P. C. Counet and U. Berges; Biblical Interpretation Series, 71; Leiden: Brill) 21–44.

Berlin, A. 2002. *Lamentations* (OLT; Louisville, KY, and London: Westminster John Knox).

Broyde, M. J. (ed.). 2011. *Contending with Catastrophe: Jewish Perspectives on September 11th* (New York: K'hal Publishing).

Calvin, J. 1855. *Commentaries on the Book of the Prophet Jeremiah and the Lamentations*, vol. 5 (trans. and ed., J. Owen; Edinburgh: Calvin Translation Society).

Cohen, C. 1973. 'The "Widowed" City', *JANESCU* 5: 75–81.

Cohen, M. E. 1988. *The Canonical Lamentations of Ancient Mesopotamia* (2 vols; Potomac, MD: Capital Decisions Limited).

Dobbs-Allsopp, F. W. 1993. *Weep, O Daughter of Zion: A Study of the City-Lament Genre in the Hebrew Bible* (Biblica et Orientalia, 44; Rome: Editrice Pontificio Instituto Biblico).

Doe, P. 1968. *Tallis* (Oxford Studies of Composers, 4; London: Oxford University Press, 2nd edn).

Exum, J. C. 1995. 'The Ethics of Biblical Violence against Women', in *The Bible in Ethics: The Second Sheffield Colloquium* (ed J. W. Rogerson, M. Davies and M. D. Carroll R.; JSOTSup, 207. Sheffield: Sheffield Academic Press) 248–71.

Forsdyke, S. 2005. *Exile, Ostracism, and Democracy: The Politics of Expulsion in Ancient Greece* (Princeton: Princeton University Press).

Gottwald, N. K. 1962. *Studies in the Book of Lamentations* (SBT, 14; London: SCM Press, 2nd edn).

Gray, A. 1995. *Five Letters from an Eastern Empire* (London: Penguin).

Guest, D. 1999. 'Hiding Behind the Naked Women in Lamentations: A Recriminative Response', *Biblical Interpretation* 7: 413–48.

Hillers, D. R. 1992. *Lamentations* (Anchor Bible, 7a; Garden City, NY: Doubleday, 2nd edn).

Hunter, J. 1996. *Faces of a Lamenting City: The Development and Coherence of the Book of Lamentations* (BEATAJ, 39; Frankfurt: Peter Lang).

Ilan, T. 2008. 'Gender and Lamentations: 4Q179 and the Canonization of the Book of Lamentations', *Lectio Difficilior: European Electronic Journal for Feminist Exegesis* 2.

Joyce, P. M. 1999. 'Sitting Loose to History: Reading the Book of Lamentations without Primary Reference to Its Original Historical Setting', in *In Search of True Wisdom: Essays in Old Testament Interpretation in Honour of Ronald E. Clements* (ed E. Ball; JSOTSup, 300; Sheffield: Sheffield Academic Press) 246–62.

Joyce, P. M. 2001. 'Lamentations', in *The Oxford Bible Commentary* (eds J. Barton and J. Muddiman; Oxford: Oxford University Press) 528–33.

Kaiser, O. 1992. 'Klagelieder', in *Das Hohelied, Klagelieder, Das Buch Ester* (ed. H. P. Müller et al.; ATD, 16/2; Göttingen: Vandenhoeck & Ruprecht, 4th edn) 91–198.

Landy, F. 1987. 'Lamentations', in *The Literary Guide to the Bible* (ed. R. Alter and F. Kermode; London: Collins) 329–34.

Leff, J. P. 1973. 'Culture and the Differentiation of Emotional States', *British Journal of Psychiatry* 123: 299–306.

Leff, J. P. 1988. *Psychiatry around the Globe: A Transcultural View* (London: Gaskell; 2nd edn).

Linafelt, T. 2000a. *Surviving Lamentations: Catastrophe, Lament, and Protest in the Afterlife of a Biblical Book* (Chicago and London: University of Chicago Press).

Mandolfo, C. R. 2007. *Daughter Zion Talks Back to the Prophets: A Dialogic Theology of the Book of Lamentations* (Semeia Studies, 58; Atlanta, GA: SBL).

Massenkeil, G. 1980. 'Lamentations', in *The New Grove Dictionary of Music and Musicians*, vol. 10 (ed. S. Sadie; London: Macmillan; New York: Grove) 410–12.

Megged, A. 2005. *The Living on the Dead* (trans. M. Louvish; New Milford, CT: Toby Press; 2nd edn). [Hebrew original, 1965]

Meverden, A. 2011. 'Daughter Zion as *Homo Sacer*: The Relationship of Exile, Lamentations, and Georgio Agamben's Bare Life Figure', in *Interpreting Exile: Displacement and Deportation in Biblical and Modern Contexts* (ed. B. E. Kelle, F. R. Ames, and J. L. Wright; Ancient Israel and Its Literature, 10; Atlanta, GA: SBL) 395–407.

Middlemas, J. 2006. 'Did Second Isaiah Write Lamentations III?', *VT* 56: 506–25.

Miller, G. D. 2011. 'Intertextuality in Old Testament Research', *Currents in Biblical Research* 9: 283–309.

Mintz, A. 1984. *Hurban: Responses to Catastrophe in Hebrew Literature* (New York: Columbia University Press).

Morgenstern, J. 1956, 1957, 1960. 'Jerusalem–485 B.C.', *Hebrew Union College Annual* 27: 101–79; 28: 15–47; 31: 1–29.

Moughtin-Mumby, S. R. 2008. *Sexual and Marital Metaphors in Hosea, Jeremiah, Isaiah, and Ezekiel* (Oxford Theological Monographs; Oxford: Oxford University Press).

Mumford, D. B. 1992. 'Emotional Distress in the Hebrew Bible. Somatic or Psychological?', *British Journal of Psychiatry* 160: 92–7.

O'Connor, K. M. 1999. '"Speak Tenderly to Jerusalem": Second Isaiah's Reception and Use of Daughter Zion', *Princeton Seminary Bulletin* 3: 281–94.

Parry, R. A. 2010. *Lamentations* (Two Horizons Old Testament Commentary; Grand Rapids, MI and, Cambridge: Eerdmans).

Parry, R. A. and H. A. Thomas (eds). 2011. *Great Is Thy Faithfulness? Reading Lamentations as Sacred Scripture* (Eugene, OR: Pickwick).

Provan, I. W. 1991. *Lamentations* (NCB; London: Marshall Pickering; Grand Rapids, MI: Eerdmans).

Pyper, H. S. 2001. 'Reading Lamentations', *JSOT* 95: 55–69.

Rooke, D. W. 2012. *Handel's Israelite Oratorio Libretti: Sacred Drama and Biblical Exegesis* (Oxford: Oxford University Press).

Rudolph, W. 1962. *Das Buch Ruth, Das Hohe Lied, Die Klagelieder* (KAT, 17; Gütersloh: Gerd Mohn, 2nd edn.).

Salters, R. B. 1986. 'Lamentations 1.3: Light from the History of Exegesis', in *A Word in Season: Essays in Honour of William McKane* (ed. J. D. Martin and P. R. Davies; JSOTSup, 42; Sheffield: JSOT Press) 73–89.

Salters, R. B. 1999. 'Using Rashi, Ibn Ezra and Joseph Kara on Lamentations', *Journal of Northwest Semitic Languages* 25: 201–13.

Salters, R. B. 2010. *Lamentations* (ICC; London and New York: Continuum).

Sawyer, J. F. A. 1989. 'Daughter of Zion and Servant of the Lord in Isaiah: A Comparison', *JSOT* 44: 89–107.

Schopf, F. J. 2011. 'Musical Responses to Lamentations', in Parry and Thomas 2011: 147–53.

Seidman, N. 1994. 'Burning the Book of Lamentations' in *Out of the Garden: Women Writers on the Bible* (ed. C. Büchmann and C. Spiegel; New York: Fawcett Columbine, London: Pandora) 278–88.

Seitz, C. R. 1998. *Word Without End: The Old Testament as Abiding Theological Witness* (Grand Rapids, MI and Cambridge: Eerdmans).

Shatz, D. '"From the Depths I Have Called You": Jewish Reflections on September 11th and Contemporary Terrorism', in Broyde 2011: 197–233.

Sommer, B. D. 1999. *A Prophet Reads Scripture: Allusion in Isaiah 40–66* (Contraversions: Jews and Other Differences; Stanford, CA: Stanford University Press).

Stiebert, J. 2003. 'Human Suffering and Divine Abuse of Power in Lamentations: Reflections on Forgiveness in the Context of South Africa's Truth and Reconciliation Process', *Pacifica* 16: 195–215.

Tiemeyer, L.-S. 2007. 'Geography and Textual Allusions: Interpreting Isaiah xl–lv and Lamentations as Judahite Texts', *VT* 57: 367–85.

Tiemeyer, L.-S. 2011. 'Lamentations in Isaiah 40–55', in Parry and Thomas 2011: 55–63.

Treves, M. 1963. 'Conjectures sur les dates et les sujets des Lamentations', *Bulletin Renan* 95: 1–4.

Van Selms, A. 1974. *Jeremia deel III en Klaagliederen* (Nijkerk: Callenbach).

Weems, R. J. 1995. *Battered Love: Marriage, Sex, and Violence in the Hebrew Prophets* (OBT; Minneapolis, MN: Fortress).

Wenthe, D. O. 2009. *Jeremiah, Lamentations* (Ancient Christian Commentary on Scripture, Old Testament, 12; Downers Grove, IL: InterVarsity Press).

Wilcox, P. 2011. 'John Calvin's Interpretation of Lamentations', in Parry and Thomas 2011: 125–30.

Willey, P. T. 1997. *Remember the Former Things: The Recollection of Previous Texts in Isaiah 40–55* (SBL Dissertation Series, 161; Atlanta, GA: Scholars Press).

Williamson, H. G. M. 1994. *The Book Called Isaiah: Deutero-Isaiah's role in Composition and Redaction* (Oxford: Clarendon; New York: Oxford University Press).

*2:1 How the Lord in his anger
humiliated daughter Zion!
He cast down from heaven to earth
the splendor of Israel;
he did not remember his footstool
on the day of his anger.*

*2:2 The Lord laid waste without pity
all the habitations of Jacob;
in his wrath he has broken down
the strongholds of daughter Judah;
he has brought to the ground in dishonor
the kingdom and its rulers.*

Babylonians and Cossacks

In the introduction to his chapter 'The Golden Age of Polish Jewry' in *Jewish Responses to Catastrophe*, David Roskies makes a fascinating and important theological point. From our modern perspective, especially looking back in the light of the Shoah (the Holocaust), he argues, we expect to find that 'the greater the catastrophe, the more it should challenge the basic theology of sin–retribution–restoration; the more it should undermine the standard rituals and liturgical formula' (Roskies 1989: 107). In fact, he claims, the textual evidence gathered in his substantial anthology, which spans the Bible to modern times, points in the opposite direction: 'the greater the catastrophe, the more it recalled the ancient archetypes; the more it brought to mind the calamity that had most recently been withstood' (107). This trend is exemplified in the first reading that Roskies presents in his chapter on Polish Jewry, a response to the Cossack revolt led by Bogdan Chmielnicki in 1648–49 written by Rabbi Nathan Nata Hanover.

Nathan Hanover was (most likely – the precise details of his life are unknown) born in Poland and, after the Cossack uprising, travelled through Europe, writing, teaching, and studying Jewish mysticism. He died in Moravia – apparently murdered by a Turkish soldier – in 1683. His best-known work of those that survived is *Yeven Metsulah*, known in English as *The Abyss of Despair* or *The Deep Mire* (first printed in Venice in 1653), a report from a Jewish perspective of the Cossack uprising in mid-seventeenth-century Poland. The account reads in some respects as historical, and indeed it has sometimes been regarded as such. But although Hanover provides some historical background, for example, on relations between Jews, Poles and Cossacks in the time leading up to the uprising (good relations between Jews and Poles were disrupted by Cossacks), and a sense of Jewish life in that period (the uprising brought to an end a period of social, economic and intellectual flourishing for Polish Jews, hence Roskies's use of the term 'Golden Age'), *Yeven Metsulah* is not a straightforward historical work, and Hanover was interested in something more than an eye-witness account. Although he does make a brief attempt to chronicle the historical causes of the catastrophe, Hanover seeks mainly to contextualize this calamity theologically in the greater scheme of Jewish disasters. His introduction to this work begins:

> 'I am the man that hath seen the affliction by the rod of his wrath' [Lam 3:1], when God smote His people Israel, His first-born. From heaven unto earth He cast down [Lam 2:1] the beautiful and glorious land of Poland, 'oh fair in situation, the joy of the whole earth' [Ps 48:3]. The Lord hath swallowed up unsparingly the habitations of Jacob [Lam 2:2], the lot of His inheritance [Deut 32:9], and hath not remembered his footstool in the day of his anger [Lam 2:2] (Roskies 1989: 110)

The biblical allusions are typical of Hanover's work and others like it. Some of them are explicit verse citations – see for example Lam 3:1 in the first line of the quotation above – and others take the form of echoes or adaptations. So although his words, 'From heaven unto earth He cast down', are a direct citation of the first clause of Lam 2:1, the sentence as a whole is an adaptation of that verse. Hanover replaces 'the splendor of Israel' (Lam 2:1b) with 'the beautiful and glorious land of Poland'. Readers familiar with the tragic history of Jewish–Polish relations (the 'Golden Age' never returned) will find it disturbing to see that Hanover equates Poland with Israel, even specifying that it is the land itself, not simply its Jewish inhabitants, that is 'beautiful and glorious'. Yet in making this equation, Hanover also makes a crucial point about Lam 2:1. The 'splendor of Israel' is not necessarily Zion; indeed, the reference in Lam 2:2 to 'the habitations of Jacob' opens the door for precisely the liberty that Hanover takes. With frightening prescience, the author of Lamentations leaves room for his work to be reapplied in cases where a catastrophe has not occurred in the land of Israel. To be sure, the language of Lam 2:1–2 points most directly and naturally to Jerusalem and Judah, yet Hanover's perspective that Poland was an example of Israel's 'splendor' among 'all Jacob's habitations' (NJPS) can find a home in this biblical text. With respect to their attitudes towards exile and diaspora, there are interesting parallels between Hanover and Ibn Ezra (see on Lam 1:13; 3:49–50). In both cases, their use of Lamentations entails an equation of, on the one hand, the destruction of Jerusalem and the exile from Judah and, on the other, persecutions and expulsions in diaspora contexts such as medieval Spain and early-modern Poland. In both cases, the typological use of biblical Lamentations helps to highlight the surprising fact that the catastrophe was not attributed directly and explicitly to the diaspora location, but rather to some of its inhabitants. As the allusions to Lamentations make clear, a national homeland is not in itself a protection against persecution. That, unfortunately, can happen anywhere.

Hanover's introduction to *Yeven Metsulah* sheds further light on biblical Lamentations in general and the verses he cites in particular. As well as attempting to explain the causes of the Cossack revolt, he states that he has 'recorded all the major and minor encounters, as well as the evil decrees and persecutions; also the days on which those cruelties occurred, so that everyone might be able to calculate the day on which his kin died, and observe the memorial properly'. The Jewish tradition of commemorating the *yahrzeit*, the annual anniversary of a death (literally, Yiddish/German for 'time of year'), functions in part to keep alive a person's memory among family members, but it serves also as the date on which survivors remind *God* of those departed. Lamentations itself is not a chronicle of catastrophe that could be used by the descendants of specific victims to commemorate their deaths. In Jewish tradition, and perhaps even in the minds of its authors, it stands rather as a memorial for those anonymous victims of collective tragedy who would otherwise be forgotten. But, like Hanover's *The Deep Mire*, Lamentations seems intended to ensure that God remembers for all eternity those who died on days when, in his anger, he 'did not remember his footstool' (Lam 2:1).

2:3 In his fierce anger he cut down
all the might of Israel;
he has withdrawn his right hand
in the face of the enemy;
he has burned like a flaming fire in Jacob,
consuming on all sides.

2:4 He bent his bow like an enemy,
with his right hand set like a foe;
he killed all in whom we took pride
in the tent of daughter Zion;
he poured out his fury like fire.

2:5 The Lord has become like an enemy;
he has laid waste Israel.
He has laid waste all its palaces,
destroyed its strongholds,
and multiplied in daughter Judah
mourning and lamentation.

Flames of Wrath

Twice in Lam 2:3–5 divine judgment is described in terms of fire: in Lam 2:3, 'he has burned like a flaming fire in Jacob, consuming on all sides' and in Lam 2:4, 'he poured out his fury like fire'. Elsewhere in the book, fire features at Lam 1:13, 'From on high he sent fire …'. and at Lam 4:11, 'The LORD gave full vent to his fury; he poured out his blazing anger, and kindled a fire in Zion that consumed its foundations.' It is not surprising, therefore, that Lamentations should have been drawn upon when London suffered the most devastating conflagration in its history, the Great Fire of London of 2–5 September 1666. Some 13,000 houses, most of the civic buildings, St Paul's Cathedral, and eighty-seven parish churches were destroyed. Though there are believed to have been relatively few deaths, thousands of people found themselves homeless and financially ruined. For the city of London, this was a disaster of unprecedented proportions. Not surprisingly, many other catastrophes were recalled at this time of great crisis. John Evelyn wrote in his diary for 3 September: 'Thus I left it this afternoon burning, a resemblance of Sodom, or the last day … the ruins resembling the picture of Troy. London was, but is no more!' (Evelyn 2006).

On 10 October 1666, little more than a month after the disaster, there took place a 'day of humiliation and fasting', an echo perhaps of the Jewish fast day of Tisha B'Av. The Revd Edward Stillingfleet (1635–99), later Bishop of Worcester, preached at St Margaret's church, Westminster, to a congregation so large that the

The *LONDONERS* Lamentation.

Wherein is contained a forrowfull Description of the dreadfull Fire which happened in Pudding-Lane, next beyond Fiſh-ſtreet-hill on the ſecond of Septemb. 1666. betwixt twelve and one of the clock in the morning, being Sunday, and continued untill the Thurſday night following: With an account of the King and the Duke of York's indevours, with ſeverall Peers of the Land, for the quenching of the ſame; Alſo the manner of doing it; and the name of every particular place where the fire did ſtop.

Tune is,　When Troy town, &c.

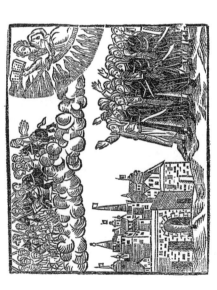

LEt better flow from every eye,
　Of all good Subjects in the Land;
Mountaines of fire were raiſed high,
　Which Londons ſtatelyeſt buildings graſp,
Welle lye thoſe buildings were ſo good,
And Aſhes lye where London ſtood.

Oh Lord! that at this ſame yeers,
　the fatteſt of time came ſuch ſtore;
Apoſt to our miſery oppreſſes,
　in five times ſpace, its burnt at laſt;
Waſte lye thoſe Fabricks were ſo good,
And Cinders lye where London ſtood.

The ſecond of September, at
　the diſmal houre ſ'twixt twelve and one,
At mid-night, up the fire gat,
　in Pudding-Lane and brought up ſtone;
Our Engines all could do no good,
Till Aſhes lay where London ſtood.

It over-flow'd from Fiſh-ſtreet-hill,
　and then gave fire to Canon-ſtreet,
then through the Lanes, about its wheel,
　untill it bathing the Thames's ſide met,
As if it would have dry'd the Flood,
And left duſt where the River ſtood.

A Strong affuaiting Eaſten-winde,
　with liberall Lungs do fan the Flame,
The Fire ſo in the water fin'd,
　you would have thought 'thad been the ſame,
The Flames which ſwallow all they mee,
Makes nothing to deſtroy a Street.

Great Congregations made of ſparks,
　fill all the Churches in the Town,
What fly up like a flock of Larks,
　the Bells and Leads are melted down;
Cauſe we from fin will not return,
Pulpits themſelves in Aſhes mourn.

With, Tar, Oyle, Flax and ancient Wood
　did make the raging Fire ſo rant,
It would not quench, unleſſe we cou'd
　at once have thrown the Thames upon't;
The fire had burnt up without fear,
Had Humber, Trent, and Tweed been there.

The Cittizens can nothing do,
　but lug their treaſure out of town,
Thirty pound Carts are hired now,
　each private man loath to his own;
But every paſſenger they grees,
With Sugar and Wine in every ſtreet.

Up to the old Exchange the fire,
　with both ambitions brings up flip,
And to the top on't that aſpire,
　untill it all do level lye;
But Greſham (he that built it) ſtands,
In ſpight of Vulcan's not commands.

The lofty front of ſtateleſs Powls,
　is now beſieged with the Flame,
In which his wonder intrails robuſt,
　but bravely doth withſtand the ſame,
And maſſy ſtones like ſhot let's fly,
Out of its own Artillery.

Women lying in, and Cripples creual
　out of their beds, into the field,
Leaſt fire ſhould conſume them all,
　'gainſt which they had no other ſhield;
In every place the fields were ſtrew'd
Which like to a great Leaguer ſhew'd.

Our gracious King, the Duke of York,
　the Life-guard and their noble Horſe,
both day and night, do watch and work;
　untill it bathing the Thames's ſtop,
London, Printed for J, Clark, at the Bible and

---

to pull down houſes, walls, and beat us
　That fire might no further go,
And ſo conſume the Suburbs too.

God gave a bleſſing to their haunes,
　for by this meanes the flames grew lower,
It bid at once obey Commands
　both at the Temple, and the Tower,
At Pie-corner, and Alderſgate,
The fire loſt his Flaming ſtate.

At Holborn-bridge and Cripple-gate,
　and in the midſt of Coleman-ſtreet,
And Baſing-hall it was ſtaid flat,
　Biſhops-gate-ſtreet and Leaden-hall,
To Cornhil-Standard are ſaved all.

Juſt at Fan-Church in Fan-Church-ſtreet,
　Cloath-workers-hall in Mincing-Lane,
The fire could no further get,
　and in Mark-Lane was quench'd again;
And now with heavy loſſes, we
Are rid of this hot miſery.

O French and Dutch many were took
　(upon ſuſpition of a plot,
That they this ruine fondly purſue
　with Fire-works) which will all be brought
Unto their tryal, but I fear,
Our ſinful hearts more guilty are.

Where of Gods wrath Arrows are
　and have ſtent at us lately ſhot,
Civil War, Peſtilence and Fire,
　for Plate and Coin, there then the Plot,
Beware the fourth, for if it fall,
Grim Famine will confound us all.

I know each Cittizen hath drank
　a ſcathing draught of this our Cup,
But let him not (to mend his baſte,)
　his grievous Crimes ſo get trap,
Let them conſider what they do,
Their Cuſtomers are ſufferers too.

When let us with hearts undefil'd,
　thank God his Mercies are ſo great,
So that the Fire hath not ſpoil'd
　the Suburbs and the Royall ſeat:
If we ſtill have each other thus,
God never will be friends with us.

Harp, in Weſt-Smithfield, Wild-Allowaine.

diarist Samuel Pepys reports that he himself was unable to get into the church and had to make do with a herring meal in a nearby pub instead (Pepys 2000). The homily survives as 'A Sermon Preached before the Honourable House of Commons at St. Margarets Westminster, Octob. 10 1666. Being the Fast-Day Appointed for the Late Dreadfull Fire in the City of London (1666)' (Stillingfleet, 1666). In this 'Fast-Sermon for the Fire of London', Stillingfleet refers to London as 'the late great and famous city' and highlights 'those sins which have brought down the Judgments of God in so severe a manner in the midst of us'. The text of the sermon is Amos 4:11 ('I have overthrown some of you, as God overthrew Sodom and Gomorrah, and ye were as a firebrand pluckt out of the burning: yet have ye not returned unto me, saith the Lord' [KJV]), but the first biblical quotation in the sermon itself is from the start of this chapter of Lamentations: 'God hath covered the daughter of Sion with a cloud in his anger, and cast down from heaven to earth the beauty of Israel, and remembred not his footstool in the day of his anger' (Lam 2:1, after KJV).

The titles of at least two prominent contemporary publications responding to the Great Fire employ the word 'Lamentation' or 'Lamentations' in their title. 'The Londoners Lamentation' is a widely circulated 'broadside' (broadsheet) ballad published in 1666 giving an account of the fire. More theological is 'London's Lamentations', by Thomas Brooks (1608–80), published in 1670 (Brooks). This work presents itself as 'a serious discourse concerning that late fiery dispensation that turned our once renowned city into a ruinous heap' (cf. Lam 1:1, 'How lonely sits the city that once was full of people! She has become like a widow who was once great among the nations. The princess among the provinces has become a vassal'). Brooks provides a series of sermons on the fire, emphasizing lessons, more religious than practical, that are to be learned from it. He draws on many biblical texts (including Ps 46:8; Ezek 26:17; and Isa 42:24–5), and not least on the biblical book of Lamentations. For example, like Stillingfleet, Brooks cites from Lam 2:1–5. He makes much of the last two words of Lam 2:5, where it is reported that God 'multiplied in daughter Judah mourning and lamentation'. Brooks writes: 'These two words, "mourning and lamentation", are joined together to note the great and eminent lamentation of the daughter of Judah upon the sight and sense of God's destroying, razing, and leveling to the ground, by the hand of the Chaldeans, etc., all the strongholds and fortresses that were built for the defence of the Israelites. Now shall the daughter of Judah greatly lament to see her strongholds laid desolate; and shall not we at all lament to see London, to see our strongholds, turned into a ruinous heap?' This is a powerful Christian case of the practice, so characteristic of Jewish tradition, of relating successive disasters to this biblical book.

In Thomas Brooks's 'London's Lamentations', as in Edward Stillingfleet's 'Fast-Sermon for the Fire of London', the disaster has happened because of the grievous sins of God's people and the deity has acted powerfully to inflict the fire as a just and fitting punishment; but now, if the people will repent, there may yet be a fresh start and new hope for the future. All the elements of such a message can indeed be found in Lamentations, but in the biblical book itself they are often accompanied by divergent perspectives. Linafelt, among others, is rightly insistent upon calling us back to the complexity of Lamentations and to the fact that in many respects it resists systematic explanation of the original disaster and its implications (Linafelt 2000a). That is indeed part of its greatness. But it must also be recognized that many of those Jews and Christians who have used the book, from the Jewish authors of the Aramaic Targum of about the fifth century CE to these seventeenth-century Christian theologians, have systematized its contents in terms of sin, judgment, repentance and new hope. This summary may not do full justice to the wonderful richness of the biblical book, but it would seem that such systematization has been one of the recurrent ways in which the book has found such an important and effective ongoing life.

[For Lam 2:6 see Lam 1:18]

2:7 *The Lord has scorned his altar,*
disowned his sanctuary;
he has delivered into the hand of the enemy
the walls of her citadels;
they raised a cry in the house of the LORD
as on a festival day.

2:8 *The* LORD *determined to lay in ruins*
the wall of daughter Zion;
he stretched the line;
he did not withhold his hand from destroying;
he caused rampart and wall to lament;
they languish together.

2:9 *Her gates have sunk into the ground;*
he has ruined and broken her bars;
her king and princes are among the nations;
guidance is no more,
and her prophets obtain
no vision from the LORD.

Lamenting Cities

The golden age of Mesopotamian city-laments predated Lamentations by some 1500 years. This means that what must be earlier examples of a similar literary genre might be said to be out of place in a reception history of the biblical book. How can what came first be understood as a comment on what came later? And yet a case can easily be made for the inclusion of the city-laments in this volume. First, the city-laments were made accessible to Hebrew Bible readers only fairly recently (see Cohen 1988 and Dobbs-Allsopp 1993). Inevitably, even those Hebrew Bible readers aware of the relative order of composition saw the city-laments as illuminating the biblical book, and not the other way around. They were affected by their own reading experience, and not by chronological considerations. To the extent, then, that reception history concerns the perceptions of readers, the Mesopotamian city-laments belong in the reception history of the book of Lamentations. Second, it can often be more useful and informative to read a given text in the light of what preceded it in its historical or literary trajectory than to read it in the light of what came after it. Indeed, there are cases – especially involving formulaic genres such as fairy tales or liturgy – when variations over time and even between cultures are negligible, and the order of composition is almost irrelevant. The case at hand is arguably one of these.

The book of Lamentations has striking parallels to Mesopotamian city-laments (see also on Lam 5:11–14). For example, both feature desolate streets, once filled with people celebrating festivals, now piled with bodies. Lamentations 1:4 reports that 'The roads of Zion mourn, empty of festival pilgrims; all her gates are desolate', while 'The Lament of Ur' describes 'the wide streets, where feasting crowds [once] gathered, jumbled they lay. In all the streets and roadways bodies lay. In open fields that used to fill with dancers, the people lay in heaps' (Jacobsen 1976). Another similarity concerns the representation of broken buildings, as highlighted by Zainab Bahrani in her discussion of 'The Lament of the Destruction of Sumer and Ur': 'When the gods left their cities, they abandoned them to the desolation and ravages of war. The desolation is described vividly in terms of the dead bodies that littered the streets, and the remaining suffering people. But the destruction of the monuments and architecture was a dominant narrative theme in the war laments' (Bahrani 2008: 166). The book of Lamentations, with its emphasis on the destruction of buildings – city fortifications as well as the Temple itself – fits almost perfectly in this context. Yet there is at least one important difference. As Bahrani shows, the city-laments describe what happens when a god abandons his or her city. In Lamentations, on the other hand, it is the people who are exiled; there is no indication whatsoever that God will leave Jerusalem. One possible explanation for this difference emerges from Bahrani's discussion of the role of city gods in Mesopotamian culture:

Deities were associated with particular cities as patron gods, and each city was the place in which that deity's house, his or her main temple, was located and where the cult statue lived. ... The cult statue was made ... using particular materials that were treated by priests. The statue was then put through a mouth-opening ceremony, in which the image was brought to life. After that, the statue was no longer an image; it was the phenomenon of the deity proper on earth. ... The removal of the god from the city had disastrous consequences. The god was exiled. He (or she) went into a form of occultation wherein divine power and protection were removed from the city (Bahrani 2008: 165).

Although the book of Lamentations contains many metaphorical descriptions of God, it at no point indicates that these found concrete representation in the city of Jerusalem. And while the destruction of the Temple is a central theme of the book, the Temple is not here presented graphically as the home of God, his former dwelling place. Perhaps the author(s) of Lamentations departed in this respect from the traditional city-lament because their understanding of God did not incorporate the idea of an image or concrete manifestation that could be physically removed from the Temple. For the Lamentations authors, those elements of devastation and destruction that Mesopotamian culture would have attributed to God's absence were attributed instead to his angry presence. At first sight, this difference between Lamentations and the city-laments might appear to reflect a theological difference between ancient Mesopotamia and ancient Israel. A second glance, however, reveals an example of inner-biblical diversity. According to Ezekiel 8–11, another biblical text by a Judahite writer of the same period, God does leave the city when it is overthrown. Indeed, the highly graphic description in Ezekiel 1 of the arrival in Babylon of something like the Ark of the Covenant can in some respects be interpreted in the light of the physical removal of Mesopotamian city gods (see Odell and Strong 2000). It is instructive to note that in this case inner-biblical diversity has been highlighted by cross-cultural comparison.

2:10 *The elders of daughter Zion*
sit on the ground in silence;
they have thrown dust on their heads
and put on sackcloth;
the young girls of Jerusalem
have bowed their heads to the ground.

Interfaith Lament?

Samira Abbassy was born in Iran, brought up in London, and lives and works in New York City. Although she is not a religious Muslim and has lived most

Samira Abbassy, *Lamentation* (2007).

of her life outside Iran, her work draws extensively on Islamic themes and
Persian iconography. Many of her paintings relate quite personally to the
religious and cultural traditions that underlie them; some, especially those
that address issues of gender, are ideological; and a few are overtly political
or deal with political themes. An example of the latter is a 2007 work called
'Lamentation', a small painting on a panel that depicts four Muslim women,
three dressed in black, and one in vibrant blue.[1] All four women are veiled, all
have visible eyes, and all have mouths that are either closed or covered by a
veil. The three dressed in black look directly out of the panel at the viewer.
The woman in blue, her bare arm extended towards the object of her gaze,
is looking at a pile of ten corpses. The painting focuses on their heads: old,
young, male, female, shaved, and with flowing locks, all with sealed living
lips and large, open, characteristically Persian eyes. Behind the four women a
recently fire-bombed car belches smoke and flames. The background is a

[1]   www.samiraabbassy.com/paintings.html

deep, warm gold, as if suffused by a gorgeous sunset but actually reflecting flames from the burning car. The faces of the corpses are also tinged with gold. The only other detail in this stylized representation of the aftermath of an act of terror is the faint imprint of a small group of men dressed all in white, hovering behind the pile of bodies. The huddled group resembles a huge hand, reminiscent of the five-fingered amulet displayed for protection in many Middle Eastern cultures. Is the impression of the hand intentional, a parody of the traditional good luck charm, the corpses testifying to its impotence, or perhaps an allusion to the hand of God, divine intervention in the world?

Samira Abbassy's memorable painting evokes many themes and images from the biblical book of Lamentations: the fire (Lam 1:13; 2:3) that consumed the foundations of the city (Lam 4:11); the young girls with heads bowed (Lam 2:10); the young and old lying dead on the streets (Lam 2:21); and even perhaps the pure gold grown dim (Lam 4:1, 2). Moreover, it implies a theological message that is as applicable to the book as to its present-day Middle Eastern context. The composition balances a burning car in the top left corner of the canvas against a pile of corpses in the bottom right corner. This could be intended to signify two different kinds of casualties of war, the inanimate, exemplified by the car, and the animate, exemplified by the corpses (see Abbassy's 2006 'Oil Vehicle' for a similar juxtaposition), but certain details point to a different reading. In the case of the car, the viewer's attention is drawn not to the vehicle itself, but to the smoke and flames that billow out of it, that is, not to the object destroyed, but to the agent of destruction. As for the ten calm faces in the bottom right corner, devoid of the blood and burning flesh we associate with fire bombs, they too deflect attention – to the faint, symbolic hand hovering above them, and to the hand of the woman dressed in blue, extended towards them. Abbassy's painting seems less interested in representing graphically the consequences of yet more violence in the Middle East – in truth, graphic representation of that kind is present in abundance on our television screens – than in exploring questions of responsibility and appropriate response. Who caused this destruction and death? The painting does not identify or even imply a specific political perpetrator, even though there must have been one. Rather, the destruction and death portrayed are associated with the fire and the hovering hand. In the book of Lamentations, too, fire and a hand are sources of destruction, the fire of God's anger (Lam 1:12–13; 2:3; 4:11) and his punishing hand (Lam 2:4, 8; 4:6). And who, the painting also demands, will challenge the destruction? Certainly not the corpses themselves – their open eyes pose a question, but their closed mouths suggest that they cannot articulate it – and not the onlooking women. Their gazes may be reproachful, implicitly demanding an account of injustices perpetrated, but their lips too are sealed: 'The elders of daughter Zion sit on the ground in silence ... the young girls of Jerusalem have bowed their heads to the ground' (Lam 2:10). In Abbassy's 'Lamentation' it is the human hand that challenges destruction, reaching out towards the corpses and towards the symbolic hand, representing divine power, which hovers above them. In biblical Lamentations, too, the response to destruction is arguably at its most intense not in words, but in gestures, above all those that involve the human hand (Lam 1:17; 2:19; 3:41; 4:10).

It is clear that the points of contact between Abbassy's 'Lamentation' and the biblical book are numerous and significant. Yet it is far from clear how, if at all, Abbassy herself was relating to the biblical text when she conceived and executed her work. She was not consciously aware of the book's existence when she painted her own 'Lamentation'. Yet surely the title she chose for it was more than a coincidence? Samira Abbassy grew up in England where, at that time, most schools had Christian components, within and beyond the curriculum. She studied at a British college of art, where she might well have been exposed to paintings on the theme of the destruction of Jerusalem. Since the language and imagery of the book of Lamentations long ago escaped the narrow confines of the Bible, she may have been responding indirectly and unknowingly to biblical ideas and images already refined by other artists when she constructed her representation of the destruction of a city. It is impossible to be sure, but the case of Samira Abbassy serves both as a cautionary tale and as an opportunity for scholars working on reception. It raises important questions about influence and inspiration, along with the possibility of some tentative answers.

A scholar who had seen 'Lamentation' hanging in a gallery but was unable to consult the artist would almost certainly have assumed an intentional allusion to the biblical book. This might have prompted the scholar to analyze its implications for Jewish-Christian-Muslim responses to sacred texts – indeed to the sacred texts of 'the other', since Lamentations is not among those biblical books that plays a role in the Quran – which would, at one level, have been undermined by the discovery that the artist did not know Lamentations. Yet at another, deeper level, the initial analysis might have survived more or less intact. Even if it could be demonstrated beyond doubt that her imagery owed no debt, however indirect, to the biblical book, the similarity of Abbassy's response to the universal theme of death and destruction following invasion, compounded by her choice of a title that evokes the Bible for many viewers, mean that her painting is at home in a reception history broadly construed.

This is good news: readers of Lamentations would have plenty to learn from Samira Abbassy even if it transpired that she learned nothing at all from Lamentations.

2:11 My eyes are spent with tears;
my stomach churns;
my bile is poured out on the ground
because of the destruction of my people,
because infants and babes faint
in the streets of the city.

2:12 They cry out to their mothers,
'Where is bread and wine?'
as they faint like the wounded
in the streets of the city,
as their life is poured out
on their mothers' bosom.

[*2:17 The LORD has done what he purposed,*
he has carried out his threat;
as he ordained long ago,
he has demolished without pity;
he has made the enemy rejoice over you,
and exalted the might of your foes.]

Short Story, Long History

Cynthia Ozick (born New York, 1928, of Russian-born parents) is an American-Jewish short story writer, novelist, poet and essayist, who has consistently won critical acclaim. Her short story *The Shawl* first appeared in the *New Yorker* magazine in 1980 and has since been reprinted often (e.g. Ozick 1990). This bleak tale tells the story of Rosa and her little girl Magda. The narrative opens with mother, baby daughter, and Rosa's teenage niece Stella on the march to who knows where. When the breasts of the famished mother cease to give milk, Magda sucks on the corner of the shawl in which she is wrapped. 'It was a magic shawl', writes Ozick, 'it could nourish an infant for three days and three nights. Magda did not die, she stayed alive, although very quiet.' Stella is jealous of her young cousin Magda, snug in her shawl, and gazes at her 'like a young cannibal'. We next see the three of them in a concentration camp, barely alive. Rosa has been hiding Magda all this time, knowing that the child would be killed if discovered. Magda is inseparable from her shawl, but one day Stella takes it away; 'I was cold', she says. Magda, by now a toddler, stumbles on her spindly legs in search of the shawl. Her mother spots her, exposed and vulnerable in the arena of the barracks. Silent no longer, the child screams for all, guards included, to hear. Rosa knows that she will need the shawl if Magda is to be quietened, and so instead of making a dash for her, she runs back into the barracks to pull the shawl off Stella. Rosa returns to the arena to see her child being carried off by a guard. The electrified fence hums like 'lamenting voices'. All at once Magda is 'swimming through the air'; she falls from her flight against the electrified fence. Rosa can only fill her own mouth with Magda's shawl, stuffing it in and stuffing it in, until she is swallowing up 'the wolf's screech ascending now through the ladder of her skeleton'.

Even if *The Shawl* is not an explicit response to the biblical book of Lamentations, the 'lamenting voices' of the electrified fence and the threat of cannibalism (cf. Lam 2:20; 4:10) are by no means the only points of contact, as Linafelt persuasively argues (Linafelt 2000a: 138–41). In both works all hope of 'pity' is extinguished (cf. Lam 2:17, 21), and in both children die in public spaces (cf. Lam 2:11–12 above). The image of Magda stumbling to her death recalls the fainting of infants and babes in the streets. Lamentations 2:12 reports that the life of infants is 'poured out on their mothers' bosom'; moreover, the Hebrew word for 'bosom', *heq*, is sometimes used of a fold of garment at the breast, indeed, one might say, a shawl. Such particular echoes lie within a broad narrative shared by the two works, a narrative of a mother's frustrated attempt to preserve her children from a violent and powerful enemy. Whether or not Ozick had Lamentations consciously in mind, readers of these two works encounter expressions of loss and trauma in words and images that witness to a tragic commonality and continuity of human experience.

The twentieth century saw horrors to equal and indeed surpass those of earlier Jewish centuries (recognizing that comparisons are fraught with difficulty – see further on Lam 2:13). The Shoah created for many a situation in which lives cannot be as they were and texts can never again be read in the same way as before. In this post-Shoah era the book of Lamentations has of necessity been read afresh in the light of new horrors, as well as serving yet again in time of tragedy (Ezrahi 1978; Linafelt 1998, 2000b; Sweeney 2008). When reading Lam 1:5 with Jannie Hunter we acknowledged the bi-directional nature of intertextual reading. Reading Ozick's searing narrative in *The Shawl* takes us back to Lamentations with new sensitivities to the human realities and the language of the biblical book, just as readers painfully familiar with the cries and the cannibalism of Lamentations bring to the experience of *The Shawl* powerful memories and echoes of a long-standing and evocative tradition.

2:13 What can I say for you, to what compare you,
O daughter Jerusalem?
To what can I liken you, that I may comfort you,
O virgin daughter Zion?
For vast as the sea is your ruin;
who can heal you?

Beyond Words?

Alan Mintz's *Hurban: Responses to Catastrophe in Hebrew Literature* (1984) is a ground-breaking thematic study of Jewish approaches across the ages to what has been, tragically, a *leitmotif* of Jewish experience: catastrophe. Mintz, a professor of modern Hebrew literature at the Jewish Theological Seminary in New York City, set out to correct an emerging scholarly trend that treated Holocaust literature as a distinct genre, intending to situate it instead within the literary tradition that preceded it and of which it is a part. Mintz soon discovered, however, that the tradition of Jewish literature that responded to catastrophe was rich and complex, demanding consideration in its own right, and not simply as a forerunner of Holocaust literature (Mintz 1984: ix). This discovery greatly affected the final form of the book, which, though in some senses permeated by the Holocaust, has other concerns.

Not surprisingly, the opening chapter of *Hurban* is on Lamentations. Mintz sees Lam 2:13 (above) as one of the most important verses in biblical literature for 'the light it casts on the dilemma of the ancient writer in the face of catastrophe' (28). What drives the poet to desperation, Mintz suggests, is the sheer incommensurability of the disaster. This is because he sees himself called upon not merely to document and memorialize the catastrophe, but also to provide consolation and healing through the vehicle of language. 'To console Zion and heal her', Mintz explains, 'would be to find something with which her ruin can be compared, likened, matched. … What the poet searches for is what we would call metaphors. For he believes that if he could find metaphors adequate to Zion's condition then her anguish could be relieved. [But] the Destruction admits of no comparisons' (29). With these words, Mintz at once crystallizes the poet's task as the poet himself might have defined it, and deftly shifts the spotlight, at least for a moment, from suffering Zion to the anguished writer of the book of Lamentations.

This transformative insight provokes many fresh reflections on the nature of the poet's task when confronting catastrophe, especially concerning the role of comparison. As much as the ancient writer struggled unsuccessfully to find fitting comparisons for Jerusalem's suffering, the modern reader is likely to find that one comparison in particular comes to mind unbidden. In terms of both the magnitude of the catastrophe and the artistic response to it, Lam 2:13 as read in the light of Mintz's interpretation evokes the Shoah. What can and cannot be said about the Shoah, in what context and by whom, have been preoccupations almost from the outset for many of those called to witness, document, memorialize, console and heal. But few writers have expressed the massively complex problem of language and the Shoah more evocatively than the Romanian-Jewish poet, Paul Celan (born Bukovina, Romania, 1920; died Paris, 1970). In an essay written in his characteristically difficult, sometimes almost impenetrable prose, Celan writes about what seems to be, on his account, the Shoah's pre-eminent survivor: language. 'Reachable, near and not lost', Celan writes, 'there remained in the midst of the losses this one thing: language. It, the language, remained, not lost, yes in spite of everything. *But it had to pass through its own answerlessness, pass through frightful muting, pass through the thousand darknesses of deathbringing speech. It passed through and gave back no words for that which happened*, yet it passed through this happening. Passed through and could come to light again, "enriched" by all this' (Celan 2000: 395 [our italics]).

Like Celan, the author of Lamentations found that he had no words capable of encapsulating or categorizing the catastrophe he was facing: 'To what can I liken you, that I may comfort you, O virgin daughter Zion?' (Lam 2:13). And yet … the very verse in which he articulates his feelings of impotence proceeds with a metaphor of the kind he feared himself unable to find: 'For vast as the sea is your ruin.' The author of Lamentations does after all have an answer to the question he has posed: 'To what can I liken you?' He compares the magnitude of Zion's suffering to the apparent infinity of the sea. Mintz reads this verse differently, seeing the sea not as an analog to Zion's suffering, but as an indication that it cannot be quantified: 'In comparing the extent of Zion's ruin to the vastness of the sea, the poet is indicating that the horror of the loss lies not in the absolute quantum of pain it has engendered but in its seeming boundlessness. Because the destruction is unprecedented, its duration and severity have no foreseeable limits; the Destruction is as unfathomable as the ocean's depths and as extensive as its unseen reaches. So when Zion cried in chapter 1, "Is there any agony like mine?" [Lam 1:12] we were meant to take this as … an accurate if frenzied statement of the fundamental problem: the incommensurability of Zion's pains' (29). What Mintz really means, perhaps, is that the Lamentations poet is unable to find another historical event or human experience that is comparable to the destruction of Jerusalem and the suffering it engendered. In this respect, the poet seems to share the sensibilities of many authors of Shoah literature who resist comparisons for fear of compromising the Shoah's unique status. Moreover, it is striking, not to say paradoxical, that Lam 2:13 contains what is arguably the book's most self-consciously 'poetic' image. Even if the sea is not a metaphor for suffering, it entails a kind of crystallization that functions similarly. Almost without exception, the imagery of Lamentations falls into three categories. First, imagery is drawn directly from the poem's physical environment: a ruined city, its impoverished inhabitants, and the world around them. Second, it is derived from the memory of what once was. Third, it emerges from a set of implied contrasts; the image of fine gold (Lam 4:1–2), for example, springs from the broken potsherds, of which it is a natural opposite. One of the few images that does not belong in any of these three categories is the sea in Lam 2:13. The sea was far from Jerusalem; the poet was surely not recalling seaside vacations in happier times; and the sea is not a natural opposite in the manner of fine gold versus potsherds. Alone in Lamentations, the sea comes 'out of the blue' or, better, directly from the poet's imagination. It is a sign that language has indeed, as Celan wrote, 'passed through and come to light again.'

2:14 Your prophets have seen for you
false and deceptive visions;
they have not exposed your iniquity
to restore your fortunes,
but have seen oracles for you
that are false and misleading.

False Prophets and Precious Vessels

In traditional Jewish Bible exegesis such as midrash it is commonplace to support an interpretation of the textual unit that is the primary focus with secondary prooftexts drawn from other parts of the Hebrew Bible. Sometimes it is possible to learn from this arrangement as much about the secondary prooftexts as about the verses that are the primary focus. Such is the case with the interpretation of Deut 1:1 in *K'li Yakar* ('Precious Vessel', an allusion to Prov 20:15), the mainly homiletical Torah commentary of Shlomo Ephraim ben Aaron Luntschitz (born Lenczyk, Poland, 1550; died [probably] Prague, 1619), the head of the yeshiva (rabbinical academy) of Lvov (Lemberg) and a leading rabbi in Prague. Less prolific Jewish commentators such as Luntschitz are often known by the name of one of their commentaries.[2] While Shlomo Ephraim ben Aaron Luntschitz might not be a household name in traditional Jewish circles, the K'li Yakar, the name by which he is known, is widely recognized. His Torah commentary was the last to be included in the *Mikraot Gedolot* ('Great

---

[2]　Others are known by what functions as a last name, e.g. Ibn Ezra (lit. Arabic 'son of Ezra'), or by an acronym consisting of the first letter of their title (Rabbi) and what function as their first and last names, e.g. Rashi (Rabbi Shlomo [ben] Isaac).

Scriptures'), the compendium of commentaries and interpretations that is an important tool in traditional Jewish learning. For reasons that need not concern us here, the K'li Yakar saw in the phrase 'between Paran and Tophel' (Deut. 1:1) – two destinations on Israel's wilderness wanderings – allusions to the spies who entered the land and delivered negative reports about the difficulties entailed in conquering it (Num 13) and to the making of the golden calf when Moses ascended Mount Sinai the first time to receive the ten commandments (Exod 32). In the case of Tophel, the site he identifies with the golden calf incident, the K'li Yakar finds a hint of idolatry in the very name itself. To demonstrate this, he invokes three biblical texts in which a Hebrew word that shares its root letters (*t-f-l*) with (and sounds like) the place name Tophel is mentioned in connection with false prophecy. His prooftexts are Jer 23:13, Lam 2:14 (above) and Ezek 13:10. Although the K'li Yakar is concerned with Deuteronomy, not with Lamentations, we reflect here on Lam 2:14 in the light of its place among the K'li Yakar's three prooftexts, and in the light of the Hebrew word that binds them to each other and to Deut 1:1, namely the root *t-f-l*.

What is wrong with false prophecy? The answer to that question varies from text to text, but the false prophets mentioned in Lam 2:14 are accused of two crimes: seeing false visions and failing to issue rebukes that might have led the people to repent. For a deeper understanding of what the author of this verse had in mind, we might naturally turn to Jeremiah, both because he is traditionally regarded as the author of the book of Lamentations and therefore an authoritative guide, and because false prophecy is an important theme in his book.[3] Yet in this case Jeremiah is not very helpful. Although false prophecy is discussed in Jer 23:13 (the K'li Yakar's prooftext), and although the key root *t-f-l* occurs in this very verse, no explicit information is forthcoming. The *t-f-l* root is not used in Jer 23:13 as a specific characteristic of false prophecy, but merely designates something distasteful (or tasteless), which happens in this case to be false prophecy. A much better guide to the significance of false prophecy in Lam 2:14 can be found in Ezekiel 13, the K'li Yakar's third prooftext, in which the root *t-f-l* is at the very heart of an extended allegory about false prophecy. Ezekiel 13 opens with a rebuke against prophets who roamed like wild jackals in the ruins (cf. Lam 5:18), and did not enter the breaches to repair the wall in readiness for the day of the LORD (Ezek 13:4–5). Instead of mending the cracks, they daub them with plaster or whitewash (*t-f-l*); when God sends rain, and wind and hailstones come, the wall will fall (Ezek 13:10–16). This imagery is picked up again in Ezek 22:28, which speaks of prophets who daub walls with plaster, *t-f-l*, and prophesy falsely, *hozim shav*, precisely the same term

---

[3] *Lamentations Rabbah* does precisely this, interpreting Lam 2:14 in light of a prooftext from Jeremiah.

used in Lam 2:14 (translated above as 'false and deceptive visions'). Ezekiel understands false prophecy as plaster applied ineffectively to a wall that needs serious structural repairs; it looks good for a while, but will be exposed for what it is – whitewash – as soon as the going gets tough.

At first glance, the reference to false prophets in Lam 2:14 seems to be unconnected to its immediate context in the chapter. However, a closer look at the verse through the lens of Ezekiel 13, with its focus on the poorly plastered wall that cannot withstand the elements, shows that Lam 2:14 fits perfectly in its broader context. The central theme of Lamentations 2 is the destruction of the physical city of Zion. God has destroyed its houses and strongholds (Lam 2:2), its palaces and ramparts (Lam 2:5, 8), his own altar and sanctuary (Lam 2:7) and, most significantly for our purposes, its walls (Lam 2:7, 8). Lamentations 2:13 asks who can repair (heal) the ruin of Zion and, as we have seen, Lam 2:14 discounts the prophets, using a word for false prophecy, *t-f-l*, that recalls Ezekiel's prophets who daub plaster, *t-f-l*, on broken walls: 'Your prophets have seen for you false and deceptive visions; they have not exposed your iniquity to restore your fortunes' (Lam 2:14). Finally, Lam 2:18 concludes that Jerusalem itself must beg to be healed: 'Cry aloud to the Lord! O *wall* of daughter Zion!' In the context – suggested by K'li Yakar's three prooftexts linked by the Hebrew root *t-f-l* – of false prophets who cover cracks in walls with plaster (*t-f-l*), this mysterious epithet, 'wall of daughter Zion' (v.18), at last makes sense.

2:15 *All who pass along the way*
clap their hands at you;
they hiss and wag their heads
at daughter Jerusalem;
'Is this the city that was called
perfect in beauty,
the joy of all the earth?'

2:16 *All your enemies*
jeer at you;
they hiss, they gnash their teeth,
they cry: 'We have consumed her!
Ah, this is the day we longed for;
at last we have seen it!'

New Testament Perspectives

Although there are no explicit citations from Lamentations in the New Testament, there are several likely allusions to the book. The language of Lam 1:15, speaking of the Lord treading 'as in a wine press the virgin daughter Judah', appears to have been taken up as an image of the wrath of God in the book of Revelation, both in Rev 14:19–20, 'So the angel swung his sickle over the earth and gathered the vintage of the earth, and he threw it into the great wine press of the wrath of God. And the wine press was trodden outside the city, and blood flowed from the wine press', and in Rev 19:15, ' he will tread the wine press of the fury of the wrath of God the Almighty'. Other possible allusions include one to Lam 3:15, 'He has filled me with bitterness, he has glutted me with wormwood', in Acts 8:23, 'For I see that you are in the gall of bitterness and the chains of wickedness', and another to Lam 3:45, 'You have made us filth and rubbish in the midst of the peoples', in 1 Cor 4:13, 'We have become like the rubbish of the world, the dregs of all things, to this very day' (cf. Webb 2000: 79–80).

More important, however, is the role Lamentations plays in the passion narrative of the gospel of Matthew. A clear allusion to Lam 2:15 (above) is found there in the context of the death of Jesus on the cross. After reference to two bandits being crucified with Jesus, the gospel narrative recounts: 'Those who passed by derided him, shaking their heads' (Matt 27:39). The following verse quotes the taunters thus: 'You who would destroy the temple and build it in three days, save yourself! If you are the Son of God, come down from the cross.' A similar allusion to Lamentations is found in Mark 15:29, but although it is likely that Mark's version is the earlier, the attention of scholars tends to focus on Matthew. This is mainly because another of the widely acknowledged allusions to Lamentations occurs in Matt 23:35 (cf. Luke 11:50–1), where a reference to the shedding of righteous blood 'from the blood of righteous Abel to the blood of Zechariah son of Barachiah' picks up Lam 4:13, which says that the enemy entered the gates of Jerusalem on account of 'the sins of her prophets and the iniquities of her priests, who shed in her midst the blood of the just'. Moffitt (2006) and also Parry (2010: 183–8) explore at length the place of Lamentations in Matthew's passion narrative, in which the themes of the shedding of righteous blood and the destruction of the Temple are brought together. Moffitt writes: 'The allusions to Lamentations function as scriptural warrant for interpreting certain historical events theologically and polemically – namely, for understanding Jesus' crucifixion as the act of righteous bloodshed par excellence that directly results in the destruction of Jerusalem and the temple' (Moffitt 2006: 319).

Matthew's gospel has sometimes been read anachronistically such that notorious later uses of this gospel in anti-Jewish polemic are simply assumed to be in keeping with the original meaning of the text. But Moffitt argues persuasively that Matthew's use of Lamentations suggests that it cannot simply be assumed that his claims are anti-Jewish: it is more likely that Matthew understands himself to be engaging in conversation and polemic within his own Jewish context. Matthew's claim that the death of Jesus at the instigation of the religious leaders led to the Temple's destruction is no more an invective against Judaism than is the similar accusation made in the Targum of Lamentations (see on Lam 5:8). Like Matthew, the Targum links Lamentations with the story of Zechariah's death (see Targum on Lam 2:20) and with the destruction of Jerusalem and its Temple by the Romans (e.g. Targum on Lam 1:19).

To return to Lam 2:15, what of the identity of the mockers who 'pass along the way'? They are presumably the same as the enemies of Lam 2:16, which continues the theme of jeering; but they are not to be taken univocally as a reference to the Babylonians or the Edomites. These taunters are best seen as a rhetorical device, not unlike the chorus in Greek tragedy. It is neither possible nor appropriate to identify these hostile onlookers, who feature as part of the presentation of the depths of Zion's anguish. In psychological terms (on which see on Lam 3:17–18), they may be read as a literary evocation of the projected self-doubt and paranoia that commonly accompany the extremes of human suffering.

[For Lam 2:17 see Lam 2:11–12]

2:18 Cry aloud to the Lord!
O wall of daughter Zion!
Let tears stream down like a torrent
day and night!
Give yourself no rest,
your eyes no respite!

God's Tears

Lamentations Rabbah (see on Lam 1:3; for the Hebrew text see *Lamentations Rabbah* 1876) features numerous *petihtot*, elsewhere usually introductory comments, literally 'openings', to individual midrashim, but here prologues or poems to the collection. Especially significant is a section near the end of the composite twenty-fourth *petihta* (Mintz 1984: 57–62; Linafelt 2000a: 100–16). It falls into two main parts. Typically for the genre, the first midrashic interpretation approaches its main theme via a related text from elsewhere in the Bible, in this case Isa 22:12, in which God instructs Israel to weep and mourn. The midrash reports that God withdrew his Shekhinah, his divine presence, the Temple was destroyed, and 'at that moment the Holy One, blessed be He, wept'. Silent no longer, God at first laments primarily over his own abject state, but gradually the divine pathos broadens out to concern for human victims, especially designated as 'children'. In his study of Lamentations and its afterlife, Linafelt identifies 'children' as Israel in relation to God: 'That is not to say that the lived suffering of 'real' children is of no account to our texts; but rather that this physical suffering was deemed as the appropriate metaphorical vehicle for the tenor of Israel' (Linafelt 2000a: 112).

A major factor in shaping *Lamentations Rabbah* is the need to address 'the … looming "gap" left by the absence of God's voice in the book of Lamentations' (Linafelt 2000a: 104). As Mintz puts it, 'since only victims speak in the text, the appropriation of their discourse means ascribing to God the voices of the very subjects His wrath has made into victims!' (Mintz 1984: 58). As the first midrash continues, the deity tells Jeremiah, understood here to be the author of Lamentations, to summon the patriarchs Abraham, Isaac and Jacob, along with Moses, 'for they know how to weep' (cf. Lam 2:18 above, 'Let tears stream down'). Wailing, the patriarchs and Moses meet God at the gates of the fallen Temple, and the deity joins them in uncontrollable weeping. This is a remarkable scene, not least in its blatant anthropomorphism. God has taken up the posture of the personified Zion of Lamentations, that of mourner (cf. Lam 2:18–19). Shaye Cohen writes that this 'becomes a source of consolation since it is God himself who is reciting the dirges and the laments' (Cohen 1982: 34). The theme of tears in Lamentations and its reception, the tears of Zion, of the world, and ultimately those of God too, have been the subject of a rich secondary literature in recent years (Fonrobert 2001; O'Connor 2002).

In a further section of the *petihta*, a second, longer portion, God is more resistant. In contrast to the first midrash, the deity is largely silent, and when he does speak (with the exception of the climax) he speaks as Israel's accuser. The patriarchs and Moses, as well as the angels, all try in vain to provoke a sympathetic response to Israel's suffering. Abraham refutes the accusations made against Israel by the Torah. In a striking image, skillfully echoing the acrostic pattern of Lamentations, all twenty-two letters of the Hebrew *alef-bet* (alphabet) give testimony against Israel, but these too are rebutted by Abraham. He begs that his own suffering faithfulness be counted in Israel's favor. Still the deity is unyielding. Finally (in what may be a supplement to the *petihta*), it is 'Rachel, our mother' who succeeds in arousing divine compassion. She achieves this success through a combination of two very different strategies. On the one hand, Rachel reasons with God, persuading him by means of an analogy with her own life that he should be capable of overcoming the jealousy that made him angry with Israel in the first place, and that in any case his jealousy was unjustified. She herself had successfully overcome her feelings of jealousy for her sister Leah (who married Jacob at the wedding that should have been hers) and moreover God's rivals, unlike hers, were mere idols, blocks of wood and stone dismissed by God himself as no-gods. On the other hand, adopting a role very similar to that of Zion in Lamentations, Rachel breaks down the deity with renewed pleas about the suffering of her children. The intertextual reference here is to Jer 31:15–16 ('A voice is heard in Ramah, lamentation and bitter weeping. Rachel is weeping for her children'), a biblical verse that would have been assumed to be from the same hand as Lamentations. Yet surely the midrashist has also in mind Lam 2:18–19, for his Rachel embodies the daughter Zion of Lamentations, whose tears stream down, and who pours out her heart like water and lifts up her hands for the lives of her children.

2:19 Arise, cry out in the night,
at the beginning of the watches!
Pour out your heart like water
before the presence of the Lord!
Lift your hands to him
for the lives of your infants,
who faint for hunger
on every street corner.

In Front of the Children

A pioneering study in the reception history of the book of Lamentations is Tod Linafelt's *Surviving Lamentations, Catastrophe, Lament and Protest in the Afterlife of a Biblical Book* (2000a). There is a great deal to be admired in this volume, which ranges from Second Isaiah through Targum, midrash and the medieval laments of Eliezer ben Kallir to Cynthia Ozick. Of particular value, however, is Linafelt's commitment to highlighting apparently unthinking endorsements by other interpreters, especially within the academy, of examples of divine injustice in the biblical text. In the book's second chapter, 'None Survived or Escaped', Linafelt explores the challenging notion that perpetrator and comforter can be one and the same. In this light, he questions an assertion made about Lam 2:19 by the influential biblical scholar Claus Westermann, whose exegesis characteristically combines technical philology of the ancient Hebrew and form criticism with interpretations drawn from Christian theology. For Westermann, Lam 2:19 constitutes a plea for 'God's gracious intervention' (Linafelt 2000a: 55). 'That is surely too benign a characterisation', Linafelt protests. 'The notion of an abused and violated woman turning for help to her abuser, and the one who abused her children, should inspire in the modern reader something less than the notion of gracious intervention' (55).

Linafelt does his best to offer a sympathetic account of Westermann's understanding of lament, specifically his view of Lam 2:19 as 'a stage through which prayer moves on the way back to a restored relationship with God' (55). Yet, as Linafelt points out, there is little in verse 19, or the verses immediately following, to signal what Westermann characterizes as patient waiting for God, still less his ideal of praise. So how can the modern reader better comprehend these verses, reading them with a keen awareness of their ancient context but without suspending all judgment of their underlying values? In order to answer this question, Linafelt focuses on their references to children. Children are first mentioned in Lam 1:5, which NRSV translates 'her children have gone away', but is better rendered by NJPS as 'Infants have gone into captivity'. The Hebrew term for 'infants' in that verse is *olal*, which, as Linafelt points out, shares a root with *alal*, to 'afflict' or 'abuse'. The same term for children (*olal*) occurs in Lam 2:19, and both verb and noun appear in Lam 2:20: 'Look, O LORD, and consider! To whom have you done (*olalta*) this? Should women eat their offspring, their new-born babes (*olalei*)?' The poet has constructed a powerful and yet appropriately subtle mechanism for confronting God with his own injustice. Not only do the children serve through their innocence as silent accusers, but the very term used to describe them reminds God that he is the author of their suffering. Because of the afflictions imposed by God upon their mothers, children are starving and dying on the streets.

To return to Lam 2:19, the lifting up of hands is a classic act of intercession (see on Lam 3:41). If Linafelt is correct, however (and his case is highly plausible), a much more powerful intercessory motif in this verse is its graphic image of children fainting from hunger in the streets. A comparison with Shakespeare's *Coriolanus* is instructive. Coriolanus has resolved to kill his family. They come before him, hoping to convince him to change his mind. No words are required; the montage itself is calculated to affect. Although no death has yet occurred, all are dressed in mourning clothes, the assembled generations of a single family, Coriolanus's own.

Enter in mourning habits, Virgilian, Volumnia, leading young Marcius, Valeria, and Attendants[4]

> My wife comes foremost; then the honour'd mould
> Wherein this trunk was framed, and in her hand
> The grandchild to her blood. But, out, affection!
> All bond and privilege of nature, break!
> Let it be virtuous to be obstinate.
> What is that curt'sy worth? Or those dove's eyes,
> Which can make gods forsworn? I melt, and am not
> Of stronger earth than others. My mother bows;
> As if Olympus to a molehill should
> In supplication nod: and my young boy
> Hath an aspect of intercession, which
> Great nature cries 'Deny not.'

---

[4] Shakespeare, *Coriolanus* V.iii.

In Coriolanus's case, the attempt to evoke compassion, represented at its most intense by his young son's 'aspect of intercession', fails. He steels himself to act as if he had no family:

> Let the Volsces
> Plough Rome and harrow Italy: I'll never
> Be such a gosling to obey instinct, but stand
> As if a man were author of himself
> And knew no other kin.

In God's case, the author of Lamentations held out hope that intercession would provoke divine compassion. Confronted not just with God's children in general, the children of Israel as it were, but with real children, infants at the breast and toddlers (the ancient Israelite equivalent of Coriolanus's young son), surely God would act to end their innocent suffering? Linafelt spells out what is problematic, from a modern, psychologically informed perspective, when victims appeal for comfort to the perpetrators of the violence committed against them. He emphasizes the danger of formulating 'too benign a characterization' of the perpetrator and rushing on to resolution and hope. Focusing on dramatic intercession involving young children, the innocent victims par excellence, by no means solves the moral problems that Linafelt raises, but it shifts the balance in the relationship between victim and perpetrator. Read in this way, the author of Lamentations is not merely seeking comfort, and he is certainly not turning a blind eye to injustices perpetrated. Rather, he is highlighting them through graphic representation in the hope that their perpetrator will bring the cycle of violence and injustice to an end.

2:20 Look, O Lord, and consider!
To whom have you done this?
Should women eat their offspring,
their new-born babes?
Should priest and prophet be killed
in the sanctuary of the Lord?

Slave Trading

André Schwarz-Bart (born Metz, France, 1928; died Guadeloupe, 2006) was a French-Jewish novelist born to Polish-Jewish parents who were deported to Auschwitz in 1941. Schwarz-Bart's parents and two brothers died in the Shoah, but he joined the resistance fighters in France, and miraculously survived. He spent his last years in Guadeloupe, the home of his wife Simone, a successful writer with whom he collaborated late in his career. His best-known work is the monumental novel *The Last of the Just* (Schwarz-Bart 2001; published first in French as *Le Dernier des Justes,*1959), which appeared to great acclaim and won the prestigious French literary award, the *Prix Goncourt*. *The Last of the Just* follows a Jewish family from Clifford's Tower, York, in the year 1190 to the crematoria of Auschwitz. *A Woman Named Solitude* (Schwarz-Bart 2002; published first in French as *La Mulâtresse Solitude*, 1972) follows a small group of slaves from West Africa to the Caribbean in the mid-eighteenth century. Schwarz-Bart has shifted his attention from one persecuted group to another, from victims of the Shoah to victims of the slave trade. This change of focus reflected the author's own life changes – a move from France under the shadow of the Shoah to the Antilles where signs of the slave trade still remained. It must also be understood in the context of a planned project between Schwarz-Bart and his wife to write a fictionalized history of the experiences of diaspora Jews on the one hand and diaspora Africans on the other.

Setting aside the personal considerations that presumably drew André and Simone Schwarz-Bart to the project, one might identify possible structural problems with such a project, regardless of the good intentions they no doubt had. Is this, for example, a case of the suffering of a woman of color from Africa that becomes visible only when juxtaposed with the suffering of a white European man? Must all suffering be classified in relation to the Shoah? Does the juxtaposition of the Shoah and the slave trade compromise the unique suffering entailed by both? These are the kinds of questions that always arise when separate catastrophes are brought together, but all the more so when race and gender are part of the equation, as here. (On that point, it is worth noting that the original French title, *La Mulâtresse Solitude*, draws attention to the race element with the term 'mulatto' or 'half-breed'.) Does Lamentations, an account of catastrophe with a strong gender element even if race is not an issue (though see discussion at Lam 5:8, 10), also suffer when it is used as a blueprint for other catastrophes, as has so often occurred? Is the woman's voice in Lamentations eclipsed, for example, or some aspect of her unique identity lost through comparison?

Solitude, the eponymous heroine of Schwarz-Bart's novel, is based on a historical figure of the same name, who played an active role in a rebellion against the owners of the plantation where she was a slave. The novel describes her birth on the slave ship that had just left the city where Bayangumay, her mother, was born free: 'When Bayangumay was born, the big city on the river, a place of shade and quiet luxury, still bore the name of Sigi, which means, Sit down. But then it became a slave port and was given the name of Sigi-Thyor: Sit down and weep' (32). Perhaps the resonances were unintended, but it is hard to read this description of Sigi-Thyor without thinking of the opening verses of Lamentations: 'How lonely sits the city that once was full of people! … She weeps bitterly in the night' (Lam 1:1–2). At first, Sigi's inhabitants have no direct contact with their white oppressors and can only imagine them: 'The common people said the whites fed on human flesh; the sages believed they offered it up to their gods' (32). Soon after the slave traders finally arrive in the city, Bayangumay has a dream about the death of her husband:

> In this nightmare that knew itself for a nightmare, she saw her aged husband standing naked in the middle of the hut, his spear upraised and his mouth open in a cry of horror, while with his free hand he hid the shame of his sexual parts. Then came a shattering sound like the crack of thunder in the dry season, when the sky cracks like a kernel of maize in the coals. Falling down on his knees, old Dyadyu thrust his spear forward and lay down on the ground to sleep, resting his head on the crook of his elbow, as men do by the fireside after days of plowing, sowing, circumcision, marriage or funeral, when everything that was to be done has been done. She decided to say nothing, to tell no-one of this dream, for she knew she did not really desire her husband's death: The plowing would soon be over and she would be able to see Komobo [her younger lover]; so why such a dream at such a time? (33)

The dream scene shares many motifs and images with the book of Lamentations, especially Lam 2:20–2, where a reference to cannibalism is likewise juxtaposed with images of swords (cf. spears in the novel), men lying prostrate on the ground, and a nod at normality with the mention of the festival day (cf. the novel's circumcision, marriage or funeral). It is not clear whether or not the similarities were intentional, but reading Lamentations through Schwarz-Bart's lens reveals a surprise in the biblical text. It is commonplace that both invaders and invaded in conquest narratives see each other as cannibals. Eating babies is an activity often attributed to the unknown or poorly understood, to the 'other', as is the case in *A Woman Named Solitude*. Lamentations, however, turns this motif upside down. Its accounts of mothers who eat their own babies cannot be dismissed as naive (or even knowing) xenophobia. The women who eat babies are far from being aliens. In this case, at least, the decision to read Lamentations alongside a novel about the slave trade seen through the lens of the Shoah by no means compromises the uniqueness of the catastrophe of the destruction of Zion. On the contrary, it reveals a unique feature of Lamentations that might otherwise be overlooked. For once it is not representatives of the 'other' that engage in sub-humanlike behavior. It is rather the ultimate insiders – the mothers and daughters of Zion.

2:21 *The young and the old are lying*
on the ground in the streets;
my young women and my young men
have fallen by the sword;
on the day of your anger you have killed them,
slaughtering without mercy.

Backchat

Sharon Moughtin-Mumby explores sexual and marital metaphors in the Bible's prophetic books, focusing on Hosea, Jer 2:1–4:4, Ezekiel 16 and 23, and selected texts in Isaiah (Moughtin-Mumby 2008). She demonstrates the diversity of such language and imagery in the prophetic books and aims to read it within the distinctive and specific literary frames in which it appears in the books themselves, rather than within the generalizing 'default frame' of some supposedly unified 'marriage metaphor'. She contends that 'the emphasis of these narratives is on the message they strive to convey, not on an abstract, hypothetical background story of *the* relationship between YHWH and the city/nation' (159).

We have seen that the personification of Zion as a woman characterizes the first two chapters of Lamentations (see on Lam 1:1). How, if at all, does this language relate to the sexual and marital metaphors in the prophetic books? This is the question directly addressed in Carleen Mandolfo's book *Daughter Zion Talks Back to the Prophets* (Mandolfo 2007). She develops (in the words of her sub-title) a 'Dialogic Theology' of the book of Lamentations, drawing upon the influence of the philosophies of Mikhail Bakhtin and Martin Buber, as well as upon feminist and postcolonial insights. Mandolfo focuses on selected prophetic texts that utilize metaphorical language to offer an account of the relationship between God and Israel from the 'husband's' perspective, and on the first two chapters of Lamentations, in which the 'wife' talks back. In these two chapters, daughter Zion enters into assertive dialogue and finds her voice, described by Mandolfo as 'the Bible's most intrepid female voice of resistance' (Mandolfo 2007: 85), over against the dominant voice of prophetic ideology. Zion, Mandolfo contends (self-critically acknowledging her own role in the reading process), crafts 'a counterstory that resists the myopic identity in which God and his prophets have confined her' (27). (For a valuable concurrent but independent study of Lamentations and the prophets that makes similar use of Bakhtin's dialogic philosophy, see Boase 2006.)

Putting flesh on these insights, Mandolfo offers a series of intertextual readings between the prophets (especially Jeremiah and Ezekiel) and Lamentations 1–2, showing how the woman reconfigures the prophets' words to construct a discourse that better reflects her experiences from her own point of view. For example, in contrast to the marital imagery of Jeremiah 2, in which God addresses the people Israel as his wife and indicts them/her for being unfaithful to him, Mandolfo highlights how in Lamentations, in phrases such as 'my young men' and 'my children', Zion constructs for herself the role of bereft mother rather than that of villainous wife: 'The LORD … has proclaimed a time against me to crush my young men; … my children are desolate, for the enemy has prevailed' (Lam 1:15–16). And whereas Ezekiel 16 accuses Jerusalem of compounding her adultery with the sin of infanticide (Ezek 16:21, 'You slaughtered my children and delivered them up as an offering to them'), in Lamentations, Zion throws back at the deity the charge made against her through the mouth of Ezekiel, suggesting that God himself is sacrificing the children in order to serve the festival day that he has called: 'my young women and my young men have fallen by the sword; on the day of your anger you have killed them, slaughtering without mercy' (Lam 2:21), and again: 'You summoned my enemies from all around as if for a festival day; and on the day of the anger of the LORD no one escaped or survived; those whom I bore and reared my enemy has consumed' (Lam 2:22). In such ways as these, daughter Zion of Lamentations 1–2 will not leave the claims of God settled or unchallenged but rather rejects the portrait painted of her in the prophets. It is interesting to note that whereas Deryn Guest advocates the removal of Lamentations from the biblical canon (see on Lam 1:1), Mandolfo, though in many ways adopting a very radical stance, writes: 'rather than expunge, whitewash, or ignore the "dangerous" books as some are wont to do (not least some feminist critics) … rather, let us embrace and resist, rejoice and weep with, and, mostly, listen respectfully to what these voices have to say for themselves' (Mandolfo 2007: 128).

²·²² *You invited my enemies from all around*
as if for a day of festival;
and on the day of the anger of the LORD
no one escaped or survived;
those whom I bore and reared
my enemy has destroyed.

History Repeats Itself

Our main source of information about the destruction of the second Temple in 70 CE is the writing of Flavius Josephus (born Judaea, 37 CE; died *c*.100). Josephus, who descended from an aristocratic priestly family, famously changed sides in the Roman–Jewish war, initially fighting with the Jewish resistance and later advocating collaboration with the Romans. He accepted imperial patronage and Roman citizenship from a Roman emperor, which was reflected in the procedure, normal at the time, of adding the name of the emperor, Titus Flavius Vespasian, to his own. For reasons including the language in which the works of Josephus were written (Greek) and transmitted (Greek and Latin), his cultural affiliation (Hellenistic), and his political identity (favorable to Roman rule), Josephus's writings were not transmitted internally in traditional Jewish contexts such as synagogues and academies. They are, however, the source of such compelling and influential – though in some cases misleading – images as the Jewish mass suicide at Masada and the triumphant Roman procession from Jerusalem, submissive Jewish captives and despoiled Temple treasures in tow (the scene visualized on the Arch of Titus in Rome). Not surprisingly, Josephus's account in *The Jewish War* of the Roman destruction of the second Temple echoes in various ways the description of the destruction of the first Temple in Lamentations. To be sure, he was in or near to Jerusalem at the time, and could therefore offer an eye-witness or at least reliable account that did not depend on biblical language and imagery. And yet the close parallels between the two events, and the Jewish inclination to interpret historical events typologically, would surely have drawn Josephus to the account in Lamentations of the first destruction when constructing his own account of the second. The influence of the biblical book seems particularly evident when Josephus negotiates between the competing factors – for example, history versus theology, objective observer versus involved participant, and self-blame versus blaming others – that drive his investigation of the causes, events and aftermath of the fall of Jerusalem. All these tensions emerge in a personal lament at the end of his account of the bloodbath in the Temple following Roman invasion (*The Jewish War* 5.11–20):

> Unhappy city! what have you suffered from the Romans to compare to this [cf. Lam 1:12]? They entered your gates to purge with fire the filthiness within you: you were no longer the place of God; you could not continue, now that you were the burial place of your own sons and could turn the Temple into a common grave for those who had slain each other. Even now you might be restored to life, if only you would make atonement to God, who destroyed you! But even the deepest emotions must be stifled in obedience to the laws of history: this is not the time for private lamentation but for a record of the facts. (*The Jewish War*, 5.19–20)

Although Josephus identifies the Romans as the perpetrators of the violence against the Jews, he makes it clear that they were agents of God. God, not the human enemy, is the real author of destruction. In Josephus's case, it can be argued that this perspective was in keeping with his political agenda. Since he was urging his fellow Jews to cooperate with Rome, it suited him to emphasize that they were acting according to divine will and not in the service of their own interests. But Josephus did not, of course, invent this presentation of a political aggressor with whom a case could be made for collaboration. The same historical/theological combination of causes and explanations is widespread in biblical and post-biblical Jewish literature, especially in relation to the Babylonian exile. Indeed, it finds one of its clearest expressions in the book of Lamentations with regard to the destruction of Jerusalem and the Temple, precisely the matters that concerned Josephus. It seems plausible that, in addition to his own political inclinations and agendas, Josephus had in mind such verses as Lam 2:22 (above) when he wrote in *The Jewish War* about the enemies who entered Jerusalem at God's invitation, and of the divine anger that would have to be appeased. Yet there is at least one significant difference between Lamentations and Josephus in this regard. Whereas the author of Lam 2:22 and other verses like it moves seamlessly between historical and theological causes, that is to say, between human and divine assailants, Josephus offers a more analytical presentation of the causes of Jewish suffering. This difference may be attributed to the contrast between poetry, the genre of Lamentations on the one hand, and Josephus's historical narrative on the other, or perhaps to the distinction between the, in some ways, non-historical or a-historical perspective of Lamentations and Josephus's highly developed sensibilities as a historian (see *The Jewish War* 1.1–12, where he discusses, in detail, the rules of the profession, the historian's need to retain a neutral position and present both sides of the conflict, and the importance of not allowing personal feelings and loyalties to cloud the historical facts).

Whatever the reason for the difference, his more nuanced outlook allows Josephus to articulate an idea that is not at all evident in Lamentations: the role of internal conflict within the Jewish community. With the exception of the syntactically difficult Lam 4:13–16 (see Hillers 1992: 141–4), which refers to priests, prophets and elders, Lamentations avoids singling out any group for special criticism. And even Lam 4:13–16 is far removed in spirit from the political analysis of Josephus, which blames the catastrophe on Jewish in-fighting. To be sure, there was no civil war in the period leading to the destruction of the first Temple, but there were certainly factions and groups representing different attitudes towards the Babylonians, not to mention the tensions between those who were exiled and those who stayed. Reading the biblical book in the light of Josephus highlights both the striking absence of references to such internal conflict in Lamentations and its unswerving insistence on collective guilt as opposed to the guilt of a particular faction.

References

Bahrani, Z. 2008. *Rituals of War: The Body and Violence in Mesopotamia* (New York: Zone; Cambridge, MA: MIT).

Boase, E. 2006. *The Fulfilment of Doom? The Dialogic Interaction between the Book of Lamentations and the Pre-Exilic/Early Exilic Prophetic Literature* (LHBOTS, 437; New York and London: T. & T. Clark).

Brooks, T. 1670. *London's Lamentations, or, A serious discourse concerning that late fiery dispensation that turned our (once renowned) city into a ruinous heap* (London: Printed for John Hancock and Nathaniel Ponder).

Celan, P. 2000. *Selected Poems and Prose of Paul Celan* (ed J. Felstiner; New York: W. W. Norton).

Cohen, M. E. 1988. *The Canonical Lamentations of Ancient Mesopotamia* (2 vols; Potomac, MD: Capital Decisions Limited).

Cohen, S. J. D. 1982. 'The Destruction: From Scripture to Midrash', *Prooftexts: A Journal of Jewish Liturgy* 2: 18–39.

Dobbs-Allsopp, F. W. 1993. *Weep, O Daughter of Zion: A Study of the City-Lament Genre in the Hebrew Bible* (Biblica et Orientalia, 44; Rome: Editrice Pontificio Instituto Biblico).

Evelyn, J. 2006. *The Diary of John Evelyn* (ed E. S. De Beer; selected and introduced by R. Strong; London: Everyman).

Ezrahi, S. D. 1978. 'The Holocaust Writer and the Lamentation Tradition: Responses to Catastrophe in Jewish Literature', in *Confronting the Holocaust: The Impact of Elie Wiesel* (ed A. H. Rosenfeld and I. Greenberg; Bloomington Indiana University Press) 133–49.

Fonrobert, C. E. 2001. 'When the Rabbi Weeps: On Reading Gender in Talmudic Aggadah', in *Nashim: A Journal of Jewish Women's Studies and Gender Issues* 4: 56–84.

Hillers, D. R. 1992. *Lamentations* (Anchor Bible, 7a; Garden City, NY: Doubleday, 2nd edn).

Jacobsen, T. 1976. *The Treasures of Darkness: A History of Mesopotamian Religion* (New Haven, CT: Yale).

Josephus, 1970. *The Jewish War* (trans. by G. A. Williamson; Penguin Classics; Harmondsworth: Penguin; rev. edn).

Lamentations Rabbah. 1876. *Lamentations Rabbah*, in *Midrash Rabbah, on the Five Books of Moses and the Five Megillot with Many Commentaries* (Standard Hebrew ed; 3 vols; Vilna).

Linafelt, T. 1998. 'The Impossibility of Mourning: Lamentations after the Holocaust', in *God in the Fray: A Tribute to Walter Brueggemann* (ed T. Linafelt and T. K. Beal; Minneapolis, MN: Fortress) 279–89.

Linafelt, T. 2000a. *Surviving Lamentations: Catastrophe, Lament, and Protest in the Afterlife of a Biblical Book* (Chicago and London: University of Chicago Press).

Linafelt, T. 2000b. 'Zion's Cause: The Presentation of Pain in the Book of Lamentations', in *Strange Fire: Reading the Bible after the Holocaust* (ed. T. Linafelt; Biblical Seminar, 71; Sheffield: Sheffield Academic Press; New York: New York University Press) 267–79.

Mandolfo, C. R. 2007. *Daughter Zion Talks Back to the Prophets: A Dialogic Theology of the Book of Lamentations* (Semeia Studies, 58; Atlanta, GA: SBL).

Mintz, A. 1984. *Hurban: Responses to Catastrophe in Hebrew Literature* (New York: Columbia University Press).

Moffitt, D. M. 2006. 'Righteous Bloodshed, Matthew's Passion Narrative, and the Temple's Destruction: Lamentations as a Matthean Intertext', *JBL* 125: 299–320.

Moughtin-Mumby, S. R. 2008. *Sexual and Marital Metaphors in Hosea, Jeremiah, Isaiah, and Ezekiel* (Oxford Theological Monographs; Oxford: Oxford University Press).

O'Connor, K. M. 2002. *Lamentations and the Tears of the World* (Maryknoll, NY: Orbis).

Odell, M. S. and J. T. Strong (eds). 2000. *The Book of Ezekiel: Theological and Anthropological Perspectives* (SBL Symposium Series, 9; Atlanta, GA: SBL).

Ozick, C. 1990. *The Shawl* (New York: Vintage).

Parry, R. A. 2010. *Lamentations* (Two Horizons Old Testament Commentary; Grand Rapids, MI, and Cambridge: Eerdmans).

Pepys, S. 2000. *The Diary of Samuel Pepys: a New and Complete Transcription* (ed. R. Latham and W. Matthews; 11 vols; London: HarperCollins).

Roskies, D. G. (ed). 1989. *The Literature of Destruction: Jewish Responses to Catastrophe* (Philadelphia, PA: Jewish Publication Society).

Schwarz-Bart, A. 2001. *The Last of the Just* (London: Vintage). (First published in French as *Le Dernier des Justes: Roman*, Paris: Éditions de Seuil, 1959.)

Schwarz-Bart, A. 2002. *A Woman Named Solitude* (London: Vintage). (First published in French as *La Mulâtresse Solitude: Roman*, Paris: Éditions de Seuil, 1972.)

Stillingfleet, E. 1666. *A Sermon Preached before the Honourable House of Commons at St. Margarets Westminster, Octob. 10 1666. Being the Fast-Day Appointed for the Late Dreadfull Fire in the City of London* (London: Printed by Robert White for Henry Mortlock).

Sweeney, M. A. 2008. *Reading the Hebrew Bible After the Shoah: Engaging Holocaust Theology* (Minneapolis, MN: Fortress).

Webb, B. G. 2000. *Five Festal Garments: Christian Reflections on the Song of Songs, Ruth, Lamentations, Ecclesiastes and Esther* (New Studies in Biblical Theology, 10; Leicester: Apollos).

> [3:1] *I am the man who has seen affliction under the rod of God's wrath.*
>
> [[3:3] *Against me alone he turns his hand, again and again, all day long.*]

Christological Lamentations

After two chapters in which personified Zion has taken center-stage, presented variously in the third, second or first person, the central chapter marks a departure in several respects. As in Chapters 1 and 2, an acrostic pattern is followed but this time there are three short verses for each of the twenty-two letters of the Hebrew alphabet, the *alef-bet* (See on Lam 1:1). And the chapter is voiced consistently in the first person (generally singular, with the exception of vv. 40–7, which employ the first-person plural), very much in the style of the

Lamentations Through the Centuries, First Edition. Paul M. Joyce and Diana Lipton.
© 2013 Paul M. Joyce and Diana Lipton. Published 2020 by John Wiley & Sons Ltd.

individual laments of the book of Psalms (see on Lam 5:1–5, 17, 20). The Hebrew of verse 1 begins *ani ha-gever*, 'I am the man …'. Some translations eclipse the speaker's gender in the pursuit of a more inclusive presentation (see, for example, the NRSV's 'I am the one'). But this is indeed a male figure, in contrast to the female Zion of Chapters 1 and 2, and the text is flattened when this distinction is blurred. The word *gever* is one of several Hebrew terms for 'man', and is often related to the notion of strength. The choice of the word may be intended to present the paradox of a strong person brought low in weakness (exemplifying reversal of fortune, a recurrent motif of the book; cf. Lam 1:1, 'The princess among the provinces has become a vassal'; Lam 4:5, 'those who were brought up in purple cling to ash heaps'). The quest for the identity of this figure has given rise to a wide range of interpretations (see Hillers 1992: 120–3 for a survey). Many exegetes have found a collective 'I', representing Zion (e.g. Albrektson 1963) or 'Everyman' (e.g. Kraus 1968), while others have identified the speaker with a specific individual, such as Jeremiah (e.g. Rudolph 1962) or the deposed king Jehoiachin (e.g. Porteous 1961).[1]

Patristic interpretation, the writings of the early Fathers of the Christian Church, features two main lines of thought about this figure. One of these patristic approaches relates to prophecy of the sufferings of Christ, and the other to the spiritual formation of the Church (Parry and Thomas 2011: 113–19). It is perhaps not surprising that from early times Christian Fathers found here an anticipation of the sufferings of Christ. For example, Irenaeus (born Izmir, Turkey, second century; died Lyons, France, *c*.202) links the experience of the suffering man in Lamentations 3 with the passion. He reads Lam 3:30, 'to give his cheek to the smiter, and be filled with insults', accordingly, combining this passage with texts from Isaiah (*Demonstration of the Apostolic Preaching*, para. 68, 129–30).[2] Later, in the fourth century, Rufinus (born Concordia, Italy, *c*.345; died Sicily, 410) read Lam 3:53 as a reference to the burial of Jesus. The NRSV is typical of modern translations in offering 'they flung me alive into a pit and hurled stones on me', but the Hebrew has *even*, 'stone', in the singular, as does the Latin, on which basis Rufinus interprets as 'they laid a stone upon me' (*Commentary on the Apostles' Creed*, para. 70, 131–2). The other patristic trend, focusing not on the death of Christ but rather on the growth of the Christian Church, is well exemplified in *Moralia in Job*, an influential work written between 578 and 595 by Pope Gregory the Great (born Rome, *c*.540; died Rome, 604), in which he employs the text as a vehicle for the Church's spiritual formation.

---

[1]   On parallels with the 'Suffering Servant' figure in Isaiah, see commentary section on Lam 1:17, addressing the relationship between Lamentations and Isaiah 40–55.

[2]   A selection of the main patristic materials on Lamentations is accessibly presented in Wenthe 2009.

Gregory interprets Lam 3:1 as a reference to the pain experienced by Jeremiah (conceived by Pope Gregory as the author of Lamentations) over the need to let go of the present life in order to gain the riches of the heavenly kingdom. The word commonly translated 'affliction' in English is understood as 'poverty' by Gregory, following Jerome's Latin: 'I am the man who sees my poverty'. Gregory appears to have in mind human awareness of spiritual shortcomings, understood as attachment to the things of this life (*Moralia in Job*, vol. 3, part 2, 622).

In a commentary that seeks to bridge the gap between biblical scholarship and Christian systematic theology, Robin Parry develops his own Christian typological reading of this chapter of Lamentations, building on patristic inter- pretation but sensitive to issues relating to Christian supersessionism (Parry 2010: 185–6). While acknowledging that the human figure in Lamentations 3 is not presented as a savior who dies to rescue an oppressed people, Parry argues that the connection between the man's suffering and the suffering of Jerusalem is much like the link between Jesus' death and the destruction of the holy city; in each case the man embodies in his own life-story the divine judgment. Parry also proposes an imaginative reading of Lam 3:1–18 as Christ's own prayer, as a way of enriching the Christian's understanding of the depths of Jesus' despair and his solidarity with suffering humanity. At the same time, by rendering the *gever* figure accessible and religiously relevant to Christians, Parry enhances their experience of the book of Lamentations.

The Soul's Dark Night

Juan de Yepes Álvarez (born near Ávila, Spain, 1542; died Ubeda, Spain, 1591) came from a Jewish *converso* family, that is, one that had converted from Judaism to Christianity before the expulsion of the Jews from Spain in 1492. He became a priest of the Carmelite order, which he reformed together with Teresa of Ávila. As a reformer and a mystic, he was eventually canonized as St John of the Cross. He is considered one of the foremost poets in the Spanish language. His allegorical poem 'The Dark Night of the Soul' ('Dark Night'), to which he provides his own commentary in a treatise bearing the same name, narrates the journey of the soul to its union with God (John of the Cross 1976; Kavanaugh and Rodriguez 1991; Thompson 2002). The night represents the hardships and difficulties the soul meets as it detaches from the world and reaches for the light of union with the Creator. The work is divided into two books reflecting the two phases of the dark night. The first phase is a purification of the senses; the second and more intense is that of the purification of the spirit.

A key biblical text for John is Lamentations 3, with its opening words, 'I am the man who has seen affliction under the rod of God's wrath' (v. 1). John makes much of this passage in Chapters 7 and 8 of Book 2 of 'Dark Night'. In Chapter 7 he laments: 'So many and so grievous are the afflictions of this night, and so many passages of Scripture are there which could be cited to this purpose, that time and strength would fail us to write of them.'[3] And so he decides: 'I shall tell what Jeremiah [regarded by John as the author of Lamentations] felt about it, which, since there is so much of it, he describes and bewails in many words after this manner ...'. He then quotes Lam 3:1–20 in full. The passage lends itself superbly to John's task, not least because it is followed almost immediately in Lamentations by the words 'The steadfast love of the LORD never ceases, his mercies are never spent; they are renewed every morning; great is your faithfulness' (Lam 3:22–3). Moreover, his purpose is helped by the fact that the sufferer in Lamentations 3 is an individual, as is the voyager of the 'dark night of the soul' in the mystic's theology. As John comments: 'All these complaints Jeremiah makes about these pains and trials, and by means of them he most vividly depicts the sufferings of the soul in this spiritual night and purgation. Wherefore the soul that God sets in this tempestuous and horrible night is deserving of great compassion.' Indeed, the outcome of the soul's journey is far from assured, on account of 'the dreadful pain which the soul is suffering, and of the great uncertainty which it has concerning the remedy for it, since it believes, as this prophet says here, that its evil will never end'.

An important passage of Chapter 8 of Book 2 of 'Dark Night' elaborates the picture, with frequent citation from and allusion to Lamentations 3:

> But there is another thing here that afflicts and distresses the soul greatly, which is that, as this dark night has hindered its faculties and affections in this way, it is unable to raise its affection or its mind to God, neither can it pray to him, thinking, as Jeremiah thought concerning himself, that God has set a cloud before it through which its prayer cannot pass [Lam 3:44]. For it is this that is meant by that which is said in the passage referred to, namely: 'He hath shut and enclosed my paths with square stones' [Lam 3:9]. And if it sometimes prays it does so with such lack of strength and of sweetness that it thinks that God neither hears it nor pays heed to it, as this Prophet likewise declares in the same passage, saying: 'When I cry and entreat, He hath shut out my prayer' [Lam 3:8]. In truth this is no time for the soul to speak with God; it should rather put its mouth in the dust, as Jeremiah says [Lam 3:29], so that perchance there may come to it some present hope and it may endure its purgation with patience.

Chapter 8 explains that the human state of inertia is the cover for divine activity: 'It is God who is passively working here in the soul; wherefore the soul can do nothing. Hence it can neither pray nor pay attention when it is present at the

---

[3]   Translations are those of E. Allison Peers in John of the Cross 1976.

divine offices, much less can it attend to other things and affairs which are temporal. Not only so, but it has likewise such distractions and times of such profound forgetfulness of the memory that frequent periods pass by without its knowing what it has been doing or thinking, or what it is that it is doing or is going to do, neither can it pay attention, although it desires to do so, to anything that occupies it.' ('Dark Night', Book 2, ch. 8.)

In such ways, with considerable pastoral and psychological insight, John interacts with the text of Lamentations 3 as he expounds the human experience of alienation from God, indeed victimization by God, accompanying this with a far-from-facile affirmation that, though the voyager can neither see nor believe it, God is at work in his travails. One turns from the Spanish mystic back to the Judahite poet with sensitivities newly attuned to the struggles of 'the man who has seen affliction under the rod of God's wrath'.

^{3:2} *He has driven and brought me*
into darkness without any light.

Festivals of Darkness and Light

Asked about religious observance, American Jewish teenagers from non-observant families are likely to claim first-hand experience of two Jewish festivals: Chanukah, the eight-day 'festival of lights' commemorating the rededication of the second Temple after the Maccabean revolt in 165 BCE, and Tisha B'Av. What attracts American teenagers to the Temple? Sadly, nothing. These festivals and fast days are familiar not because of their underlying religious or historical significance, but because of their timing. Chanukah falls every year at around the same time of year as Christmas. Its celebration is therefore widely encouraged by Jewish parents hoping to preserve their children from Christmas envy, hence the proliferation of Chanukah greeting cards, gift-giving, themed wrapping paper, gaudy decorations, catchy songs and chocolate coins. Tisha B'Av falls each year in July or August, and thus becomes a focus of activity at that great American institution, the Jewish summer camp. Even camps intended for Jewish children whose identification is more cultural than religious encourage restraint and somber reflection on Tisha B'Av, supplemented by programs on environmental destruction or contemporary catastrophe in Sudan or Haiti. Commenting on the Chanukah/Tisha B'Av phenomenon, a 2004 news report ('Tisha B'Av: remembering darkness') explains how Sharon Brous, a rabbi in Los Angeles, makes something spiritually significant out of a cultural coincidence. Tisha B'Av is the inverse of Chanukah: 'At the moment of light [mid-summer, when Tisha B'Av is observed], we have to remember darkness, and at the moment of darkness [mid-winter, when Chanukah is celebrated], we have to remember light ... Ultimately, Tisha B'Av is about emerging from the darkness into something much more whole.'

Whether or not she intended it, Sharon Brous's focus on light and darkness illuminates Lam 3:2, a verse that has been a stumbling block for more than one translator. According to NJPS, 'the man who has known affliction' (v. 1) walks in 'unrelieved darkness', while the NRSV has the afflicted person led 'in darkness without any light'. Literally translated, he is made to walk 'in darkness and not light', a formulation that seems at first glance tautologous. Once it has been established that the man walks in darkness, why was it necessary to add, 'and not light'? Read in the light of Sharon Brous's comment, we can see that far from being based on a pointless tautology, this formulation evokes a crucial contrast with considerable theological freight. On the one hand, the verse may be read as looking backwards; where now there is darkness, there was formerly light. On this reading, the afflicted man's darkness is rendered all the more impenetrable by the reminder that he once knew light. On the other hand, the verse may be read as looking forwards. On this reading, the reference to light may be taken as a hint that the afflicted man's darkness will end in the future, thus anticipating the chapter's (and even the entire book's) turning point: 'But this I call to mind ...' (Lam 3:21). When mentioned in isolation, darkness may be interminable and, worse still, empty. When mentioned in the context of light, darkness is purposeful. Not only do those suffering have the potential to emerge stronger, as Sharon Brous suggests, but, as is hinted by our verse (literally 'me he led and brought') in its wider literary context, the sufferers are being actively guided towards the light even as they appear to stumble in the dark.

³:⁴ *He has worn away my flesh and my skin,*
and shattered my bones;
³:⁵ *he has besieged and enveloped me*
with bitterness and hardship;
³:⁶ *he has made me sit in darkness*
like those long dead.

She'll Sit in the Dark

Lucette Lagnado, a reporter for the *Wall Street Journal*, was born in Cairo and spent the first nine years of her life there. Her father, immortalized by Lagnado in her evocative memoir, *The Man in the White Sharkskin Suit: My Family's Exodus from Old Cairo to the New World* (2007), loved the city and refused at first to leave along with other Jews fleeing persecution in the 1950s. By 1962, the situation was dangerous and hopeless, and there seemed to be little choice. Lagnado's father, by now ill and aging, arranged for his family to make the personal exodus to which Lagnado alludes in the subtitle of her book. They went first to Paris, a natural choice for members of the Egyptian Jewish community, whose educated elite conversed in French (not Hebrew or Arabic), but ultimately settled in Brooklyn, New York. The tone of the second volume of Lagnado's memoir is very different from the first. In *The Man in the White Sharkskin Suit*, she often wrote nostalgically, perhaps idealizing Cairo as the location of her own very young childhood, or perhaps seeing it through her father's seemingly uncritical eyes. In *The Arrogant Years: One Girl's Search for Her Lost Youth, from Cairo to Brooklyn* (2011), Lagnado's writing exudes bitterness and pessimism. Whereas the first volume focused upon her father, the second is mainly about her mother. Perhaps the difference in tone between the two volumes reflects the apparently very different characters of her parents, her father vibrant and optimistic, at least until he left Cairo, and her mother perpetually disappointed. But it may also reflect Lagnado's own growing understanding of the difficulties her family was facing – the perspective of a young woman preoccupied by her own challenges and problems, rather than the viewpoint of a half-aware child.

In *The Arrogant Years*, Lagnado describes her mother as a tragic figure who was the victim of upheavals both personal (an unhappy marriage) and political (exile from her homeland and separation from her extended family). With justification, Mrs Lagnado always feared the worst, and tried to protect herself and her family from the misfortunes she anticipated around every corner. Sometimes this involved strategic planning, but as often it involved fasting. She fasted when her children suffered routine childhood illnesses, for example, and even when they had bad dreams, which might augur unwelcome news. Fasting of this kind involves a complex blend of religious precedent, cultural practice and personal preference, but it is not mandated by Jewish law. Some of her fasts, however, were religiously mandated. Many Jews overlook some of the minor fast days in the Jewish calendar – the Fast of the Tenth of Tevet, for instance, commemorating the date when the first Temple walls were breached, or the Fast of Gedaliah, commemorating the assassination by zealots of Judah's governor a few years after the destruction of the first Temple. Lagnado's mother observed all the fast days, however minor, but the pinnacle of her Jewish festival calendar was Tisha B'Av, literally the 'Ninth [day of the Hebrew calendar month] of Av', or, as Lagnado calls it in her book, the 'Night of Lamentations'. On Tisha B'Av the book of Lamentations is recited in the synagogue, in Hebrew, to a melancholy chant. From the perspective of herself as a young girl, Lagnado describes the family's return home from the evening Tisha B'Av services at The Shield of Young David, the Brooklyn synagogue populated by Jews like them, recent exiles from Middle Eastern countries. 'The house was pitch black when we arrived', Lagnado writes.

'My father had already come back and was lying down in his room. Mom made her way directly to the bedroom and went to sleep. If the point of the holiday was to relive the despair and desolation of an ancient calamity, then my parents had done an excellent job – I felt completely bereft. I couldn't fall asleep. I had never liked the dark and always asked Mom to leave on a small light in the house, but tonight she had refused. *Haram*, she said; it's a sin' (Lagnado 2011: 165).

Behind Lagnado's speculation that the point of Tisha B'Av is to relive the despair of the original victims of the catastrophe is another idea. Rituals associated with particular Jewish festivals close the gap, as it were, between the people observing them and the event being commemorated. At Passover, Jews are instructed to feel as if they themselves were slaves in Egypt, and a range of ritual activities, mostly involving food – eating bitter herbs, for example – make this extraordinary demand for empathy easier to achieve. At Tisha B'Av, Jews should mourn the destruction of the Temples as if they were present. In this case, many of the prescribed, prohibited and recommended activities that aid them are linked to Jewish mourning rituals in general, but others can be interpreted as mechanisms to provoke an appropriately mournful mood. The tradition of keeping synagogue lights low or relying on candlelight, or even, as in the Lagnado family, keeping the whole house dark, seems to fall into this latter category. Sitting in the dark is not ritually required; it simply induces solemnity. Yet Lam 3:6 suggests that darkness may have more to do with mourning than meets the eye. One of the effects, if not intentions, of Jewish mourning rituals is to render the living – through a systematic turning away from all that is life-affirming – temporarily like the dead. The 'afflicted man' of Lamentations 3 laments that God made him sit in darkness 'like those long dead'. In other words, God was teaching him a practical lesson in empathy – this is what it is like to be dead, which is precisely one of the crucial lessons that mourners must try to learn.

3:7 He has fenced me in so that I cannot escape;
he has weighed me down with chains;
3:8 though I cry out and beg for help,
he shuts out my prayer;
3:9 he has blocked my ways with hewn stones,
he has made my paths crooked.

Lamenting Vienna

Among the many twentieth-century musical settings of Lamentations, we have thus far considered only Andrew Lovett's one-act opera *Lonely Sits the City* (see on Lam 1:1). Notable landmarks include Pablo Casals's 1932 motet for mixed choir, 'O Vos Omnes' (based on the Latin Vulgate of Lam 1:12) and Leonard Bernstein's *Jeremiah Symphony* (1942), in which verses from Lamentations are sung by a solo soprano (Lam 1:1–3; 4:14–15; 5:20–1). For Lent of 1956, Hungarian composer Lajos Bárdos wrote a musical setting for eight verses of Lamentations 5, to lament the events of the Soviet occupation of his country, while in 1958 Igor Stravinsky composed a large-scale choral work entitled *Threni* (Latin for 'Lamentations') – a pure twelve-note work in which the composer expressly avoided both liturgical and historical connotations (cf. Schopf 2011: 151–2). Here we turn to a nine-voice setting by the American composer Ernst Krenek.

The early life of Ernst Krenek (born Vienna, 1900; died Palm Springs, California, 1991) was tumultuous, both personally and politically. In 1918, he was drafted into the Austrian army, though he was able to serve in Vienna where he could continue to study. In the early 1920s he studied music and worked in Germany, and Switzerland, and in 1924 he was married briefly to Anna Mahler, the daughter of the composer Gustav Mahler. On the political front, neither his music nor his journalism found favor with the Nazi regime. In 1933, soon after the Nazis came to power in Germany, a performance in Mannheim, Germany of Krenek's setting of a prose play by Goethe was cancelled. In 1934 the Vienna State Opera gave in to pressure to cancel the premiere of his opera, or 'stage work with music', *Karl V*, which it had commissioned in 1930. The cancellation may have occurred because Krenek had been blacklisted by the Nazi regime, and the composer himself linked it to its threatening (to Nazi ideology) underlying theme: Christian universalism. In 1938, officially designated a 'degenerate artist' by the Nazis, Krenek left Europe and began a career of teaching and composition in America; there, between 1940 and 1942, he composed his highly complex a capella work for nine voices, *Lamentatio Jeremiae prophetae*, Opus 43. Krenek's choice of texts for this work followed the traditional selections for recitation in the Tenebrae services leading up to Easter in the Christian calendar (see on Lam 1:6, 10, 12). He described this as a positive act of identification with the Catholic Church, the institution in which he grew up and to which he felt an especially strong attachment from the time when its existence was threatened in Nazi Austria. Each of the selected passages ends by invoking Jerusalem and praying for its salvation. In his own mind, Krenek plausibly associated Jerusalem with Austria (or perhaps more specifically Vienna), which welcomed Hitler and fell from its former glory (Stewart 1991: 237–8). Remarkably, since Krenek must have felt pressure to make a name for himself, not to mention a living, in his new country, he did not compose Lamentations for public performance, but for personal (possibly therapeutic) benefit; he did not expect that it would ever be performed. This may explain the work's extreme complexity – the composer would more likely have adapted to the needs of a choir and simplified the music had he envisaged that it would one day be sung. Fortunately, he was wrong about the destiny of his composition; already in 1942, part his setting of Lamentations was performed by a women's choir in St Paul, Minnesota, where Krenek was teaching, and in 1958, in the Netherlands, came the first performance of the entire work (Stewart 1991: 239–40; cf. Schopf 2011: 149–50).

On 16 April 2002, Bernard Holland reviewed a performance of Krenek's *Lamentations of Jeremiah* for the *New York Times*. Holland observed that although the piece was written 'amid the violence and cataclysm of World War II … its biblical cries of pain, with their ready application to current events then and now, refine rawness and immediacy into an elegance and symmetry of great beauty'. This 'civilizing effect', wrote Holland, is achieved in part 'by the 12-tone underpinnings of Krenek's nine-part choral piece'. What the audience savored, he concluded, 'was the composer's skillful imitative counterpoint and unfailing equilibrium of design, not his connections to ruined cities and suffering citizenry'. Even if Holland is correct that Krenek's composition is in some respects far removed from ruined cities, his setting is close in form, if not in content, to the spirit of its biblical source. What Krenek achieves through orderly Renaissance polyphony, skillful design and artful symmetry is arguably the musical equivalent of the biblical poet's use of the acrostic form (see on Lam 1:1). In Lamentations 3 in particular, where the acrostic is in triplicate – three *alefs*, three *bets*, three *gimels* and so forth – it is fair to say that the measured, almost mathematical, poetic form tempers what would otherwise be the book's harshest expression of physical and mental suffering (see e.g. Lam 3:4, 11, 12–17). Most obviously, the civilizing effect of music and poetry serves to make this suffering slightly more bearable. The ordered forms, musical and poetic, help to contain emotions that might otherwise spew out of control. More interesting, the act of control through form can be understood as resistance in kind. Lamentations 3:7–9 describes the confinement of 'the man who has seen affliction' (cf. v. 1). God has walled him up and chained him, shut out his prayer, blocked his ways. By exerting *self*-restraint, walling up their *own* pain, chaining down their *own* anger, and containing their *own* emotions, poet and composer respectively have made redundant the notion of God as prison-warden. They have taken upon themselves the obligation to limit and control. At the same time, by civilizing, and even beautifying, suffering, they have made it very hard for God to stop listening to them, an occurrence that, not without justification, they feared (cf. Lam 3:8).

3:10 *He is a bear lying in wait for me,*
a lion in hiding;
3:11 *he led me off my way and tore me to pieces;*
he made me desolate;
3:12 *he bent his bow and set me*
as a mark for his arrow.

3:13 *He shot into my vitals*
the arrows of his quiver;
3:14 *I have become the laughing-stock of all my people,*
the object of their gibes all day long.

Remembering Destruction in the Midst of Rebuilding

The Jewish theologian and political activist Abraham Joshua Heschel (born Warsaw, 1907; died New York City, 1972) descended from an important rabbinical family, and began his higher education in a yeshiva, an academy of traditional higher Jewish learning. His pursuit of doctoral studies at the University of Berlin marked a significant step in a move away from his religious background, and this direction was confirmed when he received rabbinic ordination under the auspices of Germany's Jewish Liberal movement. Along with all Polish Jews living in Germany, he was deported to Poland in 1938. He left for London just before the German invasion of Poland, and from there went to America in 1940. He was one of the few members of his family to survive the Shoah. From 1946 to 1972 – most of his professional life – Heschel taught at the Jewish Theological Seminary of America. He published widely on subjects including the Bible, Jewish mysticism, Hasidism, and Jewish theology, but he is remembered almost as much for his political activism as for his scholarship. He was, for example, a committed participant in the civil rights movement, as evidenced by a well-known photograph of the 1965 civil-rights march from Selma to Montgomery, Alabama, in which Heschel walks arm-in-arm with a small group of protesters that included Martin Luther King. He drew his own ethical values in part from the teachings of the biblical prophets, but in Heschel's case this was by no means equated with a rosy view of Jeremiah, Ezekiel and the others as bastions of (left-wing) ethical universalism. On the contrary, Heschel dealt intensively, in *The Prophets* (1962), with what is sometimes called 'the dark side of God', his anger, jealousy, and other problematic 'human' emotions.

In 1967, Heschel visited Israel, not for the first time in his life, but at a critical time in the life of the fledgling Jewish state – a few weeks after the end of the Six-Day War. The book he wrote and published soon after his return to the USA, *Israel: An Echo of Eternity* (1997), suggests that his visit aroused in him a complex tangle of emotions: grief over the successive catastrophes of Jewish history, not least the one that claimed the lives of many members of his own family in 1930s and 1940s Europe, mixed with joy over the birth and survival of the state.[4] This potent mix seems to have surfaced most clearly when he visited the Western Wall, the symbolic survivor of Jerusalem's destroyed Temples, 'the old mother crying for us all', 'its face … open only to those smitten with grief' (Heschel 1997: 19). The sense of the proximity of Jewish history – destruction and redemption – that Heschel experienced in a moment at the Western Wall stayed with him in the streets of Jerusalem. He wrote that as he recalled the 'reading of the Lamentations', when the 'House of Prayer is a house of weeping' (Heschel 1997: 21), it was as though all the nights of the Fast Day of Tisha B'Av – well over two thousand since the destruction of the first Temple – had been condensed into a single night. 'It is the night', he wrote, 'on which God himself set fire to the First Temple and then to the Second Temple' (21).

It is hardly surprising that, in what Heschel would surely have experienced as the heady early days of Israel's survival, he reflected upon the destruction of his ancestors, distant and close. Nor is it surprising, especially given his physical location, that he linked their loss with the destruction of the Temple. What is surprising is that he highlighted God's role in the Temple's destruction and, by implication, in that of his ancestors, and underlined it with his citation of Lam 3:10–14. What enabled Heschel, at one and the same intense moment, to mourn the destruction of six million Jews and many others before them, to hope for the redemption of the Jewish people through the building of the state of Israel and, seemingly, to hold responsible for the destruction the very source of his hope for redemption? He answers this question himself with reference to one of the most graphically disturbing of the problematic verses of Lamentations that he cited: 'We are a people in mourning, painfully puzzled, exceedingly forthright, but neither blasphemous nor bitter. What audacity in a soul that can ardently adore God and also say of Him: He was "like a bear lying in wait, like a lion in hiding [Lam 3:10]. … The LORD had become like an enemy [Lam 2:5]"' (22). To understand Heschel's point of view here, it helps to glance back to his earlier work. One of his tasks in *The Prophets* is to offer a positive account of Jewish theology in the light of what he sees as a negative presentation that emerges from some Christian theologians. Paraphrasing L. R. Farnell in *The Attributes of God* (1925), Heschel writes: 'Jewish theology seems never to have risen above the "vindictive theory of justice, human and divine" in its exposition of the ultimate divine purpose. And the defect of the Jewish presentation of

---

[4] For a similar mix of themes and emotions, see the foreword to Chaim Raphael's *Walls of Jerusalem* (1968), a highly personal history of the legend of the Roman destruction of Jerusalem built around an annotated collection of selected passages from *Lamentations Rabbah*. The book was written over a long period, in part in response to the Shoah. Raphael notes in a preface that it reached the publisher's desk on 7 June 1967, 'the day on which Jewish soldiers marched through the city they had recaptured to pray again at the Western Wall'.

God in much of the Old Testament is the imputation to him of "strong vindictiveness with liability to such passing human emotions as rage, fury and jealousy'" (Heschel 1962: 84).

An aspect of biblical prophecy that Heschel particularly emphasized is intercession; prophets for him are middlemen between Israel and God who address both, and may even affect God more than Israel. This emphasis on intercession entails a focus on anger, divine as well as human, to which Heschel, himself in search of an enduring relationship with God, was motivated to find a constructive approach. It is against this theological background that the image of God as 'a bear … in wait' and 'a lion in hiding' (Lam 3:10) posed no threat to the ardent adoration mentioned by Heschel. But much as this answers a question about Heschel and his theology, it raises another question about Lamentations and its theological point of view. In Lamentations, as in the biblical prophets, intercession is central, and, partly as a consequence of that, God's anger features prominently. But how much evidence is contained within this biblical book of the people's passionate love of God?

3:15 He has filled me with bitterness,
he has glutted me with wormwood.

[*3:19 To recall my distress and my dislocation*
is wormwood and gall!]

The Curse of Lamentations

As Laurence Sterne's Tristram Shandy, struggling with the problem of precisely when to begin the story of his life, settles on a point before he was born, the history of interpretation must sometimes begin before a text was written. Deuteronomy 28–9 includes a catalog of crimes and the corresponding curses that will befall Israel if she commits them. The fundamental crime is infidelity, and the punishment par excellence is exile: a nation will come from the ends of the earth, bringing ruin that will lead mothers to eat their babies along with the afterbirth (Deut 28:49–57). Were these verses redacted in the light of Lamentations (cf. Lam 2:20; 4:10), providing a predictive explanation, of the kind so beloved by Deuteronomistic thinkers, for the Babylonian invasion of Jerusalem? Or does Lamentations mirror Deuteronomy, words and images reflecting the sheer predictability of the catastrophe, and demonstrating, moreover, that it was self-inflicted? Questions such as these about the order of composition and the direction of influence within the Bible itself cannot easily be resolved. For our purposes, however, there is a sense in which to dwell too much upon them is to miss their potential contribution.

From the perspective of most readers of the Bible (the point of view that is central in a reception history) Deuteronomy 28–9 and Lamentations are atemporal. They represent two sets of responses to the same eternally relevant question – why do bad things happen to good people? Read together, intertextually, in no particular chronological order, they generate a new way of thinking about the intractable problem of responsibility. Who destroyed Jerusalem? The political-historical answer to this question is that Jerusalem was destroyed by the imperial might of Babylon, but to lay the blame fully at the feet of the Babylonians represented a challenge to divine omnipotence. Accordingly, another response is offered, the standard prophetic response in the Bible: God was solely responsible. Babylon was God's agent and God was merely using it as a rod for Israel's back (cf. Isa 10:5). But if Israel is to learn from this experience, and to use it to strengthen and develop her enduring relationship with God, she must be willing to share the responsibility. The punishment of destruction and exile must have been one that she brought upon herself, and, at the same time, one that she can learn to avoid in future. And yet, as with the above-mentioned challenge posed by the role of the Babylonians, how does this fit with divine omnipotence? Is there anything at all – even that which lies deep in the human heart – that does not in the end emanate from God himself?

Reading Lamentations intertextually with Deuteronomy 28–9 brings to light an extraordinary poetic meditation on the complex, sensitive question of the interaction of divine and human responsibility for the destruction of Jerusalem and the Babylonian exile. The passage beginning with Deut 29:15 (English, v. 16) focuses on infidelity, the worship of other gods, as the main explanation for exile. Deuteronomy, 29:17 (English, v. 18) characterizes the inclination to worship idols as a sickness at the community's inner core: 'Perchance there is among you some man or woman, or some clan or tribe, whose heart is even now turning away from the LORD our God to go and worship the gods of other nations – perchance there is among you a stock sprouting gall and wormwood.' This verse contains a word pair, *rosh veanah*, 'gall and wormwood', that occurs elsewhere in the Bible (albeit in reverse, *la'anah verosh*, 'wormwood and gall') only in Lam 3:19: 'To recall my distress and my dislocation is wormwood and gall.' The clear implication of Deut 29:17 is that 'gall and wormwood' is a metaphor for a sickness that comes from within, parallel to its other image, the heart that has already begun to turn away from God to worship other gods. Lamentations, however, uses the metaphor very differently. Lamentations 3:19 does not specify the source of the 'wormwood and gall', although the fact that they have to be 'recalled' arguably hints at an external source. But one of the two terms in the word pair has occurred four verses earlier in a context that makes it clear that even this comes from God: 'He has filled me with bitterness, he has glutted me with wormwood' (Lam 3:15). As these two verses of Lamentations have it, even what is conceived in Deut 29:17 as a deeply internal inclination to worship idols, something that grows secretly in the human heart, comes in fact from outside. God himself is the source of the 'wormwood and gall' within Israel's heart; he initiated the crime for which he is punishing his people. It is at once edifying and deeply unsettling to have this particular theological message – among the Bible's most challenging – revealed so starkly by a single twisted metaphor.

3:16 *He has made my teeth grind on gravel,*
and made me cower in the dust.

The Afflicted Man as Proto-Martyr?

The *Avot de Rabbi Natan* ('Fathers according to Rabbi Nathan') is a work of uncertain authorship that emerged between the eighth and the tenth centuries CE. Although one of its two versions, known as the A version, is usually printed among the minor tractates of the Babylonian Talmud, the work shares more in common with midrash than with mainstream talmudic literature. Both versions of the *Avot de Rabbi Natan*, the A version and the B version, include an account of the deaths by martyrdom of two important figures from second-century CE Roman Palestine, Rabban Simeon ben Gamaliel and Rabbi Ishmael ben Elisha. Rabban Simeon ben Gamaliel was the second of six similarly named holders of the important political office of *Nasi* (Prince) in first- to fifth-century CE Palestine. Rabbi Ishmael was a colleague of the better-known Rabbi Akiba, with whose legal opinions he often differed. Along with Rabbi Akiba, Rabban Simeon ben Gamaliel and Rabbi Ishmael are numbered among the so-called Ten Martyrs who feature prominently in the liturgy of Yom Kippur (the Day of Atonement) and died, according to Jewish tradition, on the same day at the hands of Roman persecutors.[5]

All known manuscripts of the *Avot de Rabbi Natan*, whether version A or B, begin their account of the death scene in more or less the same way. Rabban Simeon ben Gamaliel and Rabbi Ishmael compete on the day of their deaths over which one of them is greater and therefore deserves to be executed first – the former, Rabban Simeon ben Gamaliel, a prince and son of a prince, or the latter, Rabbi Ishmael, a high priest and son of a high priest:

> When the executioner came to decapitate Rabban Simeon ben Gamaliel, Rabbi Ishmael said to him, Do not do that, I am greater than he is. Come to decapitate me first. He [the executioner] asked, Why are you greater than him? Because I am

---

[5] Accounts of their deaths appear in other rabbinic texts, including the *Mekhilta de Rabbi Ishmael* and *Seder Eliyahu Rabbah*.

a High Priest, he replied, and the son of a High Priest. So the executioner went to decapitate Rabbi Ishmael. Rabban Simeon ben Gamaliel said to him, Do not do that. I am greater than he is. Come and decapitate me first. He [the executioner] asked him in what way he was greater. He [Rabban Gamaliel] answered: I am a Prince and the son of a Prince. (*Avot de Rabbi Natan* B 41b)

Which rabbi won the debate and was decapitated first by the Roman executioner? The result differs according to the manuscript consulted. Some report that Rabban Gamaliel was acknowledged to be greater and was therefore executed first, and others report that Rabbi Ishmael was greater and was thus the first to die. In all manuscripts, though, the loser (whichever he was) kisses the winner's about-to-be-decapitated head and exclaims: 'Oh, how the mouth that engaged with Torah is now filled with gravel.' Through his death, we are told, this martyr was 'thus fulfilling what was written, "He has made my teeth grind on gravel, and made me cower in the dust" [Lam 3:16]'.

The citation of Lam 3:16 is interesting both for what it takes from its original context in Lamentations and for what it brings to it. While the *Avot de Rabbi Natan* focuses on the Roman executioner as the agent of death, the verse from Lamentations brings a divine component into the picture. God is the 'He' who made the sufferer's teeth grind on gravel. The biblical citation thus functions in the rabbinic narrative as a source of the creative tension that features in many such accounts over the ultimate cause of the martyr's death. Was it the Babylonian enemy or the divine opponent who made the 'man who has seen affliction' (Lam 3:1) bite the dust? Was it the Roman hand that wielded the axe or the divine hand that allowed it to fall? At the same time, the verse from Lam 3:16 in the *Avot de Rabbi Natan* sets the rabbinic martyr in a typological context; as the one whose teeth ground on gravel, he is now 'the man who has seen affliction' (Lam 3:1). And just as the biblical citation locates the rabbinic martyr in a typological line that includes 'the man who has seen affliction', so, reading in the other direction, it places 'the man who has seen affliction' in the line of Jewish martyrs that included Rabban Simeon ben Gamaliel, Rabbi Ishmael and their lamented peers. Scholarship on martyrdom often highlights its distinctive temporal component – the so-called concertina-ing of time. The *Avot de Rabbi Natan* achieves precisely this effect when it evokes a biblical proto-martyr, 'the man who has seen affliction', in an account of fully developed rabbinic martyrs, and thus collapses the temporal gap between them.

The reference to gravel also effects a powerful rhetorical trick in the rabbinic story. Many rabbinic texts speak of Torah in the mouth of a great sage. Readers might be more inclined in general to experience that image in terms that are auditory (words of Torah that are heard), not sensory (words of Torah that are tasted). Yet here, as juxtaposed with Lam 3:16, we can almost *feel* Torah:

not gravel but its opposite – pearls of wisdom, perhaps? This point leads directly to what the rabbinic story brings to the book of Lamentations. Temporally speaking, Lamentations 3 is mainly two-dimensional, focusing on the transition from present suffering to future hope. Its few references to the *past* are only implied and indirect. In this respect Chapter 3 contrasts starkly with other sections of Lamentations which, though also two-dimensional, focus on the glorious past as compared with the ghastly present. Lamentations 4, for example, is replete with temporal comparisons involving past and present: those who once feasted now perish; those raised in purple cling to ash heaps (Lam 4:5); snow-white princes are now blacker than soot; ruddy bodies are now dry as wood (Lam 4:7–8). The martyrdom account in the *Avot de Rabbi Natan* imports the past into Lam 3:16, thus making it three-dimensional in temporal terms. It allows the reader who knows both texts and reads them intertextually to experience sensually the pearls of wisdom that preceded, perhaps, the gravel in the mouth of 'the man who has seen affliction' (Lam 3:1). Here is another way in which the *Avot de Rabbi Natan* plays with time. It brings to Lamentations 3 a glimpse of the past as compared with the present (that was then and this is now), and with it a powerful sense of loss that is inextricably linked to the passage of time.

3:17 My life is bereft of peace;
I have forgotten what happiness is,
3:18 Therefore I say, 'Gone is my glory,
and all that I had hoped for from the Lord.'

[3:40 Let us search and examine our ways,
and return to the Lord.

3:51 My eyes cause me grief
for all the young women of my city.

5:15 Gone is the joy of our hearts;
our dancing has turned into mourning.]

Learning How to Lose

The very first words of Lamentations place center-stage the themes of loss and bereavement: 'How lonely sits the city that once was full of people! She has become like a widow who was once great among the nations' (Lam 1:1). This language has been taken as a cue to ask what light may be shed on the book from the perspective of the psychology of human loss and bereavement, as studied by modern pastoral psychologists. Some of the book's contradictions and inconsistencies may be understood more readily in the light of what has been learned about how human beings react to experiences of radical loss (Joyce 1993; Reimer 2002). The insights of Elisabeth Kübler-Ross on death and dying and Yorick Spiegel on grief and bereavement (Kübler-Ross 1969; Spiegel 1973) are especially illuminating, both for the verses cited above and for much of the rest of the book too. Kübler-Ross suggests five stages experienced by those who are dying, each of which we might discern in Lamentations: first, denial (cf. Lam 3:31, 'For the Lord does not reject forever') and isolation (cf. Lam 1:2, 'there is no one to comfort her among all her friends; all her allies have betrayed her, they have become her enemies'); second, anger (cf. Lam 2:20, 'Look, O LORD, and consider! To whom have you done this?'); third, bargaining, often including pleading for relief from pain and the prospect of death (Lam 3:40, above, can be read as an example of bargaining; cf. Lam 2:19, 'Pour out your heart like water before the presence of the Lord! Lift your hands to him for the lives of your infants'); fourth, depression (Lam 3:17–18 and 5:15, above, can both be read as examples of depression); and finally, fifth, acceptance, quiet detachment in recognition of impending death (cf. Lam 3:26. 'It is good that one should wait quietly for the salvation of the LORD').

Spiegel's paradigm assesses the psychology of bereavement by highlighting a range of four stages of grief, and these too might be discerned in Lamentations: first, shock (cf. Lam 1:1, 'How lonely sits the city …!'); second, controlled grief, often expressed through mourning rites (cf. Lam 2:10, 'The elders of daughter Zion sit on the ground in silence; they have thrown dust on their heads and put on sackcloth; the young girls of Jerusalem have bowed their heads to the ground'); third, regression, marked by a range of defense mechanisms, such as the recalling of happier times (cf. Lam 1:7, 'Jerusalem remembers, in the days of her affliction and sorrow, all the precious things that she had in days of old'); and finally, fourth, adaptation, that is, adjustment to the bereaved condition, so that eventually a new start can be made (cf. Lam 3:32, 'when he afflicts, he shows compassion according to his abundant kindness'). It is important to note that both Kübler-Ross and Spiegel observe that those affected can 'get stuck' at a particular stage or regress to an earlier stage, that the stages can in any case be encountered in varying sequences, and moreover that elements of different stages can coexist. All too often biblical criticism has been hampered by the unrealistic assumption that people react to events with a single consistent emotion or opinion. Kübler-Ross and Spiegel help us see that a person (and by extension a community) can experience and express a whole gamut of emotions within a short space of time, and this is an invaluable help in reading Lamentations. These insights can provide a framework within which the inconsistencies and ambiguities of the book might better be understood, without resorting to theories of composite authorship. This approach to Lamentations is a heuristic and exploratory one, so for example the apparently positive verses that appear in the middle section of Lamentations 3 can be read either in terms of 'acceptance/adaptation' or of 'denial/regression'.

This is but one of a range of ways in which Lamentations may be illuminated from psychology. In another example, Linafelt employs Freudian psychoanalysis in his reading of Lamentations (Linafelt 2000a: 141–3), specifically Freud's distinction between mourning and melancholia (Freud 1991a). Mourning is a positive process that brings a sense of resolution to suffering, while melancholia, on the other hand, prevents the possibility of resolution. Linafelt foregrounds the protest of personified Jerusalem in Lamentations 1 and 2, resisting the predominant theological impulses of Lamentations 3; in doing this he highlights the rhetoric of melancholia over the possibility of resolution in mourning, arguing that the poetry functions to perpetually confront God and interminably express pain. Pyper develops Linafelt's work in this area, albeit in a different direction. Using Freud's article 'The Ego and the Id' (Freud 1991b), Pyper argues that the surviving voice in Lamentations turns the anguish of survival into an attack on the mother, personified Zion, reinforced by wider biblical motifs that juxtapose women, food, and death. Ultimately, hope is projected on to the continued violence of the father, God, which is justified at the expense of the mother (Pyper 2001).

In a rather different mode, Labahn applies insights from John Archer's *The Nature of Grief* (Archer 1999) to Lamentations and argues that mourning paves the way towards a positive future with God (Labahn 2002). Archer highlights two different ways of coping with grief, a 'loss-orientated' process and a 'restoration-orientated' process. The theological tensions in the book are explained by Labahn through these differing perspectives. She suggests that Lamentations evidences both of the styles identified by Archer. Lamentations 1, 2, 4, and 5 exemplify the 'loss-orientated' style and reflect an extreme sense of loneliness and pain. However, the prominent central position of Lam 3:21–39 draws significant attention to the 'restoration-orientated' coping process, and here she locates the overall purpose of the book.

Smith-Christopher explores Lamentations through the psychological insights of refugee studies and post-traumatic stress disorder (PTSD) (Smith-Christopher 2002: 75–104). Those who experience PTSD are disoriented by recurrent intrusive memories, dreams, feelings of repetition of the destruction and violence, debilitating depression, detachment, and estrangement. Moreover, these symptoms persist to the degree that they can appear years after the event or events that triggered them, even instigating a cross-generational passing of PTSD symptoms from parents to children. Smith-Christopher recognizes the serial trauma that Lamentations depicts and relates this to PTSD. Recurring memories of destruction and brutality crop up in Lamentations, indicative of 'intrusive memories', including cannibalism (e.g. Lam 4:10), famine (e.g. Lam 2:11–12), rape (Lam 1:10; 5:11), and slaughter (e.g. Lam 2:21). Further, the sense of isolation (the absence of comfort, for example, in Lam 1:2) and depression (e.g. Lam 1:20) evidenced in the poetry are also PTSD symptoms. Smith-Christopher concludes that to read the book through the lens of PTSD 'is once again to recover Lamentations as a measure of the psychological and spiritual crisis of the exile' (104).

A valuable recent contribution is a study in which Heath Thomas relates prayer and pain through reflection on psychological analysis and Lamentations research (Thomas 2010). Surveying applications of psychological insights to studies of the book, he notes a recurrent shortcoming: these approaches consistently undervalue the crucial indicators of prayer. This leads him on to investigate the relationship between prayer and pain in the poetry by exploring the connections between Lamentations and the psychology of prayer. And so in a rich variety of ways, from the apparently secular to the overtly religious, psychological insights can be seen to shed abundant light on the book of Lamentations, providing a good example of the way that the reception of the book in the modern period has reflected the priorities and concerns of the age.

[For Lam 3:19 see Lam 3:15]

3:20 Whenever I remember them,
my soul is bowed down within me.
3:21 But this I call to mind,
and therefore I have hope.

[*3:60 You have seen all their malice,*
all their designs against me.
3:61 You have heard their taunts, O LORD,
all their plots against me.
3:62 The whispers and murmurs of my assailants
are against me all day long.
3:63 Whether they sit or rise – see,
I am the butt of their gibes.
3:64 Pay them back for their deeds, O LORD,
according to the work of their hands!
3:65 Give them anguish of heart;
your curse be on them!
3:66 Pursue them in anger and destroy them
from under the heavens of the LORD.]

No Widow but an Abandoned Bride

Lamentations Rabbah (see on Lam 1:3) tells the following parable in relation to Lam 3:21:

> Rabbi Abba bar Kahana said: It is like a king who married a woman and wrote her a large marriage-settlement contract (*ketubah*, 'document'). He wrote to her: So

many bridal chambers am I building for you; so much jewellery I make for you; so much gold and silver I give you. Then he left her for many years and journeyed to the provinces. Her neighbours used to taunt her and say to her: hasn't your husband abandoned you? Go! Marry another man. She would weep and sigh, and afterward she would enter her bridal chamber and read her marriage-settlement contract and sigh [with relief]. Many years and days later the king returned. He said to her: I am amazed that you have waited for me all these years! She replied: My master, O king! If not for the large marriage-settlement you wrote me, my neighbours long ago would have led me astray.[6]

What inspired the author of this midrash to recount a parable about an abandoned bride and her marriage-settlement contract in relation to a verse of Lamentations that has no apparent connection with brides and grooms? The first clue is the *ketubah*, the marriage-settlement document that features so prominently in the parable. In Lam 3:21, arguably the turning point of the entire book of Lamentations, the demonstrative pronoun (*zot*, Hebrew feminine, 'this') appears, tantalizingly, without a referent. What precisely is it that the poet calls to mind and therefore has hope of? To be sure, the most plausible object of *zot* is specified in the verse that follows: 'The steadfast love (*hesed*) of the LORD never ceases, his mercies are never spent' (v. 22). The source of hope is God's steadfast love. But the midrashic author – licensed by the biblical poet's decision to keep his readers in suspense and reveal only in verse 22 the referent of a pronoun mentioned in verse 21 – has other ideas.

Whenever the Torah scroll is opened and raised ceremonially in the synagogue just prior to its public recitation, the congregation stands and sings a line of liturgy drawn from the book of Deuteronomy: 'And this (*zot*) is the Torah that Moses placed before the children of Israel … (Deut 4:44)'. In one highly charged context, the word *zot* is identified with the Torah, and for this reason, according to Jewish tradition, many other instances of the Hebrew demonstrative pronoun *zot* ('this') must therefore also allude to the Torah. This is the basis of *Lamentation Rabbah*'s interpretation of Lam 3:21. Since, in another highly charged context – the turning point of the biblical book from despair to hope – the word *zot* occurs without a referent, the midrashic author supplies one: *zot* must refer to the Torah. At this point, his imagination takes over, in combination, of course, with his theological understanding of the nature of God's relationship with Israel and details drawn from the historical backdrop against which the parable was probably composed, namely tense relations in Roman Palestine. He interprets the Torah, which he sees signified

---

[6]   For an excellent analysis of this parable, see D. Stern 1991.

by *zot* in Lam 3:21, as a *ketubah*, a marriage-settlement contract. In the first instance this is simply the *ketubah* between a king and the wife he abandons soon after marrying her, but as the parable unfolds we see that it is also the contract between God and Israel: the Torah.

In the parable, the function of the marriage contract is to reassure the king's wife. During his long absence, her neighbors taunted her, telling her that her husband would not return and that she should remarry. Whenever she heard this, she read her *ketubah* and it gave her hope that her neighbors were wrong and that her husband would return to her. Given the historical context from which the midrash emanated, these neighbors probably represented those Christians who told the Jews that God had abandoned them. When the king returns, he is astonished to find that his abandoned wife has remained faithful to him. His astonishment plays a vital role. Whereas the book of Lamentations blames Israel for causing God to turn his face away, the midrash blames the king for leaving. No good reason is given for the absence, which even he knows was unacceptably long. Certainly, it was not the fault of his wife, whose faithfulness far exceeded what could have been expected of her, as we see from the king's reaction. In response to his astonishment, his wife tells him that indeed had it not been for the *ketubah* he had written, her neighbors would long ago have led her astray. The neighbors provide the punch line of the parable. As noted above, their prominence can be explained in part by the parable's historical context in Roman Palestine. But surely the taunting neighbors grew from seeds planted in Lamentations itself, where Israel's taunting enemies also play a key role (Lam 3:60–6).

This midrash, like many others, can best be interpreted in the light both of the historical context of its authors and the context of the biblical text that is its starting point. The parable's *ketubah*/Torah image reflects the biblical connection between *zot* (Lam 3:21) and God's steadfast love (Lam 3:22) as the source of Israel's hope. Its focus on the taunting neighbors underlines the role, explored in the second half of Lamentations 3, that is played by the prospect of God's rejection of Israel's enemies on his return to Israel. The parable thus brings out a crucial, albeit non-politically correct, feature of Lamentations. Israel's hope for a renewed relationship with God has both an internal, theological component symbolized by God's steadfast love (v. 22; cf. the *ketubah* in the midrash), and an external, political dimension symbolized by his commitment to vindicate her in the eyes of her enemies (Lam 3:60–6; cf. the neighbors in the midrash) and repay them according to their just deserts (v. 64). Given the historical circumstances of the Babylonian destruction of Jerusalem and the exile of its leaders, it is clear why both theological and political dimensions are required. And given the historical circumstances for Jews in Roman Palestine, it is clear why the midrashic author of the *Lamentations Rabbah* parable should have highlighted them.

3:22 The steadfast love of the Lord *never ceases,*
his mercies are never spent;
3:23 they are renewed every morning;
great is your faithfulness.
3:24 'The Lord *is my portion', says my soul,*
'therefore I will wait for him.'

New Life in the Holy Land?

Can lifeless bodies
be chambers
for hearts lashed
to eagles' wings –
a man at the end of his tether,
whose only desire
is to rub his cheeks
in chosen dust? …

I long to approach
and grow faint by their tombs
eyes brimming
at their ruins.
All my thoughts
shudder for Sinai,
my heart and eyes
for Mount Avarim.
How can I not
dissolve into tears
and hope
for the dead to revive? …

But I fear
the sins of youth
numbered
in the Lord's book,
and those of old age,
renewed
each morning,
cannot answer
for backsliding,
and put to straits
where can I go?[7]

[7]   Halevi 2002: 104–7.

Yehuda Halevi (born Spain, 1080; died Jerusalem, 1141) was perhaps the brightest luminary among Spain's medieval Jewish poets. The details of his life are not certain, but it seems that he was born in the north of Spain and spent most of his adult life in Muslim-ruled Andalusia, moving between Granada, Toledo, Seville and Cordoba, a refugee from the violent outbreaks that marred Spain's justly celebrated *convivencia*, peaceful and productive coexistence between Muslims and Jews. Like many other Jews of his generation, Yehuda Halevi came to doubt the viability of a long-term Jewish diaspora, and in the late 1130s he set out for Palestine with the unusual goal of settling there. According to popular legend, he died soon after arriving in Jerusalem, trampled by a Saracen horseman, a tragic end to a traumatic journey (about which we are well informed, thanks to documents that survived miraculously in the Cairo Geniza). Yehuda Halevi's poem 'Can Lifeless Bodies' (a title simply taken from its first line) is a travel poem about just such a journey.

Written perhaps after Halevi's failed attempt to reach Jerusalem by way of Egypt, this poem about a Jewish journey from the Spanish diaspora to the Holy Land contains little outright optimism; at best, it seems, the returnee to Zion it describes will lie next to his ancestors in the dust of a holy site. Itself a product of *convivencia*, the poetry of medieval Jewish Spain owes much to Arabic conventions, but is distinguished too by a high density of biblical allusions. The world that emerged from the pen of Yehuda Halevi is a complex tapestry whose threads comprise many examples of biblical scenes, characters, imagery and language, and his characteristic 'turn it and turn it again' approach to his biblical sources is fully evident in 'Can Lifeless Bodies'. Among the dozen or so biblical allusions in this poem is a citation from the book of Lamentations: 'renewed every morning' (Lam 3:23). Given the bleak picture that Halevi wanted to sketch in this poem, it is hardly surprising that he turned to Lamentations, one of the Bible's bleakest books. What is initially surprising, though, is that the verse to which he alludes is not bleak at all, but marks the book's turning point from despair to (admittedly) cautious hope. (This turning point was discussed above with respect to Lam 3:20-1 and *Lamentations Rabbah*.) Despite the anger and loss that has preceded these verses in their biblical context, what the author of Lamentations sees 'renewed every morning' is God's steadfast love and his unending mercies. Since the Bible has no shortage of expressions of God's love and mercy, what made Yehuda Halevi turn to Lamentations for one of them? It seems that the allusion works on two levels. On the first level, Halevi uses the biblical verse pessimistically, rendering what was positive in Lamentations as negative in his own poem. According to Halevi, it is not divine goodness but the sins of young and old alike that are 'renewed each morning' as the human soul yields to them constantly. As a measure, perhaps, of the depths of his own despair, Halevi seems to have taken the one spark of hope in the Bible's bleakest book and extinguished even that. On the second level, however, Halevi's use of the verse is more optimistic, closer to its sense in its original context. On this level, he focuses on the words themselves, their evocative power undiminished by his reinterpretation of them. Just as the reader of the biblical words 'renewed every morning' finds hope at the heart of the Bible's most relentless exploration of loss and destruction, so the despairing pilgrim to the Holy Land finds hope among the dead as he keens over graves, longing for the dead to revive and anticipating the discovery of inscribed tablets lying buried in the sacred dust. Even as he calls attention to the inevitability of human frailty, Halevi evokes the site of the miracle he expects: divine acceptance in the midst of human imperfection (the sins that are 'renewed each morning') and the restoration of the remnant of Zion from the midst of destruction.

Beginning the Christian Year

John Keble (born Fairford, Gloucestershire, 1792; died Bournemouth, 1866) was an English priest, poet and academic. He published his poetry collection *The Christian Year* in 1827, when he was thirty-five. Four years later, on the strength of it, he was appointed Professor of Poetry at the University of Oxford. In that capacity, in 1833, he preached the Assize Sermon (so-called because it was formally preached before two judges), on the theme of 'National Apostasy', which referred to the dangers that threatened the Church of England both from state interference and from decline in religious conviction. This sermon is often regarded as the starting point of the so-called Oxford, or Tractarian, Movement, a hugely significant high-church Anglican process of reform. Keble had a profound influence on his many friends and associates, who established Keble College, Oxford, in his memory soon after his death. *The Christian Year* reached a yet-wider circle, becoming the most popular volume of verse of the nineteenth century and one of the most influential works of its kind. Over the next twenty-five years it sold over 100,000 copies, and by 1873 sales in Britain had exceeded 375,000. In the main body of the volume, Keble presents poetry for every significant occasion of the liturgical year, beginning with the start of the Church's year on Advent Sunday, several weeks before Christmas. But this core is topped and tailed with material of a more thematic kind. For example, near the end there are sections on 'Visitation and Communion of the Sick', and 'Forms of Prayer to be Used at Sea'. And at the start of the volume, before the annual sequence, Keble begins with 'Morning' and 'Evening'. His very first text, for 'Morning', is taken from Lam 3:22–3, in the King James Version: 'His compassions fail not. They are new every morning.' Keble's poem on 'Morning' begins with an evocation of dawn:

> Hues of the rich unfolding morn,
> That, ere the glorious sun be born,
> By some soft touch invisible
> Around his path are taught to swell.

Later on in the poem, he picks up explicitly his Lamentations text:

> New every morning is the love
> Our wakening and uprising prove;
> Through sleep and darkness safely brought,
> Restored to life and power and thought.

It is striking to think that at the end of the Victorian era Christian believers from Canada to New Zealand, India to the Caribbean, began their day reflecting with Keble on the dawn of hope articulated at the heart of the book of Lamentations. The phrase 'new every morning' from Lam 3:23, coming after so many verses of dark lament, is powerfully evocative and it is perhaps not surprising that Keble chose it for the start of his book. Another example of the afterlife of this telling phrase is found on radio. The BBC's *The Daily Service* is the longest-running radio program of its kind anywhere in the world; this short daily Christian service has been broadcast without interruption since 1928. At various times in its history it has been called *New Every Morning* and, indeed, when a service book was produced to accompany the broadcasts the best-known version, first appearing in 1936, was also entitled *New Every Morning*.

3:25 The LORD is good to those who hope in him,
to the soul that seeks him.
3:26 It is good that one should wait quietly
for the salvation of the LORD.
3:27 It is good for a man to bear
a yoke in his youth,
3:28 to sit alone in silence
when the Lord has imposed it,
3:29 to put his mouth to the dust –
there may yet be hope;
3:30 to give his cheek to the smiter,
and be filled with insults.

Hearing the Voice of the Seeing Child

A remarkable essay by Alice Miller (born Alice Rostovski, Lwow, Poland, 1923; died Provence, France, 2010) provides a good example of a reading shaped by a particular ideological perspective, for it is profoundly influenced by the psychologist's personal commitment to the fate of abused children in modern societies. The essay, 'The Mistreated Child in the Lamentations of Jeremiah', comes from a book called *Breaking Down the Wall of Silence* (Miller 1991), written in the aftermath of the fall of the Berlin Wall and after Miller had rejected the practice of psychotherapy. Surprisingly perhaps, the essay does not focus at all on the fate of actual children within the biblical book; the two shocking references to the cannibalistic eating of babies in Lam 2:20 and Lam 4:10 go unmentioned. Instead, Miller finds in the protests of the book of Lamentations a powerful expression of rebellion against cruelty, this being the voice of the 'vital, feeling and seeing child' within each of us. This is a concept that she projects onto the text, which she reads within our modern setting. She perceives the book of Lamentations as ultimately emphasizing that suffering should be accepted. Having recounted the anguish expressed in the first part of Lamentations 3, Miller writes: 'This is more than a child can fathom, he desperately seeks consolation, finding it in his own apparent guilt, his own wickedness. This gives him hope' (120). In the verses that follow, the biblical book presents a message of calm acceptance: 'It is good that one should wait quietly for the salvation of the LORD. It is good for a man to bear a yoke in his youth' (Lam 3:26–7). Miller resists this attitude of passive or willing suffering, and instead gives a privileged status to the voice of protest that she hears within the text. Miller shares with some others (cf. Johanna Stiebert on Lam 1:15–16) an image of God as presented in Lamentations as an abusive figure. She argues that, in our situation as readers, acceptance of the unacceptable must be rejected. Miller contends that mistreated children typically cling to the hope that the torture they suffer is no more than a just and necessary response to their own guilt, that they are being chastised out of love. In so far as the book of Lamentations encourages this sad delusion, she contends, the book must be resisted. Miller is using the biblical text – powerful and well known – to articulate and explore a social problem in our own time. She does not invoke the Bible as an authoritative text. On the contrary, 'Jeremiah's consolation', she says, 'cannot be ours' (126).

So far removed is Miller's essay from the conventional concerns of historical criticism that, although this is in some respects a very radical piece, it assumes Lamentations to be written by Jeremiah (as tradition has had it). Moreover, Miller's discussion is in no way related to the historical judgments of redaction criticism. She does not claim that the voice of protest has been overlaid by later editors, but rather she makes a readerly decision to 'foreground' one feature of what she reads as a holistic text, namely the word of protest. This raises the fascinating question of who has the last word, both within the text and in the business of interpretation, and, furthermore, on what grounds such questions are to be decided. For Miller, ethical concerns are at the fore: toleration of abuse is simply unacceptable and the voice of the 'vital, feeling and seeing child' within the text must be championed.

*3:31 For the Lord does not
reject forever,
3:32 but when he afflicts, he shows compassion
according to his abundant kindness,
3:33 He does not willingly oppress
or afflict anyone.*

The Gospel according to Lamentations?

Maurice Frank Wiles (born London, 1923; died Oxford, 2005) was an Anglican priest and, from 1970 to 1991, Regius Professor of Divinity at Oxford University; he was also the father of the distinguished mathematician Sir Andrew Wiles. When researching his earlier family history, Maurice Wiles discovered, much to his surprise, that both his grandfathers had been Free-Church theologians: Joseph Pitts Wiles (1849–1929) and John Herbert Wilkinson (1862–1941) (Wiles 2003). In 1908 his paternal grandfather, Joseph Pitts Wiles, published a volume of short reflections for a popular audience, *Half-hours with the Minor Prophets and the Lamentations* (Wiles 1908). His treatment of the book of Lamentations is not untypical of Christian devotional writing of its day. It is characteristic in assuming authorship by Jeremiah, which is the main rationale for the taking of Lamentations with a collection of prophetic books (Lamentations being thought of in this case, perhaps, as a minor work by a major prophet). It is also typical in describing the contents of the book in terms borrowed from the Christian lexicon. Encountering the hopeful material in the heart of the middle chapter, Wiles describes Lam 3:19–41 as 'a sweet interlude of gospel comfort'. Lamentations is, after all, part of the Christian Bible and it is hardly surprising that these verses should strike a chord with this Christian devotional exegete (cf. Keble on Lam 3:22–3). Christian use of the Hebrew Bible, the Old Testament of the Church, has often been problematic with respect to Jews, the other faith community for whom it is a sacred text. This is especially likely to be the case where matters of Christology are concerned, bearing on the person and work of Christ, as in readings of Lam 4:20 ('The breath of our life, the LORD's anointed, was taken in their pits'). Such christological readings can raise large issues about the relationship between Judaism and Christianity, questions traditionally often answered by Christians in terms that assert the superiority of Christianity as a religion that has replaced Judaism. Those issues do not arise directly here, and it might be thought that no difficulties are posed in the present case, where one senses in the reception of Lamentations by the pastor Wiles an expression of that human craving for parental warmth and divine acceptance that unites the traditions rather than dividing them. However, even here matters are not straightforward, for it must be remembered that the theological languages of the two communities, Christian and Jewish, are often very different from each other, and that in some settings the use of the word 'gospel' can be excluding and far from uniting. It was used of Lamentations by Joseph Pitts Wiles very naturally when addressing a Christian readership, but in interfaith settings and the public domain, the sensitive use of theological language can pose more of a challenge.

By no means all interpreters have read these middle verses of Lamentations as positively as Wiles did in his summary, 'a sweet interlude of gospel comfort'. As we have seen, Stiebert claims that, given the wider context in the book, references to the deity's 'compassion' and 'kindness' (Lam 3:32) read like 'macabre sarcasm' (Stiebert 2003: 199), while Dobbs-Allsopp argues that Lamentations follows the pattern of classical tragedy and regards the central passage of Chapter 3 (vv. 19–41) as ultimately removing all traces of hope (Dobbs-Allsopp 1997). Against these views, it can be argued that the text's final form, reflecting redactional development, heightens themes of explanation, theodicy and hope, in short, that it achieves a degree of theological closure, focused here at what can be seen as the apex of the book (cf. Soggin 1976: 396–7). On such an understanding, one might trace a story of reception even within the development of the text itself.

3:34 *When all the prisoners of the land*
are crushed under his feet,
3:35 *when human rights are perverted*
in the face of the Most High,
3:36 *when a cause is subverted*
– does the Lord not see it?

3:37 *Who can speak and it will be done,*
if the Lord has not commanded it?
3:38 *Is it not from the mouth of the Most High*
that good and bad come?
3:39 *Why should any living man complain*
about the punishment of his own sins?

[3:58 *You have taken up my cause, O Lord,*
you have redeemed my life.
3:59 *You have seen the wrong done to me, O* LORD;
judge my cause.]

Metaphysical Laments

John Donne (born London, 1572; died London, 1631), metaphysical poet par excellence and Dean of St Paul's Cathedral, London, based 'The Lamentations of Jeremiah' (Donne 1896: 194–211), his poetic rendering in English of the book of Lamentations, on a Latin translation from the Hebrew and Syriac by Immanuel Tremellius (born Ferrara, Italy, 1510; died Sedan, France, 1580). Tremellius was an Italian Jewish convert to Christianity, initially Catholicism. A year after his conversion he converted again, this time to Protestantism, and was forced to leave Italy. He went on to teach at the universities of Strasbourg, Cambridge (where he was Regius Professor of Hebrew), Heidelberg, and latterly the College of Sedan in France. Tremellius's Latin translation of the Bible was published in London in 1580.

The book of Lamentations raises many theological problems, especially relating to divine responsibility for human suffering, but one of its most overtly theological discussions occurs in Lam 3:34–9 and 58–9. The hard questions these verses pose, more or less explicitly, include: Is all human suffering justified, or might people suffer unjustly? If people sometimes suffer unjustly, where does God, characterized in these verses as a judge not as the perpetrator, stand in relation to the injustice? Is God unaware of the injustice? Is he aware of injustice, but chooses to ignore it? Or does God actually cause the injustice, not directly (in these particular verses, the human enemy is the direct cause), but indirectly, by making a judgment that perverts justice and fails to support the innocent, or by failing to make any judgment at all when one is required? Depending on the answers to these questions, other questions emerge: What is the appropriate human response to suffering? Must it be assumed that all suffering is merited, in which case there are no grounds for complaint? Indeed, to go one step further, must it be assumed that God is always just, in which case not only are there no grounds for complaint, but complaint amounts to divine character defamation? The theological complexities in these verses are compounded by especially difficult Hebrew, occasioned by the demand of the acrostic in Chapter 3 to begin three consecutive verses (vv. 34–6) with the letter *lamed* (l), which is also the Hebrew preposition meaning 'to' or 'for' (see Berlin 2002 for a good account of these difficulties).

However, it seems possible to get to the heart of the problem by concentrating on verse 36, translated above as a question: 'When a cause is subverted – does the Lord not *see* it?' A key term in this verse is the word 'see', a translation of the Hebrew *ra'ah*, which is most often rendered 'see' or 'look'. The same word, in the Hebrew and in most translations, is picked up again in Lam 3:59, which answers the question posed in verse 36 with the words: 'You have *seen* the wrong done to me, O LORD; judge my cause' (v. 59). According to this verse, God certainly did see the wrong that was done, and he is again asked to judge it. Turning now to John Donne, the word 'see' occurs only in his rendition of Lam 3:35, where the Hebrew *ra'ah* does not occur and where most translations opt for phrases like 'in the face of' (NJPS, very close to the Hebrew's 'opposite the face of') or the NRSV's 'in the presence of'. In Lam 3:36, Donne takes what seems most likely to be a question (as it is translated above) and turns it into a statement, replacing its 'see' with 'allow'. And when it comes to Lam 3:59, he omits altogether the clause which contains the Hebrew word *ra'ah*, usually translated 'see':

> 34. That underfoot the prisoners stamped be,
> 35. That a man's right the judge himself doth see
> To be wrung from him;
> 36. That he subverted is
> In his just cause, the Lord allows not this.
> 37. Who then will say, that aught doth come to pass,
> But that which by the Lord commanded was?
> 38. Both good and evil from His mouth proceeds;
> 39. Why then grieves any man for his misdeeds? …
>
> 58. Thou, Lord, my soul's cause handled hast, and Thou
> Rescuest my life. 59. O Lord, do Thou judge now.

Like many other translations (e.g. NJPS and NRSV), our translation of Lam 3:36 is doubly tentative. First, it poses a question – 'Does God not see injustice?' – to which there are at least two possible answers – 'Yes, he does!' and 'No, he does not!' Second, and more important for our purposes, it uses a word, 'see', that is open to multiple interpretations. 'Not seeing' can be understood variously as 'not being aware of'; 'refusing to acknowledge'; 'paying no attention to'; 'not focusing on'; 'not caring about' or, possibly, 'not taking care of', and even 'not choosing' (NJPS) or 'not approving of' (KJV). In contrast to the author of the book of Lamentations, John Donne has no doubts: he is certain that God cannot tolerate injustice. In order to make this clear, he replaces the multivalent word 'see' in Lam 3:36 with the unambiguous word 'allow', and then omits altogether the first clause in Lam 3:59: 'You have seen the wrong done to me.' Donne has little choice in this matter. Since he had insisted that God did not 'allow' (see) injustice (cf. v. 36), he cannot easily render the biblical author's contrary insistence that God had indeed 'seen' (allowed) injustice (cf. v. 59). For the most part, Donne's rendering of Lamentations, following Tremellius's Latin translation, stays fairly close to the biblical text. In this instance, however, it is one of his infrequent departures from the text that is instructive. Since the Hebrew verb *ra'ah*, 'to see', is both common and multivalent, it is not immediately obvious that Lam 3:59 offers an answer – 'You have seen the wrong done to me, O LORD' – to a question posed twenty-three verses earlier: 'When a cause is subverted – does the Lord not see it?' (Lam 3:36). It is Donne's very omission of the words he finds difficult in verse 59 ('You have seen the wrong done to me') that draws attention to their presence in the biblical text and underlines their implications. For the author of Lamentations, unlike Donne, God does see injustice, with all that this entails.

[For Lam 3:40 see Lam 3:17–18]

3:41 Let us lift up our hearts and our hands to God in heaven.
3:42 We have transgressed and rebelled, and you have not forgiven.

Painting Lamentations

Marc Chagall (born near Vitebsk, Russia, 1887; died Paris, 1985) grew up in a region of imperial Russia with a large Jewish population. In Vitebsk and its surrounds lay the seeds of Chagall's famously colorful and vibrant depictions of Jewish life in pre-Shoah Russia – flying violinists and bearded rabbis. The inspiration for his equally well-known illustrations of the Bible seems, however, to have come from a different period of Chagall's life. He would certainly have learned biblical stories as part of his traditional Jewish education, but it was not to Jewish text study that he turned when, in the early 1930s, by now living in Paris, he was commissioned to illustrate a new edition of the Bible. Instead, he went to Palestine, drawing his inspiration from the physical landscape where the stories took place as opposed to the pages of Jewish interpretation they generated. But if the land was Chagall's muse, needless to say, the Bible itself was his primary source, and its influence is readily detected in the details.

Chagall's *The Capture of Jerusalem* (1956) appears to owe many features to the book of Lamentations. The angel of death – a sinister equivalent of the floating violinist in Chagall's Vitebsk-inspired paintings – hovers over the walled city of Jerusalem (cf. Lam 1:13, 'From on high he sent fire; it went deep into my bones'), brandishing not a violin, but the fiery torch that moments ago set light to the houses burning below (cf. Lam 2:3, 'he has burned like a flaming fire in Jacob, consuming on all sides'). At bottom left is the bowed figure of a king (cf. Lam 2:6, 'the LORD has abolished in Zion festival and sabbath, and in his fierce indignation has spurned king and priest') at the head of the procession of exiles, crown tipped forwards (cf. Lam 5:16, 'The crown has fallen from our head; woe to us that we have sinned!'). The two figures next to him, one likewise bowed, the other gazing out at the viewer,

Marc Chagall, *The Capture of Jerusalem* (1956).

both, like the king, separated slightly from the masses, could be his sons (cf. Lam 2:9, 'Her gates have sunk into the ground; he has ruined and broken her bars; her king and princes are among the nations'). The road into captivity is lined with the bodies of the dead (cf. Lam 2:21b, 'my young women and my young men have fallen by the sword; on the day of your anger you have killed them, slaughtering without mercy') or those too weak to flee (cf. Lam 2:21a,

'The young and the old are lying on the ground in the streets' and Lam 2:12, 'They cry out to their mothers, "Where is bread and wine?" as they faint like the wounded in the streets of the city, as their life is poured out on their mothers' bosom'). And we observe many pairs of upraised hands, starting with those of a bearded man we might take to be the prophet Jeremiah and extending into the line of departing exiles (cf. Lam 3:41, above). It is not certain, of course, that Chagall derived this evocative image of uplifted hands from the biblical text. First, it features in many other portrayals of Jerusalem destroyed (see e.g., Francesco Hayez, *Destruction of the Temple in Jerusalem*, 1867, and David Roberts, *The Siege and Destruction of Jerusalem by the Romans under the Command of Titus*, 1850). Perhaps Chagall was influenced by these or other earlier works. Second, it could reflect a natural response to the combination of flight and fire; many will recall the iconic 1972 Vietnam War photograph of a girl fleeing – arms outstretched if not upraised – from her napalm-bombed village near Saigon. Had Chagall himself seen victims in flight from burning villages closer to home?

Yet the particularities of Chagall's depiction suggest that his representation could indeed have been informed by the book of Lamentations. If that is the case, the most prominent pair of hands belongs to the Jeremiah figure, who stands next to and slightly above the king, in keeping with their relative status now that the city has fallen. Whereas the faces of the king and his subjects are, without exception, set between the ground and exile, the gaze of the Jeremiah figure is fixed somewhere between the burning city and the angel of death hovering over it. This is neither a Mrs Lot-like backwards glance, nor a defiant look back in anger. The direction of his gaze confirms that he has not given up on Jerusalem, and his upraised hands signify in turn his conviction that God has not abandoned its inhabitants. The place of hope in Lamentations is much debated but, through their depiction of upraised hands, Chagall and the other visual artists mentioned above reveal something important about expressions of hope and prayer – in Lamentations and beyond: they are not only verbal. Gestures and physical postures too have a crucial role to play, and to overlook them in the biblical book is to underestimate the degree of hope it contains. If it was Chagall's intention that the owner of the most prominent pair of hands was the prophet Jeremiah, he has gone one step further. Chagall would surely have identified Jeremiah as the author of Lamentations. By portraying him with hands uplifted in an act of prophetic intercession, Chagall at once highlights an expression of prayer in the biblical book and signals an essential characteristic of the book as a whole. Like its prophetic 'author', the book itself stands between God and Israel, creatively mediating and, by that means, sustaining the relationship between them, even in the midst of anger, loss and despair.

Francesco Hayez, *Destruction of the Temple in Jerusalem* (1867).

David Roberts, *The Siege and Destruction of Jerusalem by the Romans under the Command of Titus* (1850).

3:43 You have wrapped yourself with anger and pursued us;
you have slain without pity;
3:44 you have wrapped yourself with a cloud
so that no prayer can pass through.
3:45 You have made us filth and rubbish
in the midst of the peoples.

3:46 All our enemies
have opened their mouths against us;
3:47 panic and pitfall have come upon us,
devastation and destruction.
3:48 My eyes flow with rivers of tears
over the ruin of my people.

Lamenting the War against Terror

Daniel Berrigan (born Minnesota, 1921) is an American Jesuit priest, poet and peace activist, known especially for his high-profile protests against the Vietnam War, and author of *Lamentations: From New York to Kabul and Beyond* (Berrigan 2002). In the aftermath of the tragic events of 11 September 2001, Berrigan saw the book of Lamentations as a framework for a personal, political and pastoral response to what he viewed as twin catastrophes: on the one hand, the death and destruction wreaked in America when terrorists hijacked planes and flew them into the twin towers of New York City's World Trade Center and the Pentagon buildings in Washington, DC, and, on the other hand, the death and destruction caused by the retaliatory invasion of Afghanistan initiated by (then) President George W. Bush as part of America's 'war against terror'. It seems most likely to have been the first of these catastrophes – the attacks in New York and Washington, DC – that caused Berrigan to turn to Lamentations after 9/11. So many of its themes and images resonate. Above all, perhaps, is the destruction of the World Trade Center and the threatened destruction of the Pentagon, both apparently inviolable and at the same time symbolic of America's economic and military might (cf. Lam 1:10, 'The foe has laid hands on all her precious things; she has even seen the nations invade her sanctuary, those whom you forbade to enter your congregation'). Then the television footage of revellers celebrating the attacks on the streets of Gaza (cf. Lam 2:17, 'The LORD has ... made the enemy rejoice over you, and exalted the might of your foes', and Lam 2:22, 'You summoned my enemies from all around as if for a festival day'). And the political commentators eager to explain that America had brought this tragedy upon itself (Lam 1:5, 'Her foes have become the masters, her enemies are at ease, because the LORD has made her suffer for her many transgressions'), the only enemy invasion of America in living memory (cf. Lam 4:12, 'The kings of the earth did not believe, nor did any of the inhabitants of the world, that foe or enemy could enter the gates of Jerusalem'). There were the images of the victims in New York City – by no means inhabitants of the corridors of power, as outsiders might have predicted judging from the location of their workplace when viewed from afar, but rather men and women from America's lower-middle class, many of them ethnic minorities, lowly City employees, or 'back office workers' laboring behind the scenes for glamorous bosses who spent their days cutting deals in grander, if smaller, uptown locations (Lam 2:21, 'The young and the old are lying on the ground in the streets; my young women and my young men have fallen by the sword'). And finally there were New York City's firemen, who risked their own lives in the hope of finding survivors in the wreckage – fire had literally come down from above (cf. Lam 1:13, 'From on high he sent fire; it went deep into my bones') and the firemen, its human extinguishers, were on the front line of the resistance.

No wonder Berrigan wrote: 'On those raw pages [of Lamentations], I met – myself, ourselves. The poetry is a pure outcry, out of ancient Jerusalem, out of the World Trade Center less than a year past' (Berrigan 2002: xvii). But even if these were indeed the kind of parallels that led Berrigan to use Lamentations as a framework for his response to 9/11, the injustices that preoccupied him emanated primarily from the second component of the catastrophe – America's choice of Afghanistan as its target in the 'war against terror', and what he saw as the Catholic Church's complicity in the invasion: 'Fortified with the approval of the Catholic bishops and a Congress feverish with bellicosity, the president launched a new form of war' (xvii). Here, it seems, he departs from Lamentations, where no more than a few lines express the hope that Zion's enemies will suffer as Zion once suffered (cf. Lam 4:21–2). And yet there is a sense in which Berrigan remains true to the spirit of the biblical book. What stands out in his activist meditation is his focus on the confusion of war: Who is the enemy? Who are the victims? Are they 'Enemies, or God the enemy – or both mingled?' asks Berrigan. 'The people are at sea, our poet clings to a spar and cries out' (85). Paradoxically, it is perhaps the very sense of being at sea – the 'panic and pitfall' (Lam 3:47) – that enables those involved in a war, on either side, to experience most fully its injustice. Read in isolation, Lam 3:46 seems to evoke a human enemy, mocking and cursing Israel at her lowest ebb, but the verses that precede this one speak unambiguously of a divine enemy – God in heaven, who has wrapped himself with anger and slain without pity (Lam 3:43). 'All our enemies' (v. 46) must then include God, from which it follows that any claims against the human enemy should be, at the very least, nuanced. How can we wage a war against 'our enemies' when they include God?

Having established that the enemy is not readily identifiable, we must acknowledge another area of unclarity – the identity of war's victims. 'My people' in Lam 3:48 must be the residents of Jerusalem, and yet, if God is the enemy, should 'my people' be construed more broadly to include not only the residents of Jerusalem but all Israel beyond it, and, beyond that, all the human casualties of a war whose origins seem disturbingly 'other', more like an act of God than the result of human conflict? This leads to one final question that emerges from reading Lamentations through Berrigan's eyes: Who weeps for war? Here in Lam 3:48, it is the solitary lamenter – '*my* eyes', '*my* people' – in sharp contrast to the plurality of the protagonists mentioned in verses 46 and 47: '*our* enemies', 'against *us*'. Surely all those involved in a war should weep for its consequences? Berrigan puts this polemically: 'Let the poem borrow the voices of the driven and the exiled. Let us mourn for them – and for ourselves as well. For our thrice benighted leaders. Of them, no tears are recorded. "The president is on a roll," is jubilantly recorded' (85). Not all would call America's leaders at the time 'benighted' (though many would), and not all would feel comfortable with Berrigan's inclusion of the perpetrators among the victims of the 9/11 attacks: 'This land [Afghanistan] bereft of orchards and vines and forests, land of perennial victims' (85). But most would agree with his conclusion about the appropriate response to a day when, without doubt, the world changed forever for the worse: 'For the victims, tears and more tears, the human lot in a benighted age' (85).

3:49 My eyes will flow without ceasing,
without respite,
3:50 until the LORD from heaven
looks down and sees.

[*1:13 From on high he sent fire;*
it went deep into my bones;
he spread a net for my feet;
he turned me back;
he has left me stunned,
faint all day long.]

Lamenting the Expulsion from Spain

Abraham Ibn Ezra (born Navarre, Spain, 1089; died Spain?, 1164) was among the most accomplished of medieval Spain's Jewish polymaths; alongside biblical exegesis and poetry, he excelled as a philosopher, astronomer and mathematician. Like his close contemporary Yehuda Halevi (see on Lam 3:22–4), Ibn Ezra was a beneficiary of the cultural and intellectual interchange that was possible between Jews and Muslims during what became known as the medieval Spanish 'golden age'. But by 1140 he had been driven from Spain by persecution under the hostile Berber-Muslim Almohad regime, and thereafter he spent much of his life wandering from country to country in Europe, North Africa and the Middle East. In the very brief introduction to his commentary on the book of Lamentations, Ibn Ezra refers enigmatically to his own departure from Spain at the hands of unnamed angry oppressors (presumably the Almohads). This implicit equation of the expulsion of Jews from Spain with the Babylonian exile is almost explicit in a *qinah* (poem of lament) aptly entitled 'Lament for Andalusian Jewry' by its translator, Peter Cole (Cole 2007: 181–2). The most easily recognizable of several strong allusions in this poem to Lamentations occurs in the first of its four stanzas:

> *Calamity came upon Spain from the skies,*
> *and my eyes pour forth their streams of tears.*
> I moan like an owl for the town of Lucena,
> where exile dwelled, guiltless and strong,
> for a thousand and seventy years unchanged –
> until the day that she was expelled,
> leaving her like a widow, forlorn,
> deprived of the Scriptures and books of the Law.
> As the house of prayer took folly in,
> some men murdered and others sought shelter.
> For this I weep and, mourning, wail:
> If only my head were a fountain of water.

Ibn Ezra's description of the Spanish town of Lucena as 'like a widow, forlorn' after the expulsion of its Jews resonates strongly with Lam 1:1, 'How lonely sits the city that once was full of people! She has become like a widow who was once great among the nations.' Less recognizable but arguably more significant is the allusion to Lam 1:16 in the first stanza's penultimate line. Ibn Ezra's 'For this I weep …' echoes 'For these things I weep; my eyes flow with tears.' The twin themes of weeping and waters are indeed central to Ibn Ezra's poem, and each of the first three stanzas ends with a reference to one or both of them. The second stanza concludes: 'For this I wail in my grief and mourn – for they [traces of Jewish life] have melted away like water.' The third stanza closes with the words 'For Der'a [an important

Jewish community in Morocco] I put on sackcloth and mourn: their blood, on the sabbath, was spilled like water'. The water mentioned at the end of the last stanza is metaphorical – the arrows rained upon Sarah (standing here for her Jewish descendants) by Hagar (representing her Muslim descendants): 'though she'll face the hail of her handmaiden's arrows – till the Lord with compassion looks down from the skies'. But the poem's final words point back to its two-line superscription, where there were tears in abundance: 'Calamity came upon Spain from the skies, and my eyes pour forth their streams of tears.'

Peter Cole links the second clause of this line to Lam 1:16, 'For these things I weep; my eyes flow with tears.' The source of the allusion in the first clause is less obvious. For modern readers, the arresting image of calamity coming down from the skies calls to mind such catastrophes as the aerial bombing of Guernica in 1937 and the destruction wreaked in the United States by the 9/11 attacks (see on Lam 1:1 and 3:43–8). Cole reports the suggestion that it may be an inversion of a claim made in *Genesis Rabbah*, a collection of midrashic interpretations of the biblical book of Genesis emanating from fifth-century CE Palestine: 'nothing evil descends from heaven [Hebrew *shamayim*]' (51.3). Alternatively, or perhaps even complementarily, to that suggestion, Ibn Ezra's assertion that the destruction of Spanish Jewry came from heaven could be linked to Lam 1:13: 'From on high [Hebrew *marom*, a term that often signifies the heavens] he sent fire …'. Since he refers elsewhere in the poem to Lamentations, it seems plausible to see the biblical book as a source for this image too. Lamentations would also be a more satisfying source, both poetically and theologically, than *Genesis Rabbah*. As Cole observes, Ibn Ezra's poem ends with a reference to Lamentations; the cautiously optimistic 'till the Lord with compassion looks down from the skies' alludes to Lam 3:50. Thus two things that come from the skies in the book of Lamentations, namely fire sent by God (Lam 1:13) and God's compassionate gaze (Lam 3:50), may have been used by Ibn Ezra to frame his poem. At the same time he reinforces a theological message found in Lamentations, namely that everything, bad and good, comes from heaven (e.g. Lam 3:38). In some respects, this message reflects a darker worldview than that underlying *Genesis Rabbah*'s claim that nothing bad comes from heaven. Yet as disconcerting as it is to think of God as the source of evil, it is also reassuring; what God began, he can end. One question remains. By what means can God be persuaded to move from anger to compassion? The conjunction of images in the opening lines of Ibn Ezra's lament suggests his answer: human tears! And looking back now at biblical Lamentations the reader can easily identify the same conjunction there: Fire from on high (Lam 1:13) provokes floods of tears (Lam 1:16; 3:49), which will cease only when God looks down with compassion upon his people (Lam 3:50).

[For Lam 3:51 see Lam 3:17–18]

3:52 *My enemies have hunted me like a bird without cause;*
3:53 *they ended my life in a pit*
and hurled stones on me;
3:54 *water closed over my head;*
I said, 'I am lost.'

3:55 *I called on your name, O LORD,*
from the depths of the pit.
3:56 *You heard my plea. Do not close your ear*
to my cry for help, but give me relief!
3:57 *You came near on the day that I called you;*
you said, 'Do not fear!'

Out of Africa

In the thirty or so years since Zimbabwe's independence, its stone carvers – mostly from the country's largest tribe, the Shonas – have been internationally acclaimed for their distinctive, substantial and, in all senses, 'polished' stone sculptures. But more recently a new and strikingly different art form has gained popularity in Zimbabwe; local artists have begun to make sculptures of 'junk', the materials once reserved for children's toys. The turn to 'junk art' among artists in Zimbabwe is suggestive on many levels. It reflects the country's economic poverty (on the one hand stone is prohibitively expensive and, on the other, nothing can be wasted, not even rubbish), its political turmoil and social fragility (stone implies permanence, while junk implies something makeshift and temporary), and, perhaps above all, it suggests the sheer desperation of its citizens. Paradoxically, stone does *not* in this case signify 'rock-bottom'. Rock-bottom is precisely the feeling that emanates from Taurai Gondo's evocative wire and wood sculpture, *Lamentations*, a piece that was included in a 2006 contemporary art exhibition at the National Gallery of Zimbabwe in Harare. The materials are 'found objects', rough pieces of mismatched wood and thin metal rods that might have been salvaged from a dump.

Taurai Gondo, *Lamentations*. Artist's impression by Matan Sacofsky.

The sculpture depicts a caged male figure, head thrown back and face turned heavenwards in a gesture of what can only be prayer. He is tall and painfully thin, his unnaturally long, scrawny neck elongated by his head's awkward angle, and his talon-like hands clenched in urgent supplication. The cage is cylindrical, following closely the contours of his body, and resembling not so much a prison cell as a bird cage. Air passes easily through the bars, and yet this cage affords no room to breathe. The sculpture evokes at once a human being at the moment when he can hope no harder, and a turkey trapped in a cage, helplessly awaiting the butcher's knife. It may have been the desperate prayer and not the man's bird-like qualities that made Gondo entitle his work *Lamentations*, but the sculpture brings to mind Lam 3:52–7. The biblical pit has been replaced in the sculpture by a cage, not in perfect accord with the text but an image far more evocative of a trapped bird for most modern readers. Although the sculpture depicts no recently thrown stones and no water above the man's head, the aggressive angle of his neck and way that the plane of his face is tilted absolutely horizontal suggest that something hard is bearing down upon him from above, or that he is pushing upwards against an obstacle he longs to remove. His nose is only inches from the cage's roof, but we do not doubt for an instant that this man has reached his lowest ebb, the depths of despair (v. 55). And his large, wide-open mouth, at once articulate and dumb, seems silently and uncomprehendingly to implore the Lord: 'Do not close your ear to my cry for help, but give me relief!' (v. 56).

In rejecting the polished stone that reflects Zimbabwe's natural glory, and working instead with the junk that represents the abject failure of its governance, these artists are making a strong statement of resistance. They have rejected the game of keeping up appearances, and seek rather to expose the ills of the regime that keeps them on their knees. Similarly, biblical Lamentations has opted to reveal the true measure of devastation that 'Babylon' has wreaked by overlooking such images as the Temple's former glory, and dwelling instead on the city's ruined buildings, empty streets and desperate inhabitants. Yet there is an important difference. The Zimbabwe junk artists portray images of suffering and devastation using materials that are spoiled and broken. Even if the effect it produces is powerful and evocative, this junk art, unlike the Shona stone sculptures, cannot be described as beautiful. The book of Lamentations, in contrast, is beautiful. Its authors depict the suffering and devastation of their society using exquisitely crafted poetry. Are they, unlike the junk artists, 'selling out', making suffering polished and palatable for privileged armchair consumers? This is a question that is hard to answer, but it is tempting to conclude that the aesthetic value of the book of Lamentations has played no small part in its widespread popularity and its enduring appeal.

[For Lam 3:58–9 see Lam 3:34–9]
[For Lam 3:60–6 see Lam 3:20–1]

References

Albrektson, B. 1963. *Studies in the Text and Theology of the Book of Lamentations* (Studia Theologica Lundensia, 21; Lund: CWK Gleerup).

Archer, J. 1999. *The Nature of Grief: The Evolution and Psychology of Reactions to Loss* (London: Routledge).

Berlin, A. 2002. *Lamentations* (OTL; Louisville, KY, and London: Westminster John Knox).

Berrigan, D. 2002. *Lamentations: From New York to Kabul and Beyond* (Lanham, MD, and Chicago: Sheed and Ward).

Cole, P. (ed). 2007. *The Dream of the Poem: Hebrew Poetry from Muslim and Christian Spain, 950–1492* (Princeton: Princeton University Press).

Dobbs-Allsopp, F. W. 1997. 'Tragedy, Tradition and Theology in the Book of Lamentations', *JSOT* 74: 29–60.

Donne, J. 1896. *Poems of John Donne*, vol. 1 (E. K. Chambers; London: Lawrence & Bullen).

Farnell, L. R. 1925. *The Attributes of God* (Oxford: Clarendon).

Freud, S. 1991a. 'Mourning and Melancholia', in *On Metapsychology: The Theory of Psychoanalysis* (Penguin Freud Library, 11; Harmondsworth: Penguin) 245–68.

Freud, S. 1991b. 'The Ego and the Id', in *On Metapsychology: The Theory of Psychoanalysis* (Penguin Freud Library, 11; Harmondsworth: Penguin) 350–408.

Halevi, Y. 2002. *Poems from the Diwan* (trans. G. Levin; Poetica, 32; London: Anvil Press).

Heschel, A. J. 1962. *The Prophets* (New York: Harper and Row).

Heschel, A. J. 1997. *Israel: An Echo of Eternity* (Woodstock, VT: Jewish Lights Publishing). [Original, 1967]

Hillers, D. R. 1992. *Lamentations* (Anchor Bible, 7a; Garden City, NY: Doubleday, 2nd edn).

John of the Cross. 1976. *Dark Night of the Soul* (trans. by E. Allison Peers; London: Burns & Oates).

Joyce, P. M. 1993. 'Lamentations and the Grief Process: A Psychological Reading', *Biblical Interpretation* 1: 304–20.

Kavanaugh, K. and O. Rodriguez. 1991. *The Collected Works of St John of the Cross* (Washington, DC: ICS).

Kraus, H.-J. 1968. *Klagelieder (Threni)* (BKAT, 20; Neukirchen-Vluyn: Neukirchener Verlag, 3rd edn).

Kübler-Ross, E. 1969. *On Death and Dying* (New York: Touchstone).

Labahn, A. 2002. 'Trauern als Bewältigung der Vergangenheit zur Gestaltung der Zukunft. Bemerkungen zur anthropologischen Theologie der Klagelieder', *VT* 52: 513–27.

Lagnado, L. 2007. *The Man in the White Sharkskin Suit: My Family's Exodus from Old Cairo to the New World* (New York: Ecco).

Lagnado, L. 2011. *The Arrogant Years: One Girl's Search for Her Lost Youth, from Cairo to Brooklyn* (New York: Ecco).

Linafelt, T. 2000a. *Surviving Lamentations: Catastrophe, Lament, and Protest in the Afterlife of a Biblical Book* (Chicago and London: University of Chicago Press).

Miller, A. 1991. *Breaking Down the Wall of Silence to Join the Waiting Child* (London: Virago).

Parry, R. A. 2010. *Lamentations* (Two Horizons Old Testament Commentary; Grand Rapids, MI, and Cambridge: Eerdmans).

Parry, R. A. and H. A. Thomas (eds). 2011. *Great Is Thy Faithfulness? Reading Lamentations as Sacred Scripture* (Eugene, OR: Pickwick).

Porteous, N. W. 1961. 'Jerusalem–Zion: The Growth of a Symbol', in *Verbannung und Heimkehr: Beiträge zur Geschichte und Theologie Israels im 6. und 5. Jahrhundert v. Chr.* (Festschrift W. Rudolph; ed A. Kuschke; Tübingen: Mohr) 235–52.

Pyper, H. S. 2001. 'Reading Lamentations', *JSOT* 95: 55–69.

Raphael, C. 1968. *Walls of Jerusalem* (New York: Alfred Knopf).

Reimer, D. J. 2002. 'Good Grief? A Psychological Reading of Lamentations', *ZAW* 114: 542–59.

Rudolph, W. 1962. *Das Buch Ruth, Das Hohe Lied, Die Klagelieder* (KAT, 17; Gütersloh: Gerd Mohn, 2nd edn).

Schopf, F. J. 2011. 'Musical Responses to Lamentations', in Parry and Thomas (2011) 147–53.

Smith-Christopher, D. 2002. *A Biblical Theology of Exile* (OBT; Minneapolis, MN: Fortress, 2002).

Soggin, J. A. 1976. *Introduction to the Old Testament* (London: SCM Press).

Spiegel, Y. 1973. *Der Prozess des Trauerns: Analyse und Beratung* (Munich: Kaiser).

Stern, D. 1991. *Parables in Midrash: Narrative and Exegesis in Rabbinic Literature* (Cambridge, MA: Harvard University Press).

Stewart, J. L. 1991. *Ernst Krenek: The Man and His Music* (Berkeley, CA: University of California Press).

Stiebert, J. 2003. 'Human Suffering and Divine Abuse of Power in Lamentations: Reflections on Forgiveness in the Context of South Africa's Truth and Reconciliation Process', *Pacifica* 16: 195–215.

Thomas, H. A. 2010. 'Relating Prayer and Pain: Psychological Analysis and Lamentations Research', *Tyndale Bulletin* 61: 183–208.

Thompson, C. 2002. *St John of the Cross: Songs in the Night* (London: SPCK).

Wenthe, D. O. 2009. *Jeremiah, Lamentations* (Ancient Christian Commentary on Scripture, Old Testament, 12; Downers Grove, IL: InterVarsity Press).

Wiles, J. P. 1908. *Half-hours with the Minor Prophets and the Lamentations* (London: Morgan and Scott).

Wiles, M. F. 2003. *Scholarship and Faith: A Tale of Two Grandfathers* (Cambridge: Cambridge University Press).

4:1 How the gold has grown dim!
The pure gold is debased.
The sacred stones lie scattered
on every street corner.

A Girl by Any Other Name

Lamentations 4 explores the horrors of the siege and sack of Jerusalem, with a particular emphasis on the contrast between past blessing and present loss. Like Chapters 1 and 2, it is a twenty-two-verse acrostic, and opens in Hebrew with the word *eicha*. According to Jewish tradition, most books of the Bible are named after their reputed author, their central character, or their first significant word (see on Lam 1:1). The book of Lamentations follows the third model and is therefore known as *Eicha*. Translated here simply as 'How' (as, for example, in

Lamentations Through the Centuries, First Edition. Paul M. Joyce and Diana Lipton.
© 2013 Paul M. Joyce and Diana Lipton. Published 2020 by John Wiley & Sons Ltd.

NRSV), the word *eicha* conveys in Hebrew a sense of anguish and despair resonant with another popular rendition, 'Alas' (see, for example, NJPS). A short, independent Israeli film called *Eicha* (2001, Hebrew) directed by Eliezer Shapiro – who went on to direct an immensely popular Israeli soap opera about young Orthodox 'singles' in Jerusalem – revolves entirely around the significance of the name 'Eicha'. Shapiro's concern is not the title of the biblical book, but rather the name of his film's heroine, a young woman whose parents gave their daughter the lamentable name of Eicha. Eicha's parents chose this name – understandably not a popular choice for baby girls, despite its pretty, feminine sound – because she was born on Tisha B'Av. In all countries and cultures, names can be revealing about the socio-economic status, religion, geographic and ethnic origins, and cultural preferences of their owners, or at least their owner's parents. Shapiro's film asks the loaded question 'What is in a name?' in relation to the highly complex society of modern-day Israel.

The film *Eicha* opens just before its eponymous heroine's eighteenth birthday. Eicha is shown alighting from a bus along with her friends, a group of young women whose conservative, 'modest' clothes and hair-styles immediately identify them (to anyone familiar with Israeli society) as politically and religiously right-wing Jews from a settlement. The girls are on their way to a political demonstration protesting the intention of the government of the day to give up land – including the land upon which settlements such as theirs were built – for peace. But Eicha uses this rare opportunity to spend time alone in the big city for another purpose. She slips away from the demonstration to buy clothes in a decidedly non-Orthodox boutique. Seeing her traditional garb, the ultra-fashionable shop assistant – readily identifiable by *her* clothing and hair-style as a secular and probably politically left-wing Jew – has no trouble placing Eicha as a settler, but she cannot place her name. Even Eicha's reference to Tisha B'Av elicits a blank expression; the Temples and their destruction are off the radar for this young woman. The film's viewers get the message: no matter what clothes Eicha wears and how she cuts her hair, her unusual name will always stand between her and the secular Israeli society into which she yearns to blend. Eicha understands that too, and she decides to change her name at the earliest opportunity, which, according to Israeli law, is the day of her eighteenth birthday. On the ninth day of the month of Av, her eighteenth birthday according to the Hebrew calendar, Eicha arrives at the government offices where name changes are registered and approved. But, unknown to Eicha, Israeli bureaucracy runs according to the Gregorian (solar) calendar, not the Hebrew (lunar) calendar. In that particular year, the Hebrew calendar was running ahead of the

Gregorian calendar, and thus her official, Gregorian eighteenth birthday had not yet arrived. Eicha is told that she is too early, that there is nothing to be done, and that she will have to wait and come back another day.

On her way home to her settlement, Eicha passes near the *Kotel*, the Western Wall, where she encounters members of the 'Temple Mount Faithful', a group of right-wing religious fanatics who advocate the rebuilding of the Temple on its original site (now occupied, of course, by the Al Aqsa mosque and the Dome of the Rock, the third-holiest site of Islam). Eicha becomes entangled against her will with the demonstrators, and her distinctive modest attire makes it easy for the police to mistake her for one of them. When a security guard asks her name, her fate is sealed. It goes without saying that a young woman whose very name is identified with the loss of the Temple is there to demand its restoration. Eicha is arrested. Her originally American mother – half anxious about her daughter's well-being and half proud in her mistaken belief that Eicha was arrested while calling for the rebuilding of the Temple – comes to secure her daughter's release from prison. They emerge together from the police station to see their car being towed away from the spot in which it was illegally parked. The film closes with the mother's tragi-comic response to the sad chain of events: 'This is the worst Tisha B'Av I have ever had!'

The film *Eicha* is less an example of the history of interpretation of the biblical book than a snapshot of its complex place in modern Jewish culture, even – especially – in the Jewish state. The different responses to this young woman's name signify the varying responses within Israeli society to the book of Lamentations and what it represents. For Eicha's new-immigrant, religiously and politically right-wing, Orthodox Zionist parents, their daughter's name signifies their commitment to a particular vision of the Jewish state. They are seemingly oblivious or indifferent to the name's mournful associations, but think only of the future when, as they see it, the Temple will be restored along with the glory of Zion. The government employees – representing here the Jewish state – would be happy enough to change Eicha's name, but they (literally) do not recognize the date that confirms its significance. For the young, secular Israelis among whom Eicha longs to live, her name reflects incomprehension of aliens in their midst – the girl and the Temple. For the policemen assigned to guard the Temple Mount and prevent politically explosive incidents, the name Eicha conjures up a dangerous fundamentalist, someone who cannot let go of the past. And for an adolescent girl trying to find herself in a complex world that pulls in many directions, her unusual name is part and parcel of an identity she would sooner shed. In the hands of those socio-political alchemists, the movie makers, Eicha the name transmutes – from lead to gold to pure gold, and back again.

4:2 The precious children of Zion,
once worth their weight in fine gold –
how they are reckoned as earthen pots,
the work of a potter's hands!

Who Really *Destroyed the Temple?*

Lamentations Rabbah (see also at Lam 2:18; 3:20–1; and 4:21–2) offers a surprising gauge of the preciousness of Zion's children (Lam 4:2): residents of Jerusalem were so precious that they refused to attend wedding feasts unless they had been invited *not once but twice* (*Lamentations Rabbah* 4.3). The story that accompanies this surprising claim explains their need to receive two invitations; it arose from a fear that they had been invited by mistake – the invitation had been intended for someone else.[1] According to this story, which takes place shortly before the destruction of the second Temple by the Romans in 70 CE, a wealthy Jerusalemite commissioned his servant to invite his good friend Kamza to a wedding feast at his house. But instead of inviting Kamza, as the wealthy man had intended, the servant mistakenly invited a man with a very similar name, Bar Kamza. As bad luck would have it, Bar Kamza was the wealthy Jerusalemite's bitter enemy. Seeing Bar Kamza at the feast, the host got angry and asked him to leave immediately. Bar Kamza begged the host not to shame him publicly, first promising not to eat anything at all at the feast and then, when that strategy failed, offering to pay for the entire meal. (Both these offers are surprising, even comic, when coming from a man whose Aramaic name means 'son of a locust'!) But the Jerusalemite insisted that Bar Kamza must leave the feast.

Among the onlookers was an eminent guest, Rabbi Zechariah ben Avqulos, who could have intervened on Bar Kamza's behalf, but he did not. Bar Kamza exacted his revenge by meddling in a highly sensitive, not to say explosive, political issue. He approached the Emperor and told him that the animals the Romans sent to be sacrificed at the Jerusalem Temple were not being sacrificed at all, but were being eaten by Jewish priests. At first, the Emperor refused to believe him, but then Bar Kamza convinced him to put the priests to the test. Bar Kamza accompanied the next shipment of Roman animals destined for sacrifice in the Temple, and, when no one was looking, secretly injured each one of the animals, thus rendering them all unfit for sacrifice. Afraid of offending the city's Roman rulers, some Temple officials wanted to sacrifice the animals anyway. But one priest stood firm, telling the Romans that he would sacrifice their animals tomorrow. Three days passed, and still he did not

---

[1]   A very similar story is told in the Babylonian Talmud, *Gittin* 55b–56a.

sacrifice them; Bar Kamza's story to the Emperor appeared to be confirmed. Furious at having been deceived by the Jews, the angry Romans destroyed the Temple. The midrash itself concludes that the Temple was destroyed either because of the slight difference between the names 'Kamza' and 'Bar Kamza', or because Rabbi Zechariah did not intervene when Bar Kamza was insulted. But surely the story is more complicated than that. Almost any one of its cast of characters could have been held responsible for the destruction of the Temple. Was it the careless servant who invited the wrong guest? Or the wealthy Jerusalemite who, though understandably annoyed when he saw his bitter enemy at his feast, should have resisted the impulse to shame him publicly? Or the accidental guest, Bar Kamza, who went too far when he involved the Roman authorities in his private grievance? Or Rabbi Zechariah, who should have intervened on Bar Kamza's behalf? Or the Emperor who, though entitled to be angry had his sacrificial animals indeed been rejected, should not have destroyed the Temple on account of it? Or was it the priest who argued against the sacrifice of the Emperor's animals? To be sure, he was right to want to preserve the integrity of the Temple cult, but at what cost? Taking all this into account, who in the end was responsible for the destruction of the Temple?

Returning to *Lamentations Rabbah* via a completely different biblical text, we may find a surprising answer to this question. Towards the end of the Joseph narrative (Genesis 37–50), Joseph tells his brothers not to feel guilty – it was God, not them, who brought him down to Egypt as part of his divine plan (Gen 45:8). How is this compatible with the chain of events as reported in Genesis, where God is not credited with bringing Israel into Egypt, as he is credited in Exodus with bringing Israel out? Genesis 37 offers an array of competing explanations for Joseph's descent into Egypt. First, Jacob was responsible – he caused a conflict between his sons by favoring one over the others, and then sent the favored son, Joseph, to find his brothers in the remote place where they were shepherding their sheep. Second, the brothers did it – they threw Joseph into the pit. Third, it was the Midianites – they sold him to the Ishmaelites. Fourth, the Ishmaelites must take the blame – they took him down to Egypt. And fifth (some might add), Joseph himself had a part to play – he flaunted his privileged status in the family and made his brothers jealous in the first place. Paradoxically, it is the very multiplicity of causes that makes Joseph's claim about the divine plan plausible. That is, in the absence of a single clear-cut human cause, the reader is ready to believe Joseph when he tells his brothers that it was God, not them, who brought him down to Egypt.[2] In a similar way, the *Lamentations Rabbah* midrash makes it impossible to determine whose inappropriate actions caused the destruction of the Temple.

[2]   This reading of the Joseph narrative is suggested by Edward Greenstein (1982).

Perhaps the unsettling answer is that it was none of the above. A few verses later in Lamentations 4, we hear (not for the first time) that it was God who destroyed the first Temple: 'The LORD gave full vent to his fury; he poured out his blazing anger, and kindled a fire in Zion that consumed its foundations' (v. 11). In some respects, this is surprising, given that throughout the book blame for the fall of Jerusalem is divided between various parties ranging from the nations (Lam 1:10) and, specifically, the Edomites (Lam 4:21–2), through Zion's priests and prophets (Lam 4:13) to Jerusalem itself (Lam 1:8). How can all these people be responsible if God himself destroyed the city? Perhaps, as with the *Lamentations Rabbah* story about Kamza and Bar Kamza (and the biblical story of Joseph and his brothers), it is in the end the very multiplicity of guilty parties that leaves the reader with no alternative but to hold God accountable.

4:3 *Even jackals offer the breast*
and nurse their young,
but my poor people has become cruel,
like the ostriches in the wilderness.

4:4 *The tongue of the nursling sticks*
to the roof of its mouth for thirst;
the infants beg for food,
but no one gives them anything.

[5:18 *Because of Mount Zion, which lies desolate;*
jackals prowl over it.]

Weighed in the Balance?

The search for ancient Near Eastern parallels to biblical texts can be illuminating or positively misleading, depending in part on the theology, politics and ideology of the seeker. Parallels drawn from Egyptology require especially cautious scrutiny: ancient Egypt is a hobby horse for many Hebrew Bible readers. Yet, as seems to be the case here, such comparative study can be rewarding. Jackals are mentioned twice in Lamentations, once in Lam 4:3 and again in Lam 5:18. Their appearance in Lam 5:18 needs little explanation. Naturalistically, jackals are right at home in ruins, and therefore on the ruined Temple Mount, and in literary terms they make a fitting conclusion to the preceding catalogue of images of devastation. But Johan Renkema offers a parallel from ancient Egypt that makes their appearance in the vicinity of the destroyed Temple still more suggestive. In ancient Egypt, he points out (following

Keel 1977: 33, 66–7), jackals were the animals most closely identified with the dead. The jackals that roam the Temple Mount show that Jerusalem had become not just a ruined city but a necropolis, a city of the dead (Renkema 1998: 621). Clearly, Renkema's comment is addressing Lam 5:18, but his insight may also illuminate Lam 4:3, where jackals are mentioned in a very different context.

Lamentations contains many images of reversal and decline (for example, in Lam 4:1–2 what was bright gold has become tarnished and what was once precious has become worthless, while in Lam 5:2–4 those who were once propertied have been disinherited, those who had families are now alone, and those who once benefited freely from natural resources must pay for them). Likewise, there are many images of mothers unable or unwilling to care for their offspring (for example, in Lam 2:12 starving children die on their mothers' bosoms, in Lam 2:20 and 4:10 mothers eat their offspring, and here in Lam 4:3 they are likened to ostriches, birds apparently known to abandon their eggs). Yet there is no intrinsic connection between these two general ideas of drastically declined fortune on the one hand and maternal cruelty on the other. Nor is there an obvious segue between their specific expressions at the beginning of Lamentations 4, that is, formerly precious children on the one hand (v. 2) and, on the other, jackals who, unlike the mothers of Zion, suckle their young (v. 3). An insight gleaned from Egyptology may help to explain how these two ideas are connected, and why the shift to jackals from once-precious children is not necessarily a non sequitur.

Anubis, the ancient Egyptian god of the dead, was usually depicted with the head of a jackal. One of Anubis's significant roles involved weighing the heart of someone who had recently died. On the other side of the scale was a feather signifying Maat, the Egyptian goddess who represented world order, truth and justice (Keel 1998: 71). Maat is often portrayed as a woman wearing an ostrich plume on her head, but sometimes, she is depicted by a feather alone, the distinctive adornment standing for the whole (Keel 1998: 36; Keel and Uehlinger 1998: 70–1). Illustrations from the *Egyptian Book of the Dead* show the jackal-headed Anubis standing next to an elaborate weighing scale. On one side sits a human heart (presumably just removed from someone recently departed) and on the other sits the distinctive plume of Maat (Keel 1998: 73). The ultimate fate of the person who has just died literally hangs in the balance … against an ostrich feather. If the person led a virtuous life, his or her heart will be light, and the feather will keep it suspended. But if the person led a life of sin, the heart will sink, weighed down by its sins; the feather will be unable to keep it aloft.

Jackals and ostriches are paired in several places in the Bible outside the book of Lamentations. Commenting on Lam 5:18, Adele Berlin mentions Isa 34:13; Mic 1:8; and Job 30:29, and points out their natural parallels – both jackal and ostrich have eerie cries and a taste for ruins (Berlin 2002: 106). But the above-mentioned insight gleaned from Egyptology suggests that perhaps the appearance of jackals and ostriches together in Lam 4:3 was occasioned in part by images contained in the verse that precedes it. Lamentations 4:2 speaks graphically and memorably of the near-dead children of Zion who were once 'worth their weight in fine gold' (cf. Job 28:16, 19), but are now reckoned as equivalent in value to mere clay pots. This stark contrast between the formerly valuable and the currently worthless implies the presence of an assessor or evaluator. As noted above, in ancient Egypt, the role of the assessor or evaluator was played by a jackal-headed god who is described in texts and portrayed in illustrations as weighing human hearts on a scale, balanced against an ostrich feather that signified truth and justice. This pair – the jackal and the ostrich – survives in Lam 4:3 in the form of an especially ruthless beast that nevertheless cares for its own young and a cruel bird that, by implication, does not. Is it possible that the reference to jackals and ostriches in Lam 4:3 following directly after a graphic representation of a sharp decline in value is not, after all, the non sequitur it appears at first glance to be, but reflects instead a set of images that were perfectly coherent in the world of ancient Egypt, a jackal, an ostrich, and lives held in the balance?

4:5 Those who feasted on delicacies
perish in the streets;
those who were brought up in purple
cling to ash heaps.

[4:7 Her princes were purer than snow,
whiter than milk;
their bodies were ruddier than coral,
their hair like sapphire.

4:8 Now their faces are blacker than soot;
they are not recognized in the streets.
Their skin has shrivelled on their bones;
it has become as dry as wood.]

Balkan Laments

During 1996–97, the year following the end of the Bosnian war, Nancy Lee lived in Osijek, Croatia, on a Fulbright scholarship. She travelled throughout Croatia and Bosnia, listening to accounts of what had happened and collecting lament poetry. In *The Singers of Lamentations: Cities under Siege, from Ur to*

Jerusalem to Sarajevo … (2002; cf. Lee and Mandolfo 2008: 33–46, 163–76), Lee combines a scholarly analysis of the ancient text of biblical Lamentations with the study of lamentations recited in a modern context. Drawing on oral-poetic methods and socio-rhetorical approaches, Lee finds in Lamentations the voices of poetic singers in antiphonal dialogue in the context of mourning, and argues that poets through history and across cultures share common ground in how they render suffering and destruction in their war-torn cities.

Lee tells of a story as old as Ur, one that is, alas, all too likely to be repeated many times in the future, a story of cities under siege and the way human beings respond to such trauma. Of singers from modern Sarajevo she writes: 'In a sense, not unlike the suffering singers of biblical Lamentations, they gather together amidst the rubble and try to make sense of what happened' (Lee 2002: 202). She observes 'how from ancient Ur, to Jerusalem, to contemporary South Slavic lands, poets and prophets often personify their towns to render their community's suffering' (195); personification of Zion is, of course, a key element in Lamentations, notably in Chapters 1–2. Other shared features that Lee identifies include 'concerns for lack of justice for those suffering, futility of prayer, plea for the children, and accusation of God' (75).

A recurrent, indeed defining, theme of Lamentations is the sharp contrast between former blessing and present loss. The book starts on that note (Lam 1:1) and the theme also dominates much of Lamentations 4 (in addition to the present verses, see especially v. 1–4); those once well fed are reduced to starvation, those once revered are brought to humiliation. A strikingly similar motif of contrast characterizes many of the Slavic laments that Lee presents, of which Slavica Crnjac's poem 'Vukovar' (1995) serves as a powerful and poignant example (cf. Lee 2002: 1, 60; Lee 2010: 63):

> In the old town of Vukovar
> there was a sweet smell of lime-trees …
> beautiful lime-trees fell,
> 'tambura' were silenced.

The Lamentations verses cited above speak of fine food and clothes giving way to hunger among the ash heaps, and of physical beauty succumbing to desiccation. In Crnjac's poem, beautiful lime-trees become felled trees, sunshine gives way to cloud, doves disappear and a proud tower tumbles to ruins. The contrast between what once was and what now is enables both poets to convey a sense of loss in a way that would not be possible if the destruction were simply described. The passage of time and its tragic effects is conveyed in dramatic and dynamic terms, in a way that strongly evokes the brute reality that a way of life has been lost forever.

The extent to which the modern Slavic laments are influenced by biblical Lamentations, directly or indirectly, is difficult to assess, as is the precise nature and degree of the indebtedness of the biblical text to ancient Mesopotamian city-laments. It is possible that we are dealing here simply with reflections of universal human experience, but it is more likely that there are also significant elements of cultural continuity, however hard to quantify.

4:6 For the guilt of my poor people was greater
than the iniquity of Sodom,
which was overthrown in a moment,
though no hand was laid on it.

Worse than Sodom?

Do inner-biblical interpretation and intertextuality belong in a reception history? For some ancient and many modern biblical exegetes the answer is yes. Rabbinic commentators, for example, see the Bible as a timeless text with 'no early and late'. That is, for the purposes of interpretation, the rabbis allowed themselves to bring to bear any scriptural passage on any other scriptural passage, regardless of the relative dates of their composition or, more often, the relative dates of the events they describe. For reasons that are different but related, many postmodern academic interpreters privilege the reader over the possible author, and for them too there is no need to establish an order of composition. With this in mind, it is illuminating to consider the reference to the destruction of Sodom in Lam 4:6 in the light of other biblical allusions to the downfall of that doomed city.

When it comes to what God did to Sodom (and Gomorrah), the Bible is consistent and precise. Six texts outside Genesis refer explicitly to the destruction of the city (Deut 29:22 [English, v. 23]; Isa 13:19; Jer 49:18; 50:40; Amos 4:11; and Lam 4:6), and in all six cases the verb that signifies the destruction is *h-p-ch*, 'to overthrow', 'to turn upside down'.[3] Why did all these authors choose this relatively uncommon verb over the more common, generic *sh-h-t*, 'to destroy'? It is not simply a matter of reliance on the Genesis account; both verbs appear there, along with *s-p-h*, 'to sweep away', in Gen 18:23–4. Moreover, *sh-h-t* occurs eight times in the Genesis material (Gen 18:28 [twice], 31, 32; 19:13 [twice], 14, 29) versus only three occurrences of *h-p-ch* (Gen 19:21,

---

[3] Ezek 16:50 uses the verb *sur*, 'to remove', but explicitly in relation to the inhabitants of the city, not the city itself.

25, 29), and *sh-h-t* is at the heart of the memorable and theologically significant exchange between God and Abraham over Sodom's fate (Gen 18:22–3). One explanation for the choice of *h-p-ch* in those six texts outside Genesis emerges from a consideration of the context in which Sodom is mentioned in Lam 4:6. One of many strategies used by the author(s) of Lamentations to convey the immensity of the catastrophe involves reversal of fortune. The images of reversal of fortune that occur throughout the book are particularly concentrated in the first half of Lamentations 4: gold has become clay (v. 2), the formerly rich cling to ash heaps (v. 5), snow-white princes are as black as soot (vv. 7, 8), and compassionate women cook their children (v. 10). This comparative method of depicting disaster is powerful for several reasons. First, it is not static, but illustrates a movement from the very heights to the very depths. Decline and fall, elsewhere a hallmark of the genre of tragedy, is painted here in a few broad strokes: what was valuable is now worthless. Second, images of reversal of fortune contain an inbuilt mechanism for damage assessment. We can measure at a glance the gap between the norm (mothers feed their babies) and the abnormal post-destruction situation (mothers eat their babies). Third, and perhaps most important, images of reversal of fortune do not merely illustrate destruction, they are microcosms of it. Destruction at its most calamitous entails the complete inversion of world order. To claim that what was gold is now clay is not to make a socio-economic point, as justified and relevant as that might be, but to show that nothing makes sense any more. Everything is upside down, and tried and tested methods of understanding and ordering the world are rendered ineffective. Perhaps Sodom is mentioned in Lam 4:6 because in the context of the biblical world it emblematizes the inversion of world order that is described in the verses immediately around it.

Support for this claim about the significance of Sodom in Lam 4:6 can be gleaned from a consideration of the other biblical citations mentioned above. In each one, the reference to Sodom occurs in a context that emphasizes not merely destruction but also inversion, the topsy-turvy reality that comes in its wake. Deuteronomy 29:20–8 (English, vv. 21–9) explains why a fertile land becomes barren, and why residents become exiles. Isaiah 13:19–22 predicts that Babylon will be transformed from a home for tents and domestic animals to a place of ruins and wild beasts, and Jer 49:17–22 paints a similar scene for Edom. Jeremiah 50:35–40, the strongest example, tells how the wise men of Babylon will become fools, the mercenaries in its midst will become like women, its waters will be dried up, and its settled places will become desolate. And Amos 4:9–11 describes rich agricultural terrain decimated by locusts, and strong armies reduced to a stench in the nostrils. By reading Lam 4:6 intertextually with other biblical verses that mention the destruction of Sodom, we learn something profound about the poetic art, not to mention the theological and political worldview, of Lamentations itself. The line about Sodom's overthrow is far from a throwaway line.

[For Lam 4:7–8 see Lam 4:5]

4:9 Happier were those pierced by the sword
than those pierced by hunger,
who pined away, deprived
of the produce of the field.

4:10 The hands of compassionate women
have boiled their own children;
they became their food
in the destruction of my poor people.

[*5:6 We hold out a hand to Egypt,*
to Assyria, for our fill of bread.]

[*5:9 We get our bread at the peril of our lives,*
because of the sword in the wilderness.]

No Bread of Life

The theme of hunger pervades the book of Lamentations, and more often than not it causes people to act against their natures. Hungry men, who could otherwise have been expected to offer protection to weaker citizens, die in the pursuit of food: 'I called out to my friends but they deceived me; my priests and elders perished in the city while seeking food to keep themselves alive' (Lam 1:19). The search for the bread of life might end in death: 'We get our bread at the peril of our lives, because of the sword in the wilderness' (Lam 5:9). Hunger has political consequences, leading Israel to bargain with its enemies: 'We hold out a hand to Egypt, to Assyria, for our fill of bread' (Lam 5:6). Most memorably, though, the theme of hunger is articulated in Lamentations in relation to mothers and children. Children starve because their mothers cannot feed them: 'The tongue of the nursling sticks to the roof of its mouth for thirst; the infants beg for food, but no one gives them anything' (Lam 4:4). Mothers are so hungry that they cook and eat their own children: 'The hands of compassionate women have boiled their own children' (Lam 4:10, above; cf. 2:20).

Since it is hard to conceive of an act less natural, or an inversion of order more complete, than a parent's literal consumption of his or her own child, it is shocking to read, in a poem written in the Vilna ghetto on 18 January 1943, of a father who sank still lower. The Yiddish poet Abraham Sutzkever (born

Smorgon, Russia, 1913; died Tel Aviv, 2010) wrote more than eighty poems while fighting for his own survival in unimaginably horrific circumstances under Nazi occupation. In one of these poems, 'To My Child', Sutzkever writes in the voice of a man who did not merit even the appalling fate of eating his infant son. Given the traumatic events of his early life, there is reason to think that Sutzkever was writing in his own voice. In 1941 he, his widowed mother and his young wife Freydke were sent by the Nazis to the Vilna ghetto. Sutzkever and his wife escaped two years later. After a period in which he fought the occupying Nazi forces as a partisan, he and Freydke were smuggled into Russia, and they ultimately arrived in Palestine in 1947. Sutzkever's mother, however, was not with them. She had been murdered back in Vilna before their escape, along with the newborn son to whom Freydke had given birth in the ghetto. Perhaps it was of his own dead son that Sutzkever wrote:

> Because of hunger
> or because of great love …
> I wanted to swallow you, child,
> when I felt your tiny body
> cool in my hands
> like a glass
> of warm tea …
> Maybe you will blossom again
> in my veins.
> I'm not worthy of you, though.
> I can't be your grave.[4]

Although the poem does not refer explicitly to the book of Lamentations, it seems likely that Sutzkever recalled its cannibal mothers when he spoke as a father who wanted to swallow – not only or necessarily from hunger, but out of love – his own baby. Intentionally or not, this extraordinary memorial to the Shoah's youngest victims, newborn babies, suggests a reinterpretation of the Bible so unexpected that it takes the breath away. Following Sutzkever's train of thought in 'To My Child', perhaps it was not hunger that motivated the women of Lamentations to eat their offspring. Rather, these mothers longed to return their babies to the place from which they came, not to the earth, but to their own bodies. Again bearing in mind Sutzkever, perhaps they wanted to give their children a second chance. Thinking now like mothers, not like systematic theologians, they might have asked which was the more auspicious site for regenerating life, the dry dust of the ground, or the moist warmth of the womb?

[4] Cited in Roskies 1989: 494.

Where did they stand the best chance of being once again maternal – among the crumbling stones of the fortified city that had fallen before their eyes, or within their as-yet living bodies, clinging to life, to be sure, but nevertheless a fortress under their own control? And finally, in the light of Sutzkever's 'To My Child', Lam 4:10 need not imply a temporal contrast between the time in the past when these mothers were full of compassion, women of the womb ('compassion' and 'womb' share the same Hebrew root) and the present time when they act more savagely than wild beasts. Rather, impossible as it might seem to readers (most of us) who have not experienced the depths of human despair, could it be that the very act that we least expect from mothers, namely the cannibalism of their own children, may in fact be the parental instinct's dying gasp?[5]

[For Lam 4:11 see on Lam 1:8–9]

[4:12] *The kings of the earth did not believe,*
nor did any of the inhabitants of the world,
that foe or enemy could enter
the gates of Jerusalem.

The Enemy at the Gate

Peter Martyr Vermigli (born Florence, 1499; died Zurich, 1562) was an Augustinian monk who became a Protestant and spent much of his life as a theological refugee. Vermigli's wanderings through Europe included a period spent in England, initially at the invitation of Thomas Cranmer, whom he is believed to have influenced significantly. He was appointed Regius Professor of Divinity at Oxford in 1547 but left that position, and indeed England altogether, when Mary Tudor ascended the throne in 1553 and the country's theological climate changed. He settled finally in Zurich, where he was appointed to a university chair in Hebrew. Among Vermigli's influential biblical exegeses was a lecture series on Lamentations, delivered in Strasbourg in or soon after 1542[6] and published posthumously in Zurich in 1629 as *In Lamentationes Sanctissimi Ieremiae Prophetae Commentarium* (Vermigli 1629). Politics had its place alongside theology and philology in Vermigli's exposition of the Bible. The most

---

[5]   Reading Lam 4:10 in the light of Abraham Sutzkever's poem may constitute a response of a sort to Johanna Stiebert, who comments thus upon the verse: 'most chilling of all, the women cooking their own children are called compassionate (Lam 4:10) – the very quality sought from YHWH' (Stiebert 2003: 204). Here in Sutzkever is a sense in which a mother who eats her child, who draws it back into her womb, is indeed compassionate.

[6]   James 1998: 46–7.

pressing concern of the day from his perspective was the spread of the Ottoman Empire and the threat it posed to the Church; Constantinople had fallen in 1453 and Vienna had been besieged in 1529. Vermigli attributed the Turkish threat primarily to what he saw as unacceptable formalism and nominalism in eastern Christian orthodoxy, but he believed that, nevertheless, the Protestant Church was by no means immune to danger. He mentions Turkey explicitly in four places in his lectures on Lamentations. Not surprisingly, one of them alludes to Lam 4:12 (above). On Jerusalem's supposed inviolability Vermigli writes:

> These people could not persuade themselves that the enemies were going to enter Jerusalem and that they were going to overthrow that flourishing and holy state of affairs. Nor today do foolish Christians. They promise themselves that the Turks are not going to destroy them, leaning as they do on the promise that the church shall never be destroyed, and that the gates of hell shall not prevail against it, as if they themselves automatically belonged to the church.[7]

Yet even if his wake-up call failed, and the enemy once again stormed the city gates, Vermigli is convinced that the Church can survive, just as Israel survived, not as a geopolitical entity (Christendom), but as its spiritual core. He continues:

> Those who belong to this church [Israel] are not ruined utterly; for example, in former times Jeremiah, Daniel, Ezra, Zerubbabel and those who were belonging to the true church were preserved and in this way renewed the church so that in those former times it was not extinguished.[8]

As Daniel Shute puts it, Vermigli 'believed in Christendom and believed it was worth fighting for, but he also believed that, temporarily at least, the church could survive without Christendom' (Shute 2009: 279). In one respect, Vermigli's exegesis of Lam 4:12 is puzzling. By equating its disbelieving kings with complacent Christians, Vermigli implies that the 'kings of the earth' and 'inhabitants of the world' in the Lamentations verse are the people who are actually threatened by invasion, that is, the inhabitants of Jerusalem. Yet this makes no sense in relation to Lamentations itself. In their biblical context, the 'kings of the earth' and 'inhabitants of the world' must be onlookers from the surrounding nations, watching incredulously as Jews lose control of their prized possession. Was Vermigli, enthusiastic about the political message he could hang on the peg of this verse, simply untroubled by the apparent logical inconsistency of his exegesis? Or, as seems more likely, is he rather exposing a fascinating difference between biblical Jerusalem, a capital city much like any other, and

---

[7] Vermigli 1629: 167.
[8] Vermigli 1629: 167.

post-biblical Jerusalem, which was regarded in Jewish and Christian (and, of course, Muslim) traditions as a spiritual center for citizens of all the world, not just the inhabitants of one piece of land? Indeed, in line with Vermigli's emphasis above upon the temporary transformation of the Church for the purposes of survival, it can be argued that Jerusalem too survived because for much of its history it ceased to be a geopolitical entity and functioned instead as a religious-spiritual focus for the three monotheistic religions that, in their different ways, revere it. Once this conceptual transformation has occurred – from geopolitical to religious-spiritual – the 'kings of the earth' / 'inhabitants of the world' can indeed be one and the same as those who dwell within Jerusalem, just as Vermigli sees them. To be sure, they are geographically remote from each other, but they are spiritually conjoined. Any exegete who wants to explore the role of Jerusalem in the biblical text while at the same time addressing his or her own times must negotiate this conceptual shift in Jerusalem's significance from the biblical to the post-biblical world. Peter Martyr Vermigli's commentary on Lam 4:12 shines a spotlight on precisely the exegetical boundary – invisible to so many of his fellow interpreters, past, present and future – that must be crossed. A range of fascinating questions now hangs tantalizingly in the air: Are there signs that the book of Lamentations already anticipates the transformed status of the city whose destruction it is lamenting? Had the biblical book's authors already predicted how its survival might be secured? Did they imagine a Jerusalem rebuilt and, if so, what did it look like?

4:13 *It was for the sins of her prophets*
and the iniquities of her priests,
who shed in her midst
the blood of the just.

4:14 *Blindly they wandered through the streets,*
defiled with blood
so that no one was able
to touch their garments.

4:15 *'Away! Unclean!' people shouted at them;*
'Away! Away! Do not touch!'
So they became fugitives and wanderers,
for the nations resolved,
'They shall stay here no longer',

The Untouchables

Naomi Seidman, Koret Professor of Jewish Culture at the Graduate Theological Union, Berkeley, evokes poignantly the tensions between tradition and modernity, between resignation and hope, including those relating to the role of women. She recalls a story that she heard as a Jewish child growing up in New York. The story is set before the Shoah, in a small town in Poland at the end of Tisha B'Av: 'Right after they broke the fast, the Jews would light an enormous bonfire. They would throw the Tisha B'Av liturgy with all its sad poems about the destruction of the Temple into the fire and dance and sing the midsummer night away. You see, they didn't have any use for them anymore, since this was sure to be the year the Messiah would come and take all the Jews off to the Land of Israel, and instead of fasting and sitting on the floor there would be juicy portions of the Leviathan all around' (Seidman 1994: 281). 'But it was only a story', Seidman acknowledges. 'Those books, I knew even then, had gone up in a different kind of bonfire, and still the Messiah had failed to show up. And when we were finished for this year, the Artscroll Lamentations in my lap would go straight back onto the bookshelf until next year' (281). But she is not content to leave it there: 'I think of the bonfire in that little town in Poland. I wish we could have one now. I wish we could all, in our wickedness and in our faith, throw in the books we carried under our arms and join in the end-of-lamenting dance, the dance of the olden days, spinning and whirling the New York night away' (288).

Seidman takes the setting of a synagogue Tisha B'Av service as her framework for reflections on issues of Jewish identity in the modern world. Of all the tensions thrown up in reading the book of Lamentations today, among the most acute is that relating to the presentation of women and the feminine (see on Lam 1:1, 8–9, 10, 15–16). Seidman brings an incisive feminist critique to the use of the language of defilement through menstruation (cf. Lam 1:8–9, 'Jerusalem sinned greatly, so she has become a mockery; all who honored her despise her, for they have seen her nakedness; she herself groans, and shrinks back. Her uncleanness was in her skirts; she gave no thought to her future; she sank appallingly, with none to comfort her'). As Seidman sits, reluctant and yet attentive alongside her mother in the women's section of the synagogue at the height of a New York summer, she reflects: 'I refuse to see that the menstrual blood on Jerusalem's skirt is just a way of saying that her inhabitants have committed murderous acts. The city-woman's disgrace is a poor allegory for the sins of her men who take cover in these skirts [Lam 4:13–15]' (284). She continues: 'The blood of the priests and prophets is the trace of what they have done; the blood of Jerusalem, who is "as a menstruous woman," tells us nothing more than that she has a woman's body. However much the poet may imagine the city to be his larger self, he also lets us know that her blood is something utterly alien' (284). Seidman concludes with a challenge: 'Reading Lamentations in the divided synagogue, hearing a male voice intone the complaints of the widowed Jerusalem, are we really a community of mourners, the men and women who recognize how much a woman's truth has to say about the broader experiences of national degradation? Or is Lamentations itself yet another outrage, heaping a man's distaste for women onto the already painful enough outrages of Jewish history?' (284–5).

4:16 The LORD himself has scattered them,
he will look on them no more;
no honor was shown to the priests,
no favor to the elders.

4:17 Our eyes grow ever more dim
waiting vainly for help;
we watch expectantly
for a nation that cannot save.

4:18 Our steps were dogged
so that we could not walk in our streets;
our end drew near; our days were numbered;
for our end had come.

4:19 Our pursuers were swifter
than eagles in the heavens;
they chased us on the mountains,
they lay in wait for us in the wilderness.

Queer Readings

In spite of the prohibitions concerning sexual behavior enunciated in various legal texts of the Hebrew Bible (for example, Lev 18:6–23; 20:10–21; Deut 22:13–30), it is impossible to know much about the practical realities of sexuality in ancient Israel. A striking case of readerly engagement with the biblical text, in other words, one shaped crucially by the experience of modern readers, is provided by so-called 'queer' interpretation. Ken Stone has edited a collection of essays titled *Queer Commentary and the Hebrew Bible* (Stone 2001), and a commentary on the entire Bible from this perspective is provided in *The Queer Bible Commentary* (Guest, Goss, West and Bohache 2006). One of the editors, Deryn Guest, contributes the commentary on Lamentations (394–411). Guest assesses 'the usefulness of Lamentations as a resource for those who have had to endure a history of heterosexist acts and discourse' (394). The text's images of assault, abandonment, and accusation/acrimony are reviewed in turn. These three categories are used to explore experiences of the heterosexist intimidation of Jews and Christians who are described as regularly 'under siege' within society generally, and often within their faith traditions specifically, because of their decision to identify as lesbian, gay, bisexual, transgender or queer. A verse highlighted by Guest in this context is Lam 4:19, 'Our pursuers … chased us … they lay in wait for us'. Engagement with Lamentations, in which the assault, abandonment, and accusation of Zion are described and articulated so powerfully, can become the basis for an experience of solidarity.

One can see here an affinity with the feminist-critical strategy of finding in the biblical text a ground for solidarity between oppressed women, ancient and modern, in spite of the fact that the text may well include patriarchal and sexist features. Groups often excluded on the basis of their sexuality can experience a shared sense of being persecuted by the Bible, but paradoxically (as Guest shows) they can find solidarity with each other and with figures in the Bible through identifying with the Bible's persecuted people. Guest also draws analogies between her reading on the one hand and, on the other hand, the use of Lamentations by Jews in times of communal crisis and Christian liturgical application to the sufferings of Jesus. She writes: 'For the original singers of Lamentations and for its contemporary [modern] readers, this text provided/provides a most valuable resource to begin that period of recovery' (411). This is a theme fraught with complications. The positive use of the Bible by groups apparently condemned in parts of the text must be acknowledged as paradoxical, and the role of shared victimhood in identity building is a phenomenon that can raise disturbing issues. And yet Guest is able to construct a remarkably positive reading strategy: 'Basic trust had/has been broken and the survivors needed/need to find a way back into the covenant relationship that sets new boundaries and ground rules through giving vent to the experiences of assault and abandonment and working through the stages of accusation. Healing begins here' (411).

4:20 The breath of our life, the LORD's anointed,
was taken in their pits –
the one of whom we said, 'Under his shadow
we shall live among the nations',

Messianic Laments?

'The breath of our life, the LORD's anointed, was taken in their pits' represents one of a number of references within this book to the loss of the Davidic monarchy, this being one of the defining tragedies of the age (cf. Lam 2:6, 9; 5:16). The original reference was probably to the capture of King Zedekiah by the Babylonians (cf. 2 Kgs 25:3–7; Jer 39:1–5; 52:6–9). However, ancient Jewish opinion typically finds here an allusion to Josiah, perhaps encouraged by 2 Chr 35:25 ('Jeremiah also uttered a lament for Josiah, and all the singing men and singing women have spoken of Josiah in their laments to this day. They made these a custom in Israel; they are recorded in the Laments'). So, for example, the Aramaic Targum (see on Lam 5:8) here reads: 'King Josiah, who was as dear to us as the breath of the spirit of life which is in our nostrils, and [who] was installed in office with the anointing oil of the Lord, was entrapped in the snare of their corruptions' (Alexander 2008: 173–4). Although the Targum finds messianic reference in Lam 4:22 (and also in Lam 2:22), it does not offer an overtly messianic interpretation of this verse.

The ingenuity of the Church Fathers in finding Christian meanings in Old Testament texts sometimes seems boundless. But it is hardly surprising that Lam 4:20 provided a great deal of scope for christological interpretation. A survey of references and allusions in the Fathers reveals this to be far and away the most cited verse of Lamentations in the patristic period, with thirty-three clear cases. Such interpretation was facilitated by the biblical translations used by the Fathers. It is likely that the Greek Septuagint (LXX) originally read *christos kyriou*, 'the anointed of the Lord', a literal translation of the Hebrew, but in most Greek manuscripts this had become, by accident or deliberate alteration, *christos kyrios*, 'the Lord the Anointed', which obviously lent itself to interpretation by Christians with reference to Jesus, as 'the Lord Christ'. This is picked up also by the Vulgate's *Christus Dominus*. Tertullian (born Carthage, Tunisia, c.160; died Carthage, c.225), in his confrontation with Marcion, who denied the authority of the Old Testament, finds here clear evidence that Christ always spoke in the prophets, as the Spirit of the Creator: 'For so says the prophet [by which he means Jeremiah, the assumed author of Lamentations], "The person of our Spirit, Christ the Lord" [Lam 4:20, LXX], who from the beginning was both heard and seen as the Father's vicegerent in the name of God' (Tertullian, *Against Marcion* 3:6).[9]

A particularly striking example of patristic interpretation of Lam 4:20 is found in the *First Apology* of the second-century theologian Justin Martyr (born Nablus, Palestine, c.100; died Rome, 165). Justin understands the word 'breath' in this verse as a reference to the human nostrils, which – he observes – take the shape of a cross when one looks to the sky! Thus he found here a natural symbol of the cross and an anticipation of Christ's passion. He writes: 'The human form differs from that of the irrational animals in nothing else than in its being erect and having the hands extended and having on the face extending from the forehead what is called the nose through which the living creature breathes. And this takes no other form than that of the cross. And so it

---

[9]   A selection of the main patristic materials on Lam 4:20 is accessibly presented in Wenthe 2009 (299–304; cf. xxv–vi). See further Parry 2010: 188–90; Parry and Thomas 2011: 116–17.

was said by the prophet, "The breath before our face is the Lord Christ'" (Justin Martyr, *First Apology*, ch. 55).

Philip Alexander (2008: 175) interestingly suggests that the Vulgate's reference to Christ being taken not 'in their pits' but *in peccatis nostris*, 'in our sins', reflects a Christian awareness of a Jewish tradition referring to Josiah's death in battle being the result of the secret sins of his people. Be that as it may, both Augustine (born Thagaste, Algeria, 354; died Hippo, Algeria, 430) and Rufinus (born Concordia, Italy, *c*.345; died Sicily, 410) reflect on the Vulgate's words 'in our sins' as theologically significant (Augustine, *City of God*, 18.33; Rufinus, *Commentary on the Apostles' Creed*, 19).

The poignant words in the second part of Lam 4:20, 'Under his shadow we shall live among the nations', are reminiscent of the protective role of the monarch in relation to his people as presented in royal psalms such as Psalm 72 (e.g. vv. 12–14, 'For he delivers the needy when they call, the poor and those who have no helper. He has pity on the weak and the needy, and saves the lives of the needy. From oppression and violence he redeems their life; and precious is their blood in his sight'). These words too were much discussed by the Fathers, attracted not least by the ambivalence of the word 'shadow'. Irenaeus (born Izmir, Turkey, second century; died Lyons, France, *c*.202) put together this reference to 'his shadow' with the word 'breath' earlier in the verse, which he translated 'Spirit'. He took this combination of terms to prophesy the bitter, veiling incarnation (shadow) of the Spirit Christ: 'By "shadow" it also signifies the abasement and contemptibleness of his body. Just as the shadow from straight and upright bodies is on the ground and trodden under foot, so also was the body of Christ thrown to the ground and trampled under foot at his passion' (*Demonstration of the Apostolic Preaching*, 71). Origen (born Alexandria, Egypt, *c*.185; died Tyre, Lebanon, *c*.254) read the reference to 'his shadow' in a range of ways. Negatively, it refers to the mortality of the present age that clouds even the believer's partial experience of immortality in this life (*Commentary on Matthew* 15:2). Elsewhere, Origen reads it in a more positive, albeit qualified, manner. 'His shadow in which we live' is contrasted to the shadow of the Law in which the unredeemed live. In 'his shadow' the believer has a share in Christ as the way, the truth, and life, but it is dim. The believer still awaits a perfect, future redemption (*Commentary on the Song of Songs*, 3).

Are such patristic readings merely archaic and anachronistic? Many will argue that anti-Judaism and supersessionism are so intrinsic to such an approach to the biblical text that it should have no place today. However, as with 'the man who has seen affliction under the rod of God's wrath' of Lam 3:1, Robin Parry attempts a plausible and self-critical modern Christian theological reading of Lam 4:20: 'The capture of the king in Lam 4:20 is the climax of the woes in the chapter: he who embodied the whole nation representatively has fallen to the foe. Immediately after this we have the unexpected oracle of salvation (Lam 4:21–2), with no hint in the text as to how one could move from the lowest pit to the highest point of hope in the book.' He continues: 'On a christological interpretation, the move from verse 20 to verse 21 makes perfect sense. The loss of the king of Israel to the pagan foe in 4:20 is simultaneously the climax of the exilic woes *and the means by which those woes come to an end*' (Parry 2010: 190).

Charles, King and Martyr

A new use was found for Lam 4:20 in seventeenth-century England, following the cataclysmic event of the execution of King Charles I in 1649. The high ideology of kingship in England owed much to the model of Davidic kingship, from which the messianic tradition had eventually developed; indeed, many elements of this survive in the Coronation liturgy to this day. Royalists in seventeenth-century England thought of the pious Charles as 'the Lord's anointed', cruelly martyred by the regicides.

A work known as the *Eikon Basilike* (Greek for 'The Image of the King') celebrated this characterization. Subtitled 'the Portraiture of His Sacred Majesty in His Solitudes and Sufferings', this was a book of the prayers and meditations of King Charles I from his last months. It purports to be the King's spiritual autobiography, and is written in simple, direct, and moving language. It may well have been written by another hand after his death (albeit based upon the King's papers), the most likely candidate being one Dr John Gauden. First published in February 1649, the very month after the King's execution, *Eikon Basilike* proved extremely popular, running to thirty-six editions and being translated into several languages (*Eikon Basilike* 1649). It presented Charles as the victim of tyranny and as a Christian martyr. Other tributes soon followed, in which explicit parallels with the sufferings of Christ were drawn, leading to a Royalist cult of Charles the Martyr that helped sustain the Royalist cause during the years of the Commonwealth (1649–60). Because of the favorable image *Eikon Basilike* created of the King, John Milton was assigned by the regicides to reply to it, which he did in his *Eikonoklastes* (1649).

After just eleven years, that British experiment with republicanism came to an end. After the monarchy was restored in 1660, King Charles's name was added to the ecclesiastical calendar in the *Book of Common Prayer*, with an annual day of national fasting and repentance celebrated on the day of his death, 30 January. In 1859, during the reign of Queen Victoria, the feast day of King Charles was removed from the *Book of Common Prayer* at the request

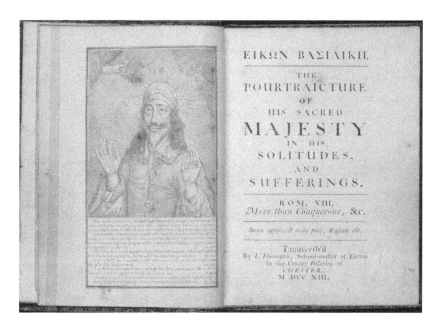

Eikon Basilike: Two examples of title page and frontispiece, dated 1648 and 1713 (Julian Calendar in both cases).

of elected representatives of the House of Commons. But that was not the end of the story. The Society of King Charles the Martyr was founded in 1894, as a High-Church Anglican devotional society. To this day it promotes of the cult of 'Saint Charles I of England, King and Martyr' and works for the full reinstatement of the feast day of King Charles.

As with the services commemorating the Great Fire of London (see on Lam 2:3–5), Lamentations was a favored text for preachers on the annual occasion of the feast day of King Charles, with far and away the commonest verse for exposition being Lam 4:20, above, with Lam 5:16, 'The crown has fallen from our head; woe to us that we have sinned!', featuring occasionally also. For example, in 1665 one Robert Twisse preached a sermon on Lam 4:20, lamenting Charles's death and developing the parallels with ancient Judah: 'England's breath stopp'd being the counter-part of Judah's miseries lamented publickly in the New-Church at Westminster on January 30: being the anniversary of the martyrdom of King Charles the First of blessed memory' (Twisse 1665). Twisse begins his sermon: 'We are met here this day to drop some Tears on the Herse of our late Martyred SOVEREIGN, who on this Day of the Month not many years agoe was basely sacrificed to the Lusts of a few Ambitious and Unreasonable men. To drop some Tears, did I say? nay rather to pour water before the Lord, to weep Streams and Rivers, if it were possible, that we might at once bewail our own unvaluable Loss in the untimely Death of so Excellent a PRINCE, and the horrid sin of those men … that were not content onely to pluck the Crown from the Head, but the Head from the Shoulders, and then glory in the committing of so great a Villany.'

There is a certain irony in this use of Lamentations. As suggested earlier, it is likely that Lam 4:20 originally made reference to the fall of a particular Judahite king. But, as we have seen, for centuries Christians read Lam 4:20 christologically, of the death of Jesus. It is a noteworthy reversal then that the King Charles theme should take Christian reading of the verse back to specific reference to a particular political monarch, albeit in a way that retains many of the symbolic associations of messianic thinking and language. It is particularly interesting that one of the earliest of the sermons, from 1649, brings in a typological parallel between the pious Charles and the ideal Judahite king Josiah, a striking echo of the typical ancient Jewish reading of Lam 4:20 as referring to Josiah. This sermon, attributed variously to William Juxon, Bishop of London, and to Robert Brown, Vicar of Sligo, is entitled *The subjects sorrow: or, Lamentations upon the death of Britain's Josiah, King Charles, most unjustly and cruelly put to death by His owne people, before His Royall Palace White-Hall* (Juxon 1649). Lamentations 4:20 is here expounded in a text 'Wherein the divine and royall prerogatives, personall virtues, and theologicall graces of His late Majesty are briefly delivered: and that His Majesty was taken away in Gods mercy unto himselfe, and for the certaine punishment of these kingdomes, from the parallel is clearly proved'. Josiah, Jesus, Charles … for the seventeenth-century English Christian the reference to 'the LORD's anointed … taken in their pits' conjured up a rich, multi-layered body of associations.

4:21 Rejoice and be glad, daughter Edom,
you that live in the land of Uz;
to you also the cup shall pass;
you shall become drunk and expose your nakedness.

4:22 The punishment of your iniquity, daughter Zion, is complete,
he will keep you in exile no longer;
but your iniquity, daughter Edom, he will repay,
he will uncover your sins.

Who Is Edom?

'*Rejoice and be glad, daughter Edom.* This is Caesarea. *You that live in the land of Uz.* This is Persia. *To you also the cup shall pass; you shall become drunk and expose your nakedness*' (*Lamentations Rabbah* 4.24, our translation). This commentary on Lam 4:21 found in the standard Hebrew edition of *Lamentations Rabbah* (*Lamentations Rabbah* 1876) is surprising in two ways. First, although rabbinic literature routinely equates Rome with Edom (following the identification of Esau/Edom as the archetypal enemy of Jacob/Israel), the equation of Edom with Caesarea in particular is unusual. Second, the reference to Persia is surprising. The connection between Uz and Persia is tenuous, and the reversal of temporal order entailed by mentioning the later empire, Rome, before the earlier one, Persia, though not unprecedented in rabbinic typologies, is confusing. The justi-fication for equating Edom with Caesarea is evidently linked to the occurrence in Lam 4:21a of the Hebrew term *bat*, literally 'daughter'. A note on *Lamentations Rabbah* 4.24 in the Jerusalem 1983 annotated Hebrew edition (*Lamentations Rabbah* 1983) observes: 'The text does not say *Edom*, but *bat Edom*. This is Caesarea, a fortified city on the coast in the west of Israel, the location of the seat of Roman government in the land' (our translation). Caesarea is known as *bat Edom* in other rabbinic texts. For the midrashic author, Lam 4:21a refers to an enemy in self-imposed exile, an imperial outpost of an occupying people.

The puzzle about Persia in 4:21b is solved easily by consulting the first printed edition of *Lamentations Rabbah* (*Lamentations Rabbah* 1519), which reads not 'This is Persia', but rather 'This is Rome'. How did the 'Rome' of the early version become 'Persia' in later versions? The transformation seems to have occurred because as well as signifying Rome for the rabbis, Edom signified Christianity. At a time when Jews feared persecution for anti-Christian teachings, this first printed edition of *Lamentations Rabbah*, along with texts of many other rabbinic works, was 'corrected', and references to Rome were replaced by Persia, far less contentious than Rome, and no longer politically sensitive. Setting Persia aside as a red herring, we can surmise that the author of *Lamentations Rabbah* 4.24, as reflected in the work's first printed edition, intended to contrast two distinct categories of a single enemy: those who occupied an imperial outpost (*bat Edom* in Lam 4:21a, read in *Lamentations Rabbah* as Caesarea), and those who lived at home in the very seat of imperial power (that is, those who according to Lam 4:21b dwell in the land of Uz, a location interpreted by *Lamentations Rabbah* as the city of Rome itself).

But is the midrash valuable only for the light it sheds on its own political context, or does it also illuminate the book of Lamentations itself? First, the typological reading highlights the peculiarity of the reference to Edom, the only enemy actually named in the book of Lamentations. Even if not overtly typological in Lamentations itself, Edom is surely viewed archetypically; in other words, Edom stands for enemies in general, not one specific enemy. Second, the midrashic emphasis on the Hebrew term *bat Edom* draws our attention to a much more common usage of the word *bat* found in the book of Lamentations, namely the phrase *bat Zion*, literally 'daughter Zion' (see Lam 1:6; 2:1, 8, 10, 13, 18). In an excursus to her commentary on Lamentations, Adele Berlin considers several interpretative options for the significance of the term *bat*. These range from simple personification ('daughter Zion') through to a designation for 'city' ('the city of Jerusalem') that emerged from the ancient Near Eastern tradition of identifying cities with their urban goddesses (Berlin 2002: 10–12), a vestige of the suggestion that the city was the daughter of a specific female sponsoring deity. Given that the term *bat Zion* occurs most frequently in texts from the exilic era, it is worth asking whether *Lamentations Rabbah*'s reading of *bat* as an imperial outpost reflects a later interpretative development or is already present in the biblical text. And if the latter, whether the biblical phrase *bat Zion*, daughter of Zion, might hint at an interest in addressing the Babylonian diaspora – members of the Jerusalem community who were deported and established themselves in Babylon – alongside the original city of Jerusalem itself.

References

Alexander, P. S. 2008. *The Targum of Lamentations* (Aramaic Bible, 17B; Collegeville, MN: Liturgical Press).

Berlin, A. 2002. *Lamentations* (OTL; Louisville, KY, and London: Westminster John Knox).

Eikon Basilike. 1649. *Eikon Basilike, vel Imago Regis Caroli, in illis suis ærumnis et solitudine* (London: J. Williams and F. Eglesfield).

Greenstein, E. L. 1982. 'An Equivocal Reading of the Sale of Joseph', in *Literary Interpretations of Biblical Narratives, II* (ed. K. R. R. Gros Louis; Nashville, TN: Abingdon Press) 114–25.

Guest, D., R. E. Goss, M. West and T. Bohache (ed.). 2006. *The Queer Bible Commentary* (London: SCM Press).

James, F. A., III. 1998. *Peter Martyr Vermigli and Predestination: The Augustinian Inheritance of an Italian Reformer* (Oxford Theological Monographs; Oxford: Clarendon).

Juxon, W. 1649. *The subjects sorrow: or, Lamentations upon the death of Britain's Josiah, King Charles, most unjustly and cruelly put to death by His owne people, before His Royall Palace White-Hall* (London).

Keel, O. 1977. *Die Welt der altorientalischen Bildsymbolik und das Alte Testament: Am Beispiel der Psalmen* (Zürich: Benziger; Neukirchen-Vluyn: Neukirchener Verlag, 2nd edn).

Keel, O. 1998. *Goddesses and Trees, New Moon and Yahweh: Ancient Near Eastern Art and the Hebrew Bible* (JSOTSup, 261; Sheffield: Sheffield Academic Press).

Keel, O. and C. Uehlinger. 1998. *Gods, Goddesses, and Images of God in Ancient Israel* (Edinburgh: T. & T. Clark).

Lamentations Rabbah. 1519. *Lamentations Rabbah*, in *Midrash Rabbah, on the Five Megillot* (Pesaro; 1st printed edn).

Lamentations Rabbah. 1876. *Lamentations Rabbah*, in *Midrash Rabbah, on the Five Books of Moses and the Five Megillot with Many Commentaries* (Standard Hebrew edn; 3 vols; Vilna).

Lamentations Rabbah. 1983. *Lamentations Rabbah* (ed. A.Z. Steinberger; annotated Hebrew edn; Jerusalem).

Lee, N. C. 2002. *The Singers of Lamentations: Cities under Siege, from Ur to Jerusalem to Sarajevo …* (Biblical Interpretation Series, 60; Leiden: Brill).

Lee, N. C. 2010. *Lyrics of Lament: From Tragedy to Transformation* (Minneapolis, MN: Fortress).

Lee, N. C. and C. Mandolfo (eds). 2008. *Lamentations in Ancient and Contemporary Cultural Contexts* (SBL Symposium Series, 43; Atlanta, GA: SBL).

Parry, R. A. 2010. *Lamentations* (Two Horizons Old Testament Commentary; Grand Rapids, MI, and Cambridge: Eerdmans).

Parry, R. A. and H. A. Thomas (eds). 2011. *Great Is Thy Faithfulness? Reading Lamentations as Sacred Scripture* (Eugene, OR: Pickwick).

Renkema, J. 1998. *Lamentations* (Historical Commentary on the Old Testament; Leuven: Peeters).

Roskies, D. G. (ed.). 1989. *The Literature of Destruction: Jewish Responses to Catastrophe* (Philadelphia, PA: Jewish Publication Society).

Seidman, N. 1994. 'Burning the Book of Lamentations', in *Out of the Garden: Women Writers on the Bible* (ed. C. Büchmann and C. Spiegel; New York: Fawcett Columbine; London: Pandora) 278–88.

Shute, D. 2009. 'Interpreting Lamentations: Theodicy and the Turks', in *A Companion to Peter Martyr Vermigli* (ed. T. Kirby, E. Campi, and F. A. James III; Leiden: Brill).

Stiebert, J. 2003. 'Human Suffering and Divine Abuse of Power in Lamentations: Reflections on Forgiveness in the Context of South Africa's Truth and Reconciliation Process', *Pacifica* 16: 195–215.

Stone, K. 2001. *Queer Commentary and the Hebrew Bible* (JSOTSup, 334; London and New York: Sheffield Academic Press).

Twisse, R. 1665. *England's breath stopp'd being the counter-part of Judah's miseries lamented publickly in the New-Church at Westminster on January 30: being the anniversary of the martyrdom of King Charles the First of blessed memory* (London: J. Flesher).

Vermigli, P. M. 1629. *In Lamentationes Sanctissimi Ieremiae Prophetae Commentarium* (Zürich). Eng. tr.: *Commentary on the Lamentations of the Prophet Jeremiah by Peter Martyr* (Sixteenth Century Essays and Studies, 55; trans. and ed. by D. Shute; Kirksville, MO: Truman State University Press, 2002).

Wenthe, D. O. 2009. *Jeremiah, Lamentations* (Ancient Christian Commentary on Scripture, Old Testament, 12; Downers Grove, IL: InterVarsity Press).

⁵:¹ Remember, O LORD, what has befallen us;
look, and see our disgrace!
⁵:² Our inheritance has been turned over to strangers,
our homes to aliens.
⁵:³ We have become orphans, fatherless;
our mothers are like widows.
⁵:⁴ We must pay to drink our own water;
gather our wood at a price.
⁵:⁵ They are always at our throats;
exhausted, we are given no rest.

[⁵:²⁰ Why have you forgotten us utterly?
forsaken us for all time?]

Forms of Lament

Lamentations 5 differs in a number of ways from the four chapters that precede it. It is the only chapter not in the form of an acrostic (though the fact that it has twenty-two verses seems most likely to reflect that form). The poem consists of verses of one line only, unlike the other chapters, and is thus much the shortest in the book. (The individual lines of Chapter 3 are in some respects similar, but there are three times as many of them!) Moreover, Chapter 5 lacks the *qinah*, 'lament', meter that characterizes most of the book, for it consists predominantly of lines whose parts

Lamentations Through the Centuries, First Edition. Paul M. Joyce and Diana Lipton.
© 2013 Paul M. Joyce and Diana Lipton. Published 2020 by John Wiley & Sons Ltd.

balance each other (three Hebrew words, followed by another three Hebrew words), rather than the unbalanced lines of the *qinah* (three words, then just two). Nonetheless, this chapter has a coherence and consistency of form unequalled in any other chapter. There is just one speaking voice: the first-person plural 'we' of the lamenting community (found elsewhere only at Lam 3:40–7). This final chapter of the book expresses the voice of the people, a collective petition for restoration.

Lamentations 5 is strikingly similar to a number of Psalms (notably Pss 44, 74, 79, 80, 83). It opens with the plea 'Remember, O LORD, what has befallen us' (v. 1). This is reminiscent of the call to the deity to remember that is found in some Psalms, for example, Ps 74:2, 'Remember your congregation'. Lamentations 5:20 picks up the theme: 'Why have you forgotten us utterly? forsaken us for all time?' (cf. Ps 44:24, 'Why do you forget our affliction and oppression?'). The second half of Lam 5:1 calls on God to 'look and see', again a feature found in the Psalms, e.g. Ps 80:14 (Hebrew v. 15), 'Turn again, O God of hosts; look down from heaven, and see'. There follows, beginning in Lam 5:2 and extending to verse 18, a description of the miserable situation that has befallen the city. This too is a typical feature of some Psalms (cf. Pss 44:9–16; 74:4–9; 79:1–4). And Lamentations 5 ends with a renewed plea for divine mercy. In Lam 5:21, the lamenting community pleads 'return us', a refrain found three times in Psalm 80, in verses 3, 7 and 19 (Hebrew vv. 4, 8 and 20). Parallels to the language of the closing verses of the chapter are found also in Pss 74:1 and 79:5.

Is it by chance that Lamentations 5 and this group of Psalms share so many features and formulae? One of many contributions made by the influential biblical scholar Hermann Gunkel (born Springe, Hanover, 1862; died Halle, 1932) was the observation that the Psalms tend to fall into certain types. Gunkel was a German Protestant and the father of form criticism, a critical methodology that attempted to categorize the forms of the biblical literature and to identify the 'life setting' in which units were produced. Gunkel's form criticism is a classic case of the historical criticism of the Bible that flourished especially the nineteenth and twentieth centuries, and whose influence is still significant. This historical criticism is a part of the long story of the reception of the biblical text. Though objectivity is a virtue that is highly acclaimed in this approach, historical criticism, like all intellectual movements, is of its time. With the passage of years we can see increasingly clearly that it is a modernist development that flourished in the very age when Darwin was developing his evolutionary theory and Sigmund Freud, somewhat later, was doing his groundbreaking work in psychoanalysis. It is striking how many features historical criticism of the Bible shares with these and other intellectual movements from the same period. For example, both Gunkel and Freud speak of 'aetiology' when addressing questions of origins and causation. And like Freud, historical critics apply a 'hermeneutic of suspicion' – psychoanalysts look for the meaning behind the slip of the tongue, while historical critics of the Bible press inconsistency or repetition for their significance. Historical critics will attempt to reconstruct what they understand as the 'real story' behind the biblical text, a history of the ideas and institutions of ancient Israel. This finds its parallel in the psychoanalyst's determination to find the 'real story' below the surface of the narrative presented by the client. And in attempting to explicate the biblical text, historical criticism often features evolutionary or developmental patterns in reconstruction of the emergence of ancient Israel's belief and practice.

One the best-known cases of Gunkel's categorization of biblical material is his extremely influential work on the Psalms. Following Gunkel, biblical scholars often describe Psalms such as 44, 74, 79, 80 and 83 as 'Communal Laments (or Complaints)'. Gunkel included Lamentations 5 in his list of such laments (Gunkel 1998 [1933]: 82). He listed three main parts into which they are divided: 'a lamenting complaint over the misfortune' (cf. Lam 5:2–18); 'a supplicational petition to Yhwh to change the misfortune' (cf. Lam 5:21); and 'types of thoughts … in which one reproaches oneself for consolation' (cf. Lam 5:16) or 'speaks before Yhwh in order that he will hear and intervene' (cf. Lam 5:1) (88). He highlighted Lamentations 5 as an example of a lament that is made up almost entirely of material reflecting the first of these three parts, namely complaint (88). With regard to 'life setting', Gunkel suggested that Lamentations 5 'may have been sung during one of the festivals at the ruins of Jerusalem, like the ones mentioned in Zech 7' (98).[1] Some skepticism about Gunkel's hypothetical settings may be in order, but, by exposing the common features shared with similar units, the categorization approach that he introduced has helped many readers to see what they are looking at in biblical texts. Such is the case with his categorization of Lamentations 5 as a song of communal lament that is perfectly at home with a group of similarly structured and motivated Psalms. Indeed, given the differences noted above between Lamentations 5 and the chapters that precede it, one might even suggest that, in some respects, the Psalms identified by Gunkel as communal laments provide as fitting an introduction to Lamentations 5 as Lamentations 1–4.

[For Lam 5:6 see Lam 4:9–10]

5:7 Our ancestors sinned; they are no more,
and we bear their guilt.

Laying the Blame

The Jewish physician and writer Solomon Ibn Verga was born into the political and religious upheaval of fifteenth-century Spain. He apparently moved to

---

[1]   Cf. Zech 7:5, 'Say to all the people of the land and the priests: When you fasted and lamented in the fifth month and in the seventh, for these seventy years, was it for me that you fasted?'

Lisbon after the expulsion of Jews from Spain in 1492, living for a time as a Marrano – a 'hidden Jew' who practiced Judaism secretly while living outwardly as a Christian – before leaving Portugal in 1506. He seems to have died in Flanders around 1530. In the 1520s, probably while living in Turkey, Ibn Verga wrote *Shevet Yehudah, The Sceptre of Judah*, which was first published in its original Hebrew in Turkey in the 1550s, and later translated into Spanish, Latin, German and Yiddish. *Shevet Yehudah* presents itself as a historical compilation that details many disputations and cases of persecution of Jews. In the early modern period the work achieved great popularity as a straightforward history, although later commentators have claimed that it has a strong literary component. This would not be surprising. Ibn Verga's task in *Shevet Yehudah* was not to document past events, but to locate the catastrophe that faced his own generation – the expulsion from Spain – within a chain of similar tragedies that began with the destruction of the first Temple. Analyzing the causes of these catastrophes, Ibn Verga asked a question that has, to this day, refused to lie down and die: Why us? Why have Jews, especially, from his own perspective, the Jews of Spain, suffered so much persecution? The source of his primary answer is the biblical book of Amos: 'You alone have I known of all the families of the earth, therefore I will visit upon you all your sins' (Amos 3:2). Subsidiary explanations offered in *Shevet Yehudah* include the Jewish failure to command Gentile respect; the blame that was attached to Jews by Christians for killing Jesus; Gentile envy of Jewish religion, women and wealth; false evidence given by Jews; and the excessive pride of some Jewish leaders. But first after the verse from Amos in Ibn Verga's list of explanations for the persecution of Jews is a verse from Lamentations: 'Our ancestors sinned; they are no more, and we bear their guilt' (Lam 5:7). This verse is a classic biblical statement of transgenerational punishment, in keeping with, for example, Exod 20:5–6: 'For I the LORD your God am a jealous God, punishing children for the iniquity of parents, to the third and the fourth generation of those who reject me, but showing steadfast love to the thousandth generation of those who love me and keep my commandments'.

Speaking for a moment in general terms, it is hard to know whether to think negatively or positively about transgenerational punishment. On the negative side, it promotes feelings of inevitability and helplessness – why should people make an effort to correct their behavior and improve themselves if their destiny is determined by the actions of their ancestors? This may explain in part the rejection of postponed punishment by Ezekiel (Ezek 18:2) and Jeremiah (Jer 31:29–30), both of whom refer to the parable about the children whose teeth were set on edge (punished) when their fathers ate sour grapes (sinned). Adherence by the exiles to the notion of transgenerational punishment diminished the chances that they would take responsibility for their own actions. On the positive side, transgenerational punishment means that victims need no longer beat their own breasts when bad things happen to them; they are simply settling someone else's bill, and it can be a plausible (if, or perhaps because, unfalsifiable) strategy for sustaining a theodicy. In Lam 5:7, this 'positive' reading prevails; the very point of these verses of the book's closing chapter is to emphasize the people's utter helplessness and the depths of their despair (cf. 'we have become orphans', v. 3; 'slaves rule over us', v. 8; 'women are raped', v. 11), in the hope that God will relent and bring an end to their suffering. As a rhetorical strategy, it had more than a chance of proving effective, and, psychologically speaking, there is a sense in which blaming a third party who no longer exists is less damaging than self-blame for events beyond the actor's own control.

Yet it must be said that both self-blame and blaming guilty ancestors have the potential for considerable damage when turned by others against the party that formulated them. The Jews of Jerusalem – however badly they might have behaved – did not cause the Babylonian exile and the destruction of the Temple, and nor were these catastrophes caused by the sins of their ancestors. Likewise, neither the Jews of Spain nor their ancestors caused the expulsion from Spain in 1492. In the wrong hands – that is, the hands of the very anti-Semites inclined to persecute Jews – 'theological' histories such as Ibn Verga's that attempt to schematize catastrophe can inadvertently fuel hatred and self-hatred. The same can, unfortunately, be said of the book of Lamentations itself.

5:8 Slaves rule over us;
there is no one to rescue us from their hand.

[For 5:9 see Lam 4:9–10]

5:10 Our skin is scorched like an oven
from the fever of famine.

[*4:7 Her princes were purer than snow,*
whiter than milk;
their bodies were ruddier than coral,
their hair like sapphire.

4:8 Now their faces are blacker than soot;
they are not recognized in the streets.
Their skin has shrivelled on their bones;
it has become as dry as wood.]

Found in Translation?

The Targum of Lamentations is a translation into Aramaic, the spoken language (or more accurately languages, since it is more like a group of closely related dialects) of Yehud/Palestine in the second Temple period, and the lingua franca throughout much of the Middle East until the seventh century CE, when it was gradually superseded by Arabic. Aramaic translations of the Bible played an important role in Jewish liturgy; it made sense to recite scriptural passages related to the synagogue service in question in a language that the congregation could easily understand. *Masachet Soferim*, a (non-canonical) Talmudic tractate from the seventh century CE concerning the proper writing and reading of sacred texts, mentions that an Aramaic translation of Lamentations (not necessarily the text that survived as the Targum of Lamentations) was recited during Tisha B'Av services commemorating the destruction of the first and second Temples.

In the commentary on his 2008 edition and translation of the text of the Targum of Lamentations, Philip Alexander observes that the Aramaic 'translation' of the biblical book of Lamentations employs a range of interpretative strategies that closely resemble rabbinic midrash. When we encounter an expansion that moves well beyond the Hebrew original, such as that which occurs in the Targum in relation to Lam 5:8, it is tempting to offer an explanation of the kind that so often makes sense of the midrashic enterprise: here is a Jewish writer viewing the past in the light of his own times and concerns. The Targum of Lamentations exhibits two central concerns of this kind. First, it attempts to account for the historical phenomenon that the Temple was destroyed, twice, and the people of Judah exiled and ruled by foreigners. Second, it responds theologically to what its author(s) understood as an attack on divine justice in the biblical book of Lamentations by emphasizing the role of human sin, and thus demonstrating that the punishment was deserved. The rendering of Lam 5:8 in the Targum of Lamentations addresses the historical question of foreign rulers. It expands significantly the biblical verse; in place of 'Slaves rule over us; there is no one to rescue us from their hand' (Lam 5:8), the Targum offers, 'The sons of Ham, who were given as slaves to the sons of Shem, rule over us; there is no one to redeem us from their hand' (Alexander 2008: 182). What explains this expansion? In keeping with the observation made above that midrash often addresses the concerns of its age, we might speculate that in rendering 'slaves' as 'the sons of Ham', the Aramaic translator intended to identify them with the ruling powers of his own time. Assuming that Philip Alexander is correct to date the Targum of Lamentations to the late fifth century CE, the ruling power in question would have been the surviving Roman Empire. Yet the Romans, equated in Jewish texts from this period with Edom (and thus with Esau), are not the sons of Ham but the sons of Shem.

What then did the Targumist intend? Alexander offers a fascinating reconstruction. The primary source of the Targum's expansion is Gen

9:20–8, where Ham sees his father Noah's nakedness and his descendants are condemned to serve those of Shem. The secondary source is the table of nations in Gen 10:6–12, 'which states that Babylon was founded by Nimrod, who was a son of Cush, the son of Ham. In other words, the Babylonians were Hamites. ... The allusion, therefore, is learned and historical' (Alexander 2008: 182, n. 14). The Targumist has no interest at this point in locating his own subjugators (Rome) in the text. Rather, he wants to locate the oppressors that would have preoccupied the author of Lamentations, namely, the Babylonians. As well as showing historical insight in relation to the biblical text, the Targumist intensifies its already dominant theme of reversal of fortune: 'The slaves who rule over the Jews ("the sons of Shem") are precisely those slaves who had been condemned by ancient curse to serve them' (182, n. 14).

This is an elegant explanation by any measure, and may suffice to account for the translator's decision to render 'slaves' as 'the sons of Ham'. It is possible, though, that yet another reversal brought the sons of Ham to the Targumist's mind. Lamentations 5 continues its catalogue of catastrophes with a reference to the physical appearance of the inhabitants of Jerusalem. The term that we have rendered above as 'scorched' is often translated as 'black'. So NRSV, for example, has 'Our skin is black as an oven from the scorching heat of famine' (Lam 5:10, cf. Lam 4:8), while Alexander uses 'black' in his translation into English of this verse in the Targum (Alexander 2008: 182, n. 17), even though the translation 'black' is contested for both the Hebrew *nichmaru* and the Targum's *itk'dru*. Alexander observes that rabbinic literature identifies the sons of Ham with 'the black-skinned, negroid peoples of the south, who would regularly have appeared in the Mediterranean slavemarkets of late antiquity' (Alexander 2008: 182, n. 14). He is correct that, historically speaking, the sons of Ham 'do not fit here', but from a literary and theological perspective the image of Ham's dark skin fits perfectly. The Jews of Jerusalem, the sons of Shem, are slaves to the sons of Ham, the people they were destined to enslave (cf. Gen 9:20–8), and, in a final reversal of fortune, their own faces are now darkened by the famine inflicted upon them by the Hamite Babylonians.

It goes without saying that this last point about Ham's 'black' skin raises a number of sensitive issues for our own time. Lamentations 5:10, especially when read alongside Lam 4:7–8, can be seen to express a value judgment about skin color: white denotes privilege, health and wealth, while black or dark (scorched) skin denotes deprivation, sickness and poverty. Is the Bible exhibiting tendencies that would now be identified as racist, as some scholars have suggested in relation to such texts as Num 12:1 ('Miriam and Aaron spoke against him [Moses] because of the Cushite woman he had married'); S of

S 1:5 ('I am black, but/and beautiful'); and Amos 9:7a ('Are you not like the Ethiopians to me, O people of Israel?')?[2] And if translators perpetuate these tendencies, are they, too, open to accusations of racism? These are difficult questions to answer, but they are crucial for readers, as well as translators (not to mention translators of translations such as the work of the Targumists), to bear in mind.[3]

> [5:11] *Women are raped in Zion,*
> *virgins in the towns of Judah.*
> [5:12] *Princes are hung up by their hands;*
> *no respect is shown to the elders.*
> [5:13] *Young men must carry millstones,*
> *and boys stagger under loads of wood.*
> [5:14] *The old men are gone from the city gate,*
> *the young men from their music.*

Cultural Memory?

The issue of the reception of Lamentations in the later Hebrew Bible is a fascinating one. Elsewhere we have noted that Lamentations seems to have been known by the anonymous exilic poet from whom Chapters 40–55 of the book of Isaiah derive (see on Lam 1:17, 21). Another case is that of the late work of skeptical wisdom known variously as Qohelet and Ecclesiastes. In her monograph *The Story of Israel in the Book of Qohelet*, Jennie Barbour examines a series of correspondences between motifs in the biblical city-lament tradition, chiefly exemplified by Lamentations, and in Qohelet's closing poem (Qoh 11–12) (Barbour 2012: 143–56). This is part of her broader aim of showing that this wisdom work is more indebted to Israelite tradition than is generally allowed (recognizing, of course, that the city-lament in the Bible is in turn heir to an older, international tradition).[4] Barbour acknowledges that there are many central city-lament traits missing from Qohelet's poem, such as the personification of the city, the issue of God's agency, the direct address to the deity, and the question of the city's sin and restoration. Nonetheless, the resemblances at the level of

---

[2]   See Rice 1978 and Sadler 2005.

[3]   For a discussion of precisely these questions in the context of a broader treatment of the intersection of race and slavery in the ancient world, see Goldenberg 2003.

[4]   See Cohen 1988; Dobbs-Allsopp 1993.

scenery and atmosphere are such as to suggest that Qohelet, while being a very different type of literature, does draw on city-lament material such as Lamentations as part of its literary heritage and stylistic vocabulary.

The urban landscape is at the heart of what makes a city-lament, and the minds of both poets keep returning to the city streets (Lam 2:11–12: 'infants and babes faint in the streets of the city … they faint like the wounded in the streets of the city …'; we may compare Qoh 12:5, 'the mourners will go about the streets'). Desertion and desolation are prominent themes in both contexts (Lam 1:1, 'How lonely sits the city that once was full of people!'; Lam 5:18, 'Mount Zion, which lies desolate…'; we may compare Qoh 12:4, 'when the doors on the street are shut, and the sound of the grinding is low', and Qoh 12:6, 'the pitcher is broken at the fountain, and the wheel broken at the cistern'). Another city-lament characteristic picked up in Qohelet is the motif of sharp contrast between 'then' and 'now' (as in Lam 4:1, 'How the gold has grown dim! The pure gold is debased'; cf. Qoh 12:6, 'the silver cord is snapped, and the golden bowl is broken'). And a further shared theme is that of darkness (Lam 3:2, 'He has driven and brought me into darkness without any light'; Lam 3:6, 'he has made me sit in darkness like those long dead'. With these we may compare Qoh 12:2, 'the sun and the light and the moon and the stars are darkened and the clouds return with the rain').

Both texts hold up one group after another as representatives of general suffering. Barbour notes that 'the merismus of ages and social classes – from guards to patricians, from mill women to ladies of leisure – is a trope that city-lament uses to register catastrophe at every level' (149). Examples include Lam 1:4, 'her priests groan; her young girls grieve', and Lam 1:18, 'my young women and young men have gone into captivity!' The best example from Lamentations is provided by Lam 5:11–14, above, which recounts that women are raped, princes hung up, elders humiliated; young men and boys stagger under loads; and old men and young have departed. With this we may compare Qoh 12:3, 'in the day when the guards of the house tremble, and the strong men are bent, and the women who grind cease working because they are few, and those who look through the windows see dimly'.

In these and other ways, Qohelet's final poem evokes the Israelite tradition of city-lament best exemplified in Lamentations. As Barbour concludes, 'When Qohelet speaks of trouble in an individual life, the phrases that lie immediately to hand bring with them memories of the great trouble in his and his readers' common literary history' (166). It is no accident that the subtitle of Barbour's monograph is *Ecclesiastes as Cultural Memory*. How are we to conceive the relationship between Qohelet and Lamentations with regard to the language considered here? Barbour expresses this eloquently: 'The fall of Jerusalem to the Babylonians became a template for speaking of calamity in the Jewish writing that followed it. … The classic expression of the trauma of that disaster, the endlessly reusable Book of Lamentations, was itself initially shaped by popular recollection of the experience in antiquity, and then subsequently came to shape that recollection, as these laments were repeated and internalized in annual commemoration' (139). The motifs of Qohelet that she reviews, Barbour argues, 'together draw it into the pattern of biblical dirges over fallen cities, especially Jerusalem, which was made normative by the Book of Lamentations and which grew over time to become the standardized way of speaking of national disaster in Second Temple Judaism' (156).

'The Crown of our Head has Fallen'. Photograph of public death announcements posted on the streets of Meah Shearim, Jerusalem, April 2012.

[For Lam 5:15 see Lam 3:17–18]

5:16 The crown has fallen from our head;
woe to us that we have sinned!

Announcing Death

Visitors to Meah Shearim, the dilapidated, overcrowded, maze-like Jerusalem neighborhood that is home to the city's most isolated ultra-Orthodox Jewish sects, may be struck by the many posters that are plastered haphazardly on walls, doors, and any other available surface. In a community that makes little use of modern technology, these posters take the place of the myriad modes of instant communication upon which much of the rest of the world depends. More or less uniform in size and design, the striking black and white posters – known by their Modern Hebrew name (taken from the Yiddish), *pashkevilim* – impart information on a wide range of topics of importance to the local community. Their subjects range from opportunities to learn Torah from great rabbis, through warnings about moral threats to the community (usually emanating from the outside world) and condemnations of members who have gone off the straight and narrow (as perceived by community leaders), to information about where to buy *arbah minim*, the four types of branches and fruit required to celebrate the festival of *Sukkot* (Tabernacles).

But the posters that are seen most often on the streets of Meah Shearim are death announcements. Posters reporting that a member of the community has passed away are immediately recognizable (to a Hebrew reader) by their formulaic headings. In most cases, the heading consists of the phrase used according to Jewish tradition to report or respond to news of a death: *Baruch Dayan Emet*, 'Blessed be the True Judge' (a shortened form of a blessing that asserts God's justice). But when the person was a great teacher or highly respected in the community for his Torah learning, the poster announcing that he has passed away begins with half a verse from Lamentations: 'The crown has fallen from our head' (perhaps better read in this context as 'The crown of our head has fallen') (Lam 5:16).[5] In its biblical context, the 'crown' should probably be read as a generic symbol of honor or glory (see Hillers 1992: 159, on v. 16). The *pashkevilim* are quite specific: the crown of a Jewish community such as those in Meah Shearim – the source of its honor and glory – are its great teachers and scholars. The sense of loss to the community when such a person

---

[5]   Words extracted from this verse may also appear on the gravestones of important Jewish teachers and leaders.

passes away is often extremely intense, and it is no accident that the words chosen to announce it are drawn from the biblical book most closely identified with collective calamity.

[For Lam 5:17 see on Lam 1:19–20, 22]

[For Lam 5:18 see Lam 4:3]

5:19 *But you, O LORD, are enthroned forever;*
your throne endures for all generations.

Protesting against God

The notion of protest against God – especially complaint against certain manifestations of divine justice – is complex. On the one hand, protest has a long history that starts with the Bible itself and is amply developed in rabbinic texts, for example, especially midrash. On the other hand, protest has negative connotations ranging from ingratitude through hubris to heresy. It has accordingly played a minor role in some religious traditions, and even traditions in which it is prominent often feature counter-voices, proclaiming God's perfect justice as an antidote to those who dare to question it. In *Protest against God: The Eclipse of a Biblical Tradition* (2006), William Morrow makes a fascinating point: in every book of the Hebrew Bible bar one, complaints against God are almost always framed in a political or institutional as opposed to a domestic context (118–19). In other words, when God is being praised or thanked, or when his commitment to his enduring relationship with Israel is being affirmed, the range of appellations used might include 'husband' or 'father'. But when God's actions (or, as is often the case, his lack of action) are being questioned or criticized, he is almost never presented as a husband or a father, but rather in some formal, 'professional' role such as king or shepherd or judge. By the same token, God's petitioners in the context of protest will be subjects or subordinates of some kind, but they will not be wives or children.

The one book that fails to conform to this striking pattern is the book of Lamentations, where protests against God are almost always offered in a domestic context. God's petitioners represent figures from a family not an institution, so that Israel is a widow or an abandoned virgin daughter, but almost never a subject or subordinate. And at the same time God is almost never described or addressed using a term of political office. In those few cases in Lamentations where protest is framed in explicitly political language, such as the complaint against national defeat in Lam 3:42–5, the protest is counter-balanced and muted by 'images of suffering and disgrace' and 'we-complaint', self-blame that mitigates the accusations (Morrow 2006:118). In the Hebrew Bible as a whole, then, protest is reserved almost exclusively for those contexts in which the relationship between God and Israel is conceived politically or institutionally. In stark contrast to this, Lamentations resists complaining in a political or institutional context, and where that occurs, tempers the complaint with self-blame. Instead, in Lamentations, the most vociferous protest is reserved for the domestic arena, when the relationship between Israel and God is expressed as parent/child or husband/wife.

What can explain this general feature of Lamentations? Morrow identifies two main locations for this biblical book's unique preference to focus on the domestic context rather than the national arena when it comes to complaint: first, the psychology of trauma, in which lowered self-esteem and self-blame characterize victims of violence, and second, the theology of prophecy in which 'YHWH was entitled to exercise abusive violence towards a community perceived as a wayward child and adulterous wife' (Morrow 2006: 119). An additional motivation for the rule that the focus for complaint is domestic in Lamentations is suggested by the one exception, Lam 5:19: 'But you, O LORD, are enthroned forever; your throne endures to all generations'. It is easy to see why this allusion to royal status appears in the context of the note of cautious optimism that emerges at the end of the book (see on Lam 5:21–2). First, Israel lacks a human king; in Lamentations, as elsewhere in the Bible, divine kingship is increasingly emphasized in the absence of a king of flesh and blood. Second, the world as it was has been perverted or destroyed: slaves rule over citizens, women are raped, old men have left, young men are silent, joy has ceased, Mount Zion is desolate (vv. 8–18). The only hope of restoration lies with that which is eternal and thus cannot be perverted or destroyed: God's rule. Yet eternity implies immutability, and here, perhaps, is a reason in addition to those mentioned by Morrow for the striking general absence in Lamentations of direct references to God as king. With respect to destruction, identified throughout Lamentations with divine anger, immutability would be a curse, hence, perhaps, the references to God as husband and father, for whom anger has the potential to end. In the domestic sphere, anger, in all its manifestations, need not be lasting. Angry people can change their minds, change their behavior, even change their personalities; anger in humans is an emotion, not an attribute. When God enters the domestic sphere, as in the rest of Lamentations, his anger takes on a human form; painful as it is, it may not last. When God is called king, on the other hand, he is identified with an office, and the qualities inherent in the office – high among them consistency and stability – come to the fore. With respect to restoration, God's immutability is a source of optimism, hence perhaps the allusion to kingship only close to the end of the book of Lamentations.

[For Lam 5:20 see on Lam 5:1–5]

[5:21] *Return us, O LORD, to yourself, that we may return;*
renew our days as of old!

All's Well that Ends Well

In two very different Jewish liturgical contexts, the penultimate verse of the book of Lamentations serves as a grand finale. The first is on Tisha B'Av.[6] In this context, the entire book of Lamentations, including verse 22, is chanted in the synagogue to a traditional tune, and then verse 21 is repeated. It is no small matter to omit a scriptural verse that has been prescribed for a particular occasion, so verse 22 must be read. But a tradition emerged long ago in relation to the *haftarot* – the cycle of readings from the Prophets that accompany the formal recitation of the Torah (Pentateuch) in synagogue on Shabbat and festivals – that it is permissible to return to an earlier verse so that the selected scriptural reading will end on a positive note. The decision to end the recitation of Lamentations on Tisha B'Av with verse 21 instead of verse 22 was presumably made in this same spirit. The second liturgical context in which Lam 5:21 functions as a grand finale is at the end of the Torah service on every occasion, Shabbat and festival, when the Torah is recited ceremonially in synagogue. The *Sefer Torah*, the scroll from which the Torah is read, resides in a cupboard, often highly decorated and usually curtained, known as the *Aron ha'kodesh* (Holy Ark) or *Heichal* (Palace). In preparation for the reading, the scroll – either clothed in fabric or encased, according to local custom – is removed from the Ark and paraded around the synagogue with great pomp and circumstance. The process is repeated at the end of the recitation, and at precisely the moment when the scroll has been replaced and the designated individual is poised to close the curtain, the congregation sings a prayer, probably of medieval origin, comprising a selection of biblical verses: 'Whenever the Ark rested, Moses used to say, 'O LORD may You dwell among the myriad families of the people Israel' (Num 10:36); 'Return O LORD to your sanctuary, You and Your glorious Ark. Let your priests be clothed in righteousness, let your faithful sing for joy. For the sake of David your servant, do not forget your anointed' (Ps 132:8–10); 'Precious teaching I give you; never forget my Torah' (Prov 4:2); 'Its ways are pleasantness and all its paths are peace' (Prov 3:17); 'Return us, O LORD, to yourself, that we may return; renew our days as of old!' (Lam 5:21). The melody to which these verses are sung varies hugely from one synagogue to another, but the last line is typically rousing.

---

[6]   At present, Yom HaShoah, the day on which Jews throughout the world remember the Shoah, is commemorated on a separate day.

One factor in the choice of this verse as a grand finale was surely its ebullient optimism. The second half of the verse offers in one breath – and a little enigmatically once it is unpacked – both the promise of the unknown (renew our days *and* the security of the familiar (as of old). Added to this, when read in Hebrew, the first half of the verse implies repentance as well as restoration; the verb meaning 'to return' (or 'to restore', according to NRSV) also means 'to repent'. On this multivalent reading, those praying are offered not just a restoration, but also the chance to begin again with a clean slate; their sins will have been erased by repentance. And, finally, if that is not enough, God will take the active step: 'Cause us to return to you / repent, O LORD, and we will return/repent.' Bearing all this in mind, it is small wonder that the liturgical framers of the Tisha B'Av prayers and the weekly Torah service chose to use Lam 5:21 as a climax. But why did the authors of Lamentations decide differently? On one reading, the book's final four verses can be seen to form two conceptual couplets, each couplet containing a note of optimism (God's eternity and his willingness to restore, respectively) and a note of despair (you have forgotten us and rejected us, respectively). According to this reading, hope and despair are two sides of the same coin in the Lamentations world-view, and the only question is whether the head or the tail will be visible at the end. Most people, in most contexts, would probably prefer to see the head, but it is hard not to respect anew the poet-theologian of Lamentations who resolved to remove the escapist hatch and leave his readers looking dejectedly at the tail.

5:22 *For if truly you have rejected us,*
raged bitterly against us –

The Bitter End

The concluding verse of Lamentations represents a well-known challenge for Bible translators and commentators. As noted earlier, the book's final four verses form two conceptual couplets, each pair containing a note of optimism (God's eternity and his willingness to restore in vv. 19 and 21, respectively) and a note of despair (God forgetting and God rejecting in vv. 20 and 22, respectively). But the meaning of the two words that introduce this final verse (*ki im*) is very far from clear. Some scholars have suggested that Lamentations ends on a confident note (e.g. Kraus 1968: 91), judging the book as a whole to be essentially positive (cf. Johnson 1985). For these scholars, it has often been important to emphasize that God's anger is a thing of the past. For example, Robert Gordis wrote, 'The closing verse in Lamentations is crucial for the meaning and spirit of the entire poem. In spite of the simplicity of its style and the familiarity of its vocabulary, it has long been a crux' (Gordis 1974). Gordis himself ingeniously proposed taking the verbs in verse 22 as pluperfects, introduced by 'even though', with verse 22 in a subordinate relationship to the petition of verse 21 and stating its background, namely God's wrath. Thus he translated: 'Turn us to yourself, O LORD ..., even though you had despised us greatly and were very angry with us.'

The precise meaning of the opening words of verse 22 is a very old problem, and there have been numerous attempts to explain it. The ancient translations tell a story of early puzzlement. For example, the Latin Vulgate begins verse 22 with *sed*, 'but', whereas the Old Greek, Old Latin and Syriac have a causal clause, 'because ...' The modern English versions similarly represent a range of options. RSV turns verse 22 into questions: 'Or hast thou utterly rejected us? Art thou exceedingly angry with us?' NRSV takes the words *ki im* to mean 'unless'; but elsewhere in the Hebrew Bible they are used to mean 'unless' only when preceded by a negative statement. KJV (like the Vulgate) translates with an adversative: 'But you have utterly rejected us ...' NEB reads: 'If thou hast utterly rejected us, then great has been thy anger against us', consistent with the observation made by several commentators that the words *ki im* often introduce a conditional statement.

The insight that the words *ki im* can be expected to introduce a conditional statement provides the starting point for an article by Tod Linafelt (2001). He understands *ki im* as introducing only the protasis (condition) of a conditional sentence, pointing to the fact that there exists a class of conditionals in which the apodosis (the consequence clause) is missing. Linafelt thus suggests that we find in Lam 5:22 a protasis without an apodosis, or, in other words, an 'if' with the 'then' left unstated. The reason that this has been overlooked is, in Linafelt's view, that most examples of this class of conditionals occur as oaths or curses; the fact that this same arrangement occurs in non-oath formulas has been largely unacknowledged. There are non-oath examples of understood (rather than stated) apodoses in, for example, Gen 38:17, Num 5:20, and Exod 32:32. In support of including Lam 5:22 in this category Linafelt adds that in conditional clauses beginning with *im* the infinitive absolute quite often follows immediately after *im*, as it does in verse 22. Linafelt therefore takes *ki im* in the most natural sense of 'for if ...' and understands all of verse 22 as the protasis of a conditional sentence in which the apodosis is understood rather than stated: 'For if truly you have rejected us, raging bitterly against us ...'

As in his important volume *Surviving Lamentations* (Linafelt 2000a), so in this article Linafelt displays an interpretative awareness influenced to a significant degree by immersion in literature that has emerged in the wake of the Shoah. In Linafelt's case, this has led him to resist readings of Lamentations that move too readily away from the articulation of raw pain, typically in his view towards theological rationale and the emergence of hope. His work provides a good example of the way that sensitivity to the afterlife of a text can help hone the tools used in rigorous exegetical work. Linafelt writes in the article: 'Rendered thus, the final line of verse 22 is a poignantly appropriate way to end the book of Lamentations, indicating by its very incompleteness a refusal to move – in the face of YHWH's lack of response – beyond lament to praise, but also a refusal to conclude at all. The ending of the book is, then, a willful *non-ending*. The poetry is left opening out into the emptiness of God's non-response' (Linafelt 2001: 343). He continues: 'By leaving a conditional statement dangling, the final verse leaves open the future of the ones lamenting. It is hardly a hopeful ending, for the missing but implied apodosis is surely negative; yet it does nevertheless defer that apodosis. And by arresting the movement from an "if" to a "then" the incomplete clause allows the reader, for a moment, to imagine a possibility of a different "then", and therefore a different future' (343). Optimistic, pessimistic or agnostic, the book's capacity to accommodate these three diverse approaches may explain in part its enduring significance for the religious traditions that hold it sacred and the cultures they have affected.

References

Alexander, P. S. 2008. *The Targum of Lamentations* (Aramaic Bible, 17B; Collegeville, MN: Liturgical Press).

Barbour, J. 2012. *The Story of Israel in the Book of Qohelet: Ecclesiastes as Cultural Memory* (Oxford Theological Monographs; Oxford: Oxford University Press).

Cohen, M. E. 1988. *The Canonical Lamentations of Ancient Mesopotamia* (2 vols; Potomac, MD: Capital Decisions Limited).

Dobbs-Allsopp, F. W. 1993. *Weep, O Daughter of Zion: A Study of the City-Lament Genre in the Hebrew Bible* (Biblica et Orientalia, 44; Rome: Editrice Pontificio Instituto Biblico).

Goldenberg, D. M. 2003. *The Curse of Ham: Race and Slavery in Early Judaism, Christianity and Islam* (Princeton: Princeton University Press).

Gordis, R. 1974. 'The Conclusion of the Book of Lamentations (5.22)', *JBL* 93: 289–93.

Gunkel, H. (with J. Begrich). 1998. *Introduction to the Psalms: The Genres of the Religious Lyric of Israel* (Mercer Library of Biblical Studies; Macon, GA: Mercer University Press). [German original, 1933]

Hillers, D. R. 1992. *Lamentations* (Anchor Bible, 7a; Garden City, NY: Doubleday, 2nd edn).

Johnson, B. 1985. 'Form and Message in Lamentations', *ZAW* 97: 58–73.

Kraus, H.-J. 1968. *Klagelieder (Threni)* (BKAT, 20; Neukirchen-Vluyn: Neukirchener Verlag, 3rd edn).

Linafelt, T. 2000a. *Surviving Lamentations: Catastrophe, Lament, and Protest in the Afterlife of a Biblical Book* (Chicago and London: University of Chicago Press).

Linafelt, T. 2001. 'The Refusal of a Conclusion in the Book of Lamentations', *JBL* 120: 340–3.

Morrow, W. S. 2006. *Protest against God: The Eclipse of a Biblical Tradition* (Sheffield: Sheffield Phoenix Press).

Rice, G. 1978. 'Was Amos a Racist?', *Journal of Religious Thought* 35: 35–44.

Sadler, R. S., Jr. 2005. *Can a Cushite Change His Skin?* (LHBOTS, 425; New York: T. & T. Clark).

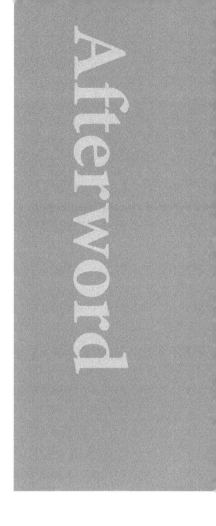

Afterword

In more ways than one, writing this commentary has been a voyage of discovery for us, and we hope that our readers too will have found ideas and insights here. In particular, we hope that they will have internalized a point that became ever more important to us as our commentary evolved: biblical scholars have no monopoly on illuminating exegesis. Time and again, we found that material from the history of reception sensitized our reading of Lamentations and generated insights that provided fresh options for understanding the ancient text. This was the process that we termed 'reception exegesis'. To be sure, it is difficult or impossible to generate certain kinds of insights – for example, those concerning Hebrew grammar or ancient Israelite history – without specialized

Lamentations Through the Centuries, First Edition. Paul M. Joyce and Diana Lipton.
© 2013 Paul M. Joyce and Diana Lipton. Published 2020 by John Wiley & Sons Ltd.

expertise of one kind or another, but readers across the generations can work in virtual partnership, as we have tried to do with the readers ancient and modern whose fruits are presented here, one producing the key that allows the other to unlock the door. We hope we have offered ample evidence of how reception exegesis can spotlight themes and patterns, elucidate difficult concepts and terms, and generally enhance our understanding of the ancient text. Examples that stood out for us include the meaning of exile (see Lam 1:3 and 1:5); the externalization of mental states (see Lam 1:20); the significance and location of 'Zion' (see Lam 2:1 and 4:12); the source and type of poetic images (see Lam 2:13); the use of non-verbal mechanisms of intercession, including children (see Lam 2:19), gestures (see Lam 3:41–2) and tears (see Lam 3:49); the role of time in describing loss (see Lam 3:16); the use of mourning rituals (see Lam 3:6); perspectives on divine justice and injustice (see Lam 2:7 and 3:15); the representation of loss by reversal and inversion (see Lam 4:6); the striking absence of claims that the people love God (see Lam 3:14); the juxtaposition of jackals and ostriches (see Lam 4:3); the meaning of the Hebrew word *bat* ('daughter') (see Lam 4:21); shared responsibility for catastrophe (see Lam 3:15 and 4:2); the absence of 'factions' (see on Lam 2:22); the meaning of 'compassionate women' (see Lam 4:10); and the use of the term 'wall of daughter Zion' in Lam 2:18 (see on Lam 2:14). From these and many other examples of reception exegesis presented in this volume, we hope that our readers will learn, as we did, that truly transformational exegesis depends less exclusively than might be supposed upon academic expertise and a great deal more than might be expected upon human experience.

In the end, this has been a book about readers, broadly construed. The book of Lamentations addresses several distinct communities of readers, or perhaps better 'hearers', of its own, from the enemies of Zion through passive onlookers to Zion herself. The use of direct speech, underlined by the explicit naming of the addressee (Zion/Jerusalem in Lam 2:13, 18 and Lam 4:22; Edom in Lam 4:21; onlookers in Lam 1:18; and 'us' in Lam 3:40–1), suggests that the biblical authors wanted their audiences to pay attention. More than that, we might infer that they sought a response, hoping to affect their audiences and, as a result, change for the better the catastrophic scene they were describing. Anthropocentric as we are, we are inclined to privilege human audiences, such as those just mentioned above, but the book of Lamentations also addresses a non-human hearer. For the authors of Lamentations, God is numbered among their intended audience and perhaps, as the most powerful and effective agent of change from their perspective, they privileged him above all others (see Lam 1:9, 11, 20, 22; 2:20; 3:42–5, 55–66; and 5:1, 19–22). In this sense, the book of Lamentations may be read as a prayer as well as a lament and, as with the Psalms, it is thus perfectly at home in the liturgical settings it has been given by Jewish and Christian traditions.

But what of the readers that the authors of Lamentations could not so easily have envisaged or imagined? The creative interpreters of the text that we have presented in this volume are themselves readers of the biblical book. At the same time, they address readers of their own, those who experience Lamentations through these later works. Reception historians, gathering all these together, create a virtual reading room in which their own contemporary readers enter into dialogue with readers throughout the centuries and from every corner of the globe. To borrow a phrase often used in the tradition of rabbinic midrash, the creative interpretation of the Bible that has featured so often in our volume, 'What is this like?' Some readers of our volume will be familiar with the appearance of a page of the Babylonian Talmud presented in its traditional format. At the center of the page is a short section of the Mishna, the second-century CE law code assembled in Roman Palestine in the aftermath of the destruction of the second Temple, and almost certainly in response to it. Surrounding the passage of Mishna, in the form of something like an elaborate floor plan with multiple rooms leading from a central vestibule, is an array of comments and explanations. Immediately surrounding the Mishna is the Gemara, a commentary on the Mishna from fifth to seventh century CE Babylonia (but incorporating much older material) that reports diverse opinions assembled over several hundred years as if it were recording the discussion in one room on a single day. And surrounding the Gemara is a range of other texts, from the Tosefta, a selection of material that originated in a similar context at the same time as the Mishna, to the commentary of the famous medieval French commentator Rashi (Rabbi Solomon ben Isaac). A central motivation for most if not all of these commentaries on the Mishna was the desire to work out how to interpret its teachings and apply them in later generations and new circumstances. A single page of the Babylonian Talmud achieves something extraordinary. It preserves a community of readers – geographically and temporally disparate and dispersed – who read, wrestled with, and applied in their own times its underlying text, the Mishna. And, needless to say, they also read and wrestled with each other. All subsequent readers of the Babylonian Talmud may join this community in its talmudic reading room as they too engage with its foundational text and interpreters. In this respect, a biblical reception history is like the Babylonian Talmud. It provides a record of a community of readers of a foundational text, in our case the book of Lamentations, showing how they interpreted it and applied it in their own lives, through many generations, around the world, and (unlike the Babylonian Talmud) across religious divides. We hope that readers of our contribution to the evolving genre of biblical reception history will have found their own places in the extraordinary community we have tried to present and preserve: readers through the centuries.

Bibliography

Agamben, G. 1998. *Homo Sacer: Sovereign Power and Bare Life* (Stanford, CA: Stanford University Press). [Italian original, 1995.]

Albrektson, B. 1963. *Studies in the Text and Theology of the Book of Lamentations* (Studia Theologica Lundensia, 21; Lund: CWK Gleerup).

Alexander, P. S. 2008. *The Targum of Lamentations* (Aramaic Bible, 17B; Collegeville, MN: Liturgical Press).

Allen, L. C. 2011. *A Liturgy of Grief: A Pastoral Commentary on Lamentations* (Grand Rapids, MI: Baker Academic).

Alter, R. 1985. *The Art of Biblical Poetry* (New York: Basic Books).

Archer, J. 1999. *The Nature of Grief: The Evolution and Psychology of Reactions to Loss* (London: Routledge).

Bahrani, Z. 2008. *Rituals of War: The Body and Violence in Mesopotamia* (New York: Zone; Cambridge, MA: MIT).

Barbour, J. 2012. *The Story of Israel in the Book of Qohelet: Ecclesiastes as Cultural Memory* (Oxford Theological Monographs; Oxford: Oxford University Press).

Berges, U. 2005. 'The Violence of God in the Book of Lamentations', in *One Text, A Thousand Methods: Studies in Memory of Sjef van Tilborg* (ed. P. C. Counet and U. Berges; Biblical Interpretation Series, 71; Leiden: Brill) 21–44.

Berlin, A. 2002. *Lamentations* (OTL; Louisville, KY, and London: Westminster John Knox).

Berrigan, D. 2002. *Lamentations: From New York to Kabul and Beyond* (Lanham, MD, and Chicago: Sheed and Ward).

Boase, E. 2006. *The Fulfilment of Doom? The Dialogic Interaction between the Book of Lamentations and the Pre-Exilic/Early Exilic Prophetic Literature* (LHBOTS, 437; New York and London: T. & T. Clark).

Boer, R. 2011. 'Against "Reception History"', contribution to 'In My View', on *The Bible and Interpretation* (posted May 2011), at http://www.bibleinterp.com/opeds/boe358008.shtml.

Brady, C. M. M. 2003. *The Rabbinic Targum of Lamentations: Vindicating God* (Studies in the Aramaic Interpretation of Scripture, 3; Leiden and Boston: Brill).

Brooks, T. 1670. *London's Lamentations, or, A serious discourse concerning that late fiery dispensation that turned our (once renowned) city into a ruinous heap* (London: Printed for John Hancock and Nathaniel Ponder).

Broyde, M. J. (ed.). 2011. *Contending with Catastrophe: Jewish Perspectives on September 11th* (New York: K'hal Publishing).

Brueggemann, W. 1986. 'The Costly Loss of Lament', *JSOT* 36: 57–71.

Calvin, J. 1855. *Commentaries on the Book of the Prophet Jeremiah and the Lamentations*, vol. 5 (trans. and ed. J. Owen; Edinburgh: Calvin Translation Society).

Celan, P. 2000. *Selected Poems and Prose of Paul Celan* (ed. J. Felstiner; New York: W. W. Norton).

Coggins, R. J. and J. L. Houlden (eds). 1990. *A Dictionary of Biblical Interpretation* (London: SCM Press; Philadelphia, PA: Trinity Press International).

Cohen, C. 1973. 'The "Widowed" City', *JANESCU* 5: 75–81.

Cohen, M. E. 1988. *The Canonical Lamentations of Ancient Mesopotamia* (2 vols.; Potomac, MD: Capital Decisions Limited).

Cohen, S. J. D. 1982. 'The Destruction: From Scripture to Midrash', *Prooftexts: A Journal of Jewish Liturgy* 2: 18–39.

Cole, P. (ed.). 2007. *The Dream of the Poem: Hebrew Poetry from Muslim and Christian Spain, 950–1492* (Princeton: Princeton University Press).

Dobbs-Allsopp, F. W. 1993. *Weep, O Daughter of Zion: A Study of the City-Lament Genre in the Hebrew Bible* (Biblica et Orientalia, 44; Rome: Editrice Pontificio Instituto Biblico).

Dobbs-Allsopp, F. W. 1997. 'Tragedy, Tradition and Theology in the Book of Lamentations', *JSOT* 74: 29–60.

Dobbs-Allsopp, F. W. 2002. *Lamentations* (Interpretation Commentary; Louisville, KY: John Knox).

Dobbs-Allsopp, F. W. and T. Linafelt. 2001. 'The Rape of Zion in Thr 1,10', *ZAW* 113: 77–81.

Doe, P. 1968. *Tallis* (Oxford Studies of Composers, 4; London: Oxford University Press, 2nd edn).

Donne, J. 1896. *Poems of John Donne*, vol. 1 (ed. E. K. Chambers; London: Lawrence & Bullen).

Eikon Basilike. 1649. *Eikon Basilike, vel Imago Regis Caroli, in illis suis ærumnis et solitudine* (London: J. Williams and F. Eglesfield).

Evelyn, J. 2006. *The Diary of John Evelyn* (ed. E. S. De Beer; selected and introduced by R. Strong; London: Everyman).

Exum, J. C. 1995. 'The Ethics of Biblical Violence against Women', in *The Bible in Ethics: The Second Sheffield Colloquium* (ed. J. W. Rogerson, M. Davies and M. D. Carroll R.; JSOTSup, 207. Sheffield: Sheffield Academic Press) 248–71.

Exum, J. C. 2012. 'Toward a Genuine Dialogue between the Bible and Art', in *Congress Volume: Helsinki, 2010* (ed. M. Nissinen; VTSup, 148; Leiden: Brill) 473–503.

Ezrahi, S. D. 1978. 'The Holocaust Writer and the Lamentation Tradition: Responses to Catastrophe in Jewish Literature', *Confronting the Holocaust: The Impact of Elie Wiesel* (ed. A. H. Rosenfeld and I. Greenberg; Bloomington, IN: Indiana University Press) 133–49.

Farnell, L. R. 1925. *The Attributes of God* (Oxford: Clarendon).

Flesher, L. S., M. J. Boda and C. J. Dempsey (eds). 2012. *Why? How Long? Studies on Voice(s) of Lamentation Rooted in Biblical Hebrew Poetry* (LHBOTS, 552; New York: T. & T. Clark).

Fonrobert, C. E. 2001. 'When the Rabbi Weeps: On Reading Gender in Talmudic Aggadah', in *Nashim: A Journal of Jewish Women's Studies and Gender Issues* 4: 56–84.

Forsdyke, S. 2005. *Exile, Ostracism, and Democracy: The Politics of Expulsion in Ancient Greece* (Princeton: Princeton University Press).

Freud, S. 1991a. 'Mourning and Melancholia', in *On Metapsychology: The Theory of Psychoanalysis* (Penguin Freud Library, 11; Harmondsworth: Penguin) 245–68.

Freud, S. 1991b. 'The Ego and the Id', in *On Metapsychology: The Theory of Psychoanalysis* (Penguin Freud Library, 11; Harmondsworth: Penguin) 350–408.

Gadamer, H.-G. 2004. *Truth and Method* (London: Continuum; New York: Crossroad; 2nd rev. edn). [German original, 1960.]

Goldenberg, D. M. 2003. *The Curse of Ham: Race and Slavery in Early Judaism, Christianity and Islam* (Princeton: Princeton University Press).

Gordis, R. 1974. 'The Conclusion of the Book of Lamentations (5.22)', *JBL* 93: 289–93.

Gottwald, N. K. 1962. *Studies in the Book of Lamentations* (SBT, 14; London: SCM Press, 2nd edn).

Gray, A. 1995. *Five Letters from an Eastern Empire* (London: Penguin).

Greenstein, E. L. 1982. 'An Equivocal Reading of the Sale of Joseph', in *Literary Interpretations of Biblical Narratives, II* (ed. K. R. R. Gros Louis; Nashville, TN: Abingdon Press) 114–25.

Greenstein, E. L. 2004. 'The Wrath of God in the Book of Lamentations', in *The Problem of Evil and Its Symbols in Jewish and Christian Tradition* (ed. H. G. Reventlow and Y. Hoffman; JSOTSup, 366; London and New York: T. & T. Clark) 29–42.

Guest, D. 1999. 'Hiding Behind the Naked Women in Lamentations: A Recriminative Response', *Biblical Interpretation* 7: 413–48.

Guest, D., R. E. Goss, M. West and T. Bohache (eds.). 2006. *The Queer Bible Commentary* (London: SCM Press).

Gunkel, H. (with J. Begrich). 1998. *Introduction to the Psalms: The Genres of the Religious Lyric of Israel* (Mercer Library of Biblical Studies; Macon, GA: Mercer University Press). [German original, 1933.]

Halevi, Y. 2002. *Poems from the Diwan* (trans. by G. Levin; Poetica, 32; London: Anvil Press).

Harasta, E. and B. Brock (eds.). 2009. *Evoking Lament: A Theological Discussion* (New York and London: T. & T. Clark).

Heschel, A. J. 1962. *The Prophets* (New York: Harper & Row).

Heschel, A. J. 1997. *Israel: An Echo of Eternity* (Woodstock, VT: Jewish Lights Publishing). [Original, 1967.]

Hillers, D. R. 1992. *Lamentations* (Anchor Bible, 7a; Garden City, NY: Doubleday, 2nd edn).

Holub, R. C. 2003. *Reception Theory: A Critical Introduction* (London: Routledge; 2nd edn).

House, P. R. 2004. 'Lamentations', in *Song of Songs / Lamentations* (WBC, 23B; Nashville, TN: Thomas Nelson) 267–473.

Hunter, J. 1996. *Faces of a Lamenting City: The Development and Coherence of the Book of Lamentations* (BEATAJ, 39; Frankfurt: Peter Lang).

Ilan, T. 2008. 'Gender and Lamentations: 4Q179 and the Canonization of the Book of Lamentations', *Lectio Difficilior: European Electronic Journal for Feminist Exegesis* 2.

Jacobsen, T. 1976. *The Treasures of Darkness: A History of Mesopotamian Religion* (New Haven, CT: Yale University Press).

James, F. A., III. 1998. *Peter Martyr Vermigli and Predestination: The Augustinian Inheritance of an Italian Reformer* (Oxford Theological Monographs; Oxford: Clarendon).

Jauss, H. R. 1982. *Toward an Aesthetic of Reception* (Theory and History of Literature, 2; Brighton: Harvester; Minneapolis: University of Minnesota Press).

John of the Cross. 1976. *Dark Night of the Soul* (trans. E. Allison Peers; London: Burns & Oates).

Johnson, B. 1985. 'Form and Message in Lamentations', *ZAW* 97: 58–73.

Josephus. 1970. *The Jewish War* (trans. by G. A. Williamson; Penguin Classics; Harmondsworth: Penguin; rev. edn).

Joyce, P. M. 1993. 'Lamentations and the Grief Process: A Psychological Reading', *Biblical Interpretation* 1: 304–320.

Joyce, P. M. 1999. 'Sitting Loose to History: Reading the Book of Lamentations without Primary Reference to Its Original Historical Setting', in *In Search of True Wisdom: Essays in Old Testament Interpretation in Honour of Ronald E. Clements* (ed. E. Ball; JSOTSup, 300; Sheffield: Sheffield Academic Press) 246–62.

Joyce, P. M. 2001. 'Lamentations', in *The Oxford Bible Commentary* (ed. J. Barton and J. Muddiman; Oxford: Oxford University Press) 528–33.

Joyce, P. M. 2011. 'Psychological Approaches to Lamentations', in Parry and Thomas (2011) 161–5.

Juxon, W. 1649. *The subjects sorrow: or, Lamentations upon the death of Britain's Josiah, King Charles, most unjustly and cruelly put to death by His owne people, before His Royall Palace White-Hall* (London).

Kaiser, O. 1992. 'Klagelieder', in *Das Hohelied, Klagelieder, Das Buch Ester* (ed. H. P. Müller et al.; ATD, 16/2; Göttingen: Vandenhoeck & Ruprecht, 4th edn) 91–198.

Kavanaugh, K. and O. Rodriguez. 1991. *The Collected Works of St John of the Cross* (Washington, DC: ICS).

Keel, O. 1977. *Die Welt der altorientalischen Bildsymbolik und das Alte Testament: Am Beispiel der Psalmen* (Zürich: Benziger; Neukirchen-Vluyn: Neukirchener Verlag, 2nd edn).

Keel, O. 1998. *Goddesses and Trees, New Moon and Yahweh: Ancient Near Eastern Art and the Hebrew Bible* (JSOTSup, 261; Sheffield: Sheffield Academic Press).

Keel, O. and C. Uehlinger. 1998. *Gods, Goddesses, and Images of God in Ancient Israel* (Edinburgh: T. & T. Clark).

Kochanowski, J. 1995. *Laments* (trans. S. Heaney and S. Baranczak; London: Faber and Faber). [Polish original, *Treny*, 1580.]

Kraus, H.-J. 1968. *Klagelieder (Threni)* (BKAT, 20; Neukirchen-Vluyn: Neukirchener Verlag, 3rd edn).

Kübler-Ross, E. 1969. *On Death and Dying* (New York: Touchstone).

Labahn, A. 2002. 'Trauern als Bewältigung der Vergangenheit zur Gestaltung der Zukunft. Bemerkungen zur anthropologischen Theologie der Klagelieder', *VT* 52: 513–27.

Lagnado, L. 2007. *The Man in the White Sharkskin Suit: My Family's Exodus from Old Cairo to the New World* (New York: Ecco).

Lagnado, L. 2011. *The Arrogant Years: One Girl's Search for Her Lost Youth, from Cairo to Brooklyn* (New York: Ecco).

Lamentations Rabbah. 1519. *Lamentations Rabbah,* in *Midrash Rabbah, on the Five Megillot* (Pesaro; 1st printed edn).

Lamentations Rabbah. 1876. *Lamentations Rabbah,* in *Midrash Rabbah, on the Five Books of Moses and the Five Megillot with Many Commentaries* (Standard Hebrew edn; 3 vols; Vilna).

Lamentations Rabbah. 1983. *Lamentations Rabbah* (ed. A. Z. Steinberger; annotated Hebrew edn; Jerusalem).

Landy, F. 1987. 'Lamentations', in *The Literary Guide to the Bible* (ed. R. Alter and F. Kermode; London: Collins) 329–34.

Lee, N. C. 2002. *The Singers of Lamentations: Cities under Siege, from Ur to Jerusalem to Sarajevo …* (Biblical Interpretation Series, 60; Leiden: Brill).

Lee, N. C. 2010. *Lyrics of Lament: From Tragedy to Transformation* (Minneapolis, MN: Fortress).

Lee, N. C. and C. Mandolfo (eds). 2008. *Lamentations in Ancient and Contemporary Cultural Contexts* (SBL Symposium Series, 43; Atlanta, GA: SBL).

Leff, J. P. 1973. 'Culture and the Differentiation of Emotional States', *British Journal of Psychiatry* 123: 299–306.

Leff, J. P. 1988. *Psychiatry around the Globe: A Transcultural View* (London: Gaskell; 2nd edn).

Lieb, M., E. Mason and J. Roberts (eds). 2011. *The Oxford Handbook of the Reception History of the Bible* (Oxford: Oxford University Press).

Linafelt, T. 1998. 'The Impossibility of Mourning: Lamentations after the Holocaust', in *God in the Fray: A Tribute to Walter Brueggemann* (ed. T. Linafelt and T. K. Beal; Minneapolis, MN: Fortress) 279–89.

Linafelt, T. 2000a. *Surviving Lamentations: Catastrophe, Lament, and Protest in the Afterlife of a Biblical Book* (Chicago and London: University of Chicago Press).

Linafelt, T. 2000b. 'Zion's Cause: The Presentation of Pain in the Book of Lamentations', in *Strange Fire: Reading the Bible after the Holocaust* (ed. T. Linafelt; The Biblical Seminar, 71; Sheffield: Sheffield Academic Press; New York: New York University Press) 267–79.

Linafelt, T. 2001. 'The Refusal of a Conclusion in the Book of Lamentations', *JBL* 120: 340–3.

Mandolfo, C. R. 2007. *Daughter Zion Talks Back to the Prophets: A Dialogic Theology of the Book of Lamentations* (Semeia Studies, 58; Atlanta, GA: SBL).

Mandolfo, C. R. 2009. 'Lamentations', in *Theological Bible Commentary* (ed. G. R. O'Day and D. L. Petersen; Louisville, KY: Westminster John Knox) 237–9.

Martinez, R. L. 1997. 'Lament and Lamentations in "Purgatorio" and the Case of Dante's Statius', *Dante Studies* 115: 45–88.

Massenkeil, G. 1980. 'Lamentations', in *The New Grove Dictionary of Music and Musicians*, vol. 10 (ed. S. Sadie; London: Macmillan; New York: Grove) 410–12.

Megged, A. 2005. *The Living on the Dead* (trans. M. Louvish; New Milford, CT: Toby Press; 2nd edn). [Hebrew original, 1965]

Mein, A. and P. M. Joyce (eds). 2011. *After Ezekiel: Essays on the Reception of a Difficult Prophet* (LHBOTS, 535; New York and London: T. & T. Clark/Continuum).

Meverden, A. 2011. 'Daughter Zion as *Homo Sacer*: The Relationship of Exile, Lamentations, and Georgio Agamben's Bare Life Figure', in *Interpreting Exile: Displacement and Deportation in Biblical and Modern Contexts* (ed. B. E. Kelle, F. R. Ames, and J. L. Wright; Ancient Israel and Its Literature, 10; Atlanta, GA: SBL) 395–407.

Middlemas, J. 2005. *The Troubles of Templeless Judah* (Oxford Theological Monographs; Oxford: Oxford University Press).

Middlemas, J. 2006. 'Did Second Isaiah Write Lamentations III?', *VT* 56: 506–25.

Miller, A. 1991. *Breaking Down the Wall of Silence to Join the Waiting Child* (London: Virago).

Miller, G. D. 2011. 'Intertextuality in Old Testament Research', *Currents in Biblical Research* 9: 283–309.

Mintz, A. 1984. *Hurban: Responses to Catastrophe in Hebrew Literature* (New York: Columbia University Press).

Moffitt, D. M. 2006. 'Righteous Bloodshed, Matthew's Passion Narrative, and the Temple's Destruction: Lamentations as a Matthean Intertext', *JBL* 125: 299–320.

Morgan, R., with J. Barton. 1988. *Biblical Interpretation* (Oxford Bible Series; Oxford: Oxford University Press).

Morgenstern, J. 1956, 1957, 1960. 'Jerusalem–485 B.C.', *Hebrew Union College Annual* 27: 101–79; 28: 15–47; 31: 1–29.

Morrow, W. S. 2006. *Protest against God: The Eclipse of a Biblical Tradition* (Sheffield: Sheffield Phoenix Press).

Morse, B. 2003. 'The Lamentations Project: Biblical Mourning through Modern Montage', *JSOT* 28: 113–27.

Moughtin-Mumby, S. R. 2008. *Sexual and Marital Metaphors in Hosea, Jeremiah, Isaiah, and Ezekiel* (Oxford Theological Monographs; Oxford: Oxford University Press).

Mumford, D. B. 1992. 'Emotional Distress in the Hebrew Bible. Somatic or Psychological?', *British Journal of Psychiatry* 160: 92–7.

O'Connor, K. M. 1999. '"Speak Tenderly to Jerusalem": Second Isaiah's Reception and Use of Daughter Zion', *Princeton Seminary Bulletin* 3: 281–94.

O'Connor, K. M. 2002. *Lamentations and the Tears of the World* (Maryknoll, NY: Orbis).

Odell, M. S. and J. T. Strong (eds). 2000. *The Book of Ezekiel: Theological and Anthropological Perspectives* (SBL Symposium Series, 9; Atlanta, GA: SBL).

Ozick, C. 1990. *The Shawl* (New York: Vintage).

Parris, D. P. 2009. *Reception Theory and Biblical Hermeneutics* (Princeton Theological Monograph Series, 107. Eugene, OR: Pickwick).

Parry, R. A. 2006. 'Prolegomena to Christian Theological Interpretations of Lamentations', in *Canon and Biblical Interpretation* (ed. C. Bartholomew et al. Scripture and Hermeneutics Series, 7; Milton Keynes: Paternoster; Grand Rapids, MI: Zondervan) 393–418.

Parry, R. A. 2010. *Lamentations* (Two Horizons Old Testament Commentary; Grand Rapids, MI, and Cambridge: Eerdmans).

Parry, R. A. and H. A. Thomas (eds). 2011. *Great Is Thy Faithfulness? Reading Lamentations as Sacred Scripture* (Eugene, OR: Pickwick).

Patrick, D. 1999. *The Rhetoric of Revelation in the Hebrew Bible* (OBT; Minneapolis, MN: Fortress) 163–78.

Pepys, S. 2000. *The Diary of Samuel Pepys: A New and Complete Transcription* (ed. R. Latham and W. Matthews; 11 vols; London: HarperCollins).

Perdue, L. G. and A. Lee (eds). 2013. *A Postcolonial Commentary on the Old Testament* (Bible and Postcolonialism; New York: T. & T. Clark).

Pham, X. H. T. 2000. *Mourning in the Ancient Near East and the Hebrew Bible* (JSOTSup, 302; Sheffield: Sheffield Academic Press).

Porteous, N. W. 1961. 'Jerusalem–Zion: The Growth of a Symbol', in *Verbannung und Heimkehr: Beiträge zur Geschichte und Theologie Israels im 6. und 5. Jahrhundert v. Chr.* (Festschrift W. Rudolph; ed. A. Kuschke; Tübingen: Mohr) 235–52.

Provan, I. W. 1990. 'Reading Texts against an Historical Background: The Case of Lamentations 1', *Scandinavian Journal of the Old Testament* 1: 130–43.

Provan, I. W. 1991. *Lamentations* (NCB; London: Marshall Pickering; Grand Rapids, MI: Eerdmans).

Pyper, H. S. 2001. 'Reading Lamentations', *JSOT* 95: 55–69.

Raphael, C. 1968. *Walls of Jerusalem* (New York: Alfred Knopf).

Reimer, D. J. 2002. 'Good Grief? A Psychological Reading of Lamentations', *ZAW* 114: 542–59.

Renkema, J. 1998. *Lamentations* (Historical Commentary on the Old Testament; Leuven: Peeters).

Rice, G. 1978. 'Was Amos a Racist?', *Journal of Religious Thought* 35: 35–44.

Roberts, J. 2011. 'Introduction', in Lieb, Mason and Roberts 2011: 1–8.

Rooke, D. W. 2012. *Handel's Israelite Oratorio Libretti: Sacred Drama and Biblical Exegesis* (Oxford: Oxford University Press).

Roskies, D. G. (ed.). 1989. *The Literature of Destruction: Jewish Responses to Catastrophe* (Philadelphia, PA: Jewish Publication Society).

Rowland, C. C. and I. Boxall. 2013. 'Reception Criticism/Theory', in *The Oxford Encyclopedia of Biblical Interpretation*, vol. 2 (ed. S. McKenzie; New York and Oxford: Oxford University Press).

Rudolph, W. 1962. *Das Buch Ruth, Das Hohe Lied, Die Klagelieder* (KAT, 17; Gütersloh: Gerd Mohn, 2nd edn).

Sadler, R. S., Jr. 2005. *Can a Cushite Change His Skin?* (LHBOTS, 425; New York: T. & T. Clark).

Salters, R. B. 1986. 'Lamentations 1.3: Light from the History of Exegesis', in *A Word in Season: Essays in Honour of William McKane* (ed. J. D. Martin and P. R. Davies; JSOTSup, 42; Sheffield: JSOT Press) 73–89.

Salters, R. B. 1999. 'Using Rashi, Ibn Ezra and Joseph Kara on Lamentations', *Journal of Northwest Semitic Languages* 25: 201–13.

Salters, R. B. 2010. *Lamentations* (ICC; London and New York: Continuum).

Salters, R. B. 2011. 'Acrostics and Lamentations', in *On Stone and Scroll: Essays in Honour of Graham Ivor Davies* (eds J. K. Aitken, K. J. Dell and B. A. Mastin; BZAW, 420; Berlin: De Gruyter) 425–40.

Sawyer, J. F. A. 1989. 'Daughter of Zion and Servant of the Lord in Isaiah: A Comparison', *JSOT* 44: 89–107.

Sawyer, J. F. A. 2009. *A Concise Dictionary of the Bible and Its Reception* (Louisville, KY: Westminster John Knox).

Sawyer, J. F. A. 2011. 'Ezekiel in the History of Christianity', in Mein and Joyce 2011; 1–9.

Schopf, F. J. 2011. 'Musical Responses to Lamentations', in Parry and Thomas 2011; 147–53.

Schüssler Fiorenza, E. 1988. 'The Ethics of Biblical Interpretation: Decentering Biblical Scholarship', *JBL* 107: 3–17.

Schwarz-Bart, A. 2001. *The Last of the Just* (London: Vintage). (First published in French as *Le Dernier des Justes: Roman*, Paris: Éditions de Seuil, 1959.)

Schwarz-Bart, A. 2002. *A Woman Named Solitude* (London: Vintage). (First published in French as *La Mulâtresse Solitude: Roman*, Paris: Éditions de Seuil, 1972.)

Seidman, N. 1994. 'Burning the Book of Lamentations', in *Out of the Garden: Women Writers on the Bible* (ed. C. Büchmann and C. Spiegel; New York: Fawcett Columbine; London: Pandora) 278–88.

Seitz, C. R. 1998. *Word Without End: The Old Testament as Abiding Theological Witness* (Grand Rapids, MI and Cambridge: Eerdmans).

Shatz, D. 2011 '"From the Depths I Have Called You": Jewish Reflections on September 11th and Contemporary Terrorism', in Broyde 2011: 197–233.

Sherwood, Y. 2000. *A Biblical Text and Its Afterlives: The Survival of Jonah in Western Culture* (Cambridge: Cambridge University Press).

Shute, D. 2009. 'Interpreting Lamentations: Theodicy and the Turks', in *A Companion to Peter Martyr Vermigli* (ed. T. Kirby, E. Campi, and F. A. James III; Leiden: Brill).

Slavitt, D. R. 2001. *The Book of Lamentations: A Meditation and Translation* (Baltimore, MD, and London: Johns Hopkins University Press).

Smith-Christopher, D. 2002. *A Biblical Theology of Exile* (OBT; Minneapolis, MN: Fortress, 2002).

Soggin, J. A. 1976. *Introduction to the Old Testament* (London: SCM Press).

Sommer, B. D. 1999. *A Prophet Reads Scripture: Allusion in Isaiah 40–66* (Contraversions: Jews and Other Differences; Stanford, CA: Stanford University Press).

Spiegel, Y. 1973. *Der Prozess des Trauerns: Analyse und Beratung* (Munich: Kaiser).

Stern, D. 1991. *Parables in Midrash: Narrative and Exegesis in Rabbinic Literature* (Cambridge, MA: Harvard University Press).

Stewart, J. L. 1991. *Ernst Krenek: The Man and His Music* (Berkeley, CA: University of California Press).

Stiebert, J. 2003. 'Human Suffering and Divine Abuse of Power in Lamentations: Reflections on Forgiveness in the Context of South Africa's Truth and Reconciliation Process', *Pacifica* 16: 195–215.

Stillingfleet, E. 1666. *A Sermon Preached before the Honourable House of Commons at St. Margarets Westminster, Octob. 10 1666. Being the Fast-Day Appointed for the Late Dreadfull Fire in the City of London* (London: Printed by Robert White for Henry Mortlock).

Stone, K. 2001. *Queer Commentary and the Hebrew Bible* (JSOTSup, 334; London and New York: Sheffield Academic Press).

Sweeney, M. A. 2008. *Reading the Hebrew Bible After the Shoah: Engaging Holocaust Theology* (Minneapolis, MN: Fortress).

Thomas, H. A. 2008. 'The Liturgical Function of the Book of Lamentations', in *Thinking Towards New Horizons: Collected Communications to the XIXth Congress of the International Organization for the Study of the Old Testament, Ljubljana, 2007* (ed. M. Augustin and H.M. Niemann; BEATAJ; Frankfurt am Main: Lang) 137–47.

Thomas, H. A. 2010. 'Relating Prayer and Pain: Psychological Analysis and Lamentations Research', *Tyndale Bulletin* 61: 183–208.

Thomas, H. A. 2011a. 'Lamentations in the Patristic Period', in Parry and Thomas 2011; 113–19.

Thomas, H. A. 2011b. 'Lamentations in Rembrandt van Rijn: "Jeremiah Lamenting the Destruction of Jerusalem"', in Parry and Thomas 2011; 154–60.

Thomas, H. A. 2013. *Poetry and Theology in Lamentations: The Aesthetics of an Open Text* (Sheffield: Sheffield Phoenix Press).

Thompson, C. 2002. *St John of the Cross: Songs in the Night* (London: SPCK).

Tiemeyer, L.-S. 2007. 'Geography and Textual Allusions: Interpreting Isaiah XL-LV and Lamentations as Judahite Texts', *VT* 57: 367–85.

Tiemeyer, L.-S. 2010. *For the Comfort of Zion: The Geographical and Theological Location of Isaiah 40–55* (VTSup, 139. Leiden: Brill).

Tiemeyer, L.-S. 2011. 'Lamentations in Isaiah 40–55', in Parry and Thomas 2011; 55–63.

Treves, M. 1963. 'Conjectures sur les dates et les sujets des Lamentations', *Bulletin Renan* 95: 1–4.

Twisse, R. 1665. *England's breath stopp'd being the counter-part of Judah's miseries lamented publickly in the New-Church at Westminster on January 30: being the anniversary of the martyrdom of King Charles the First of blessed memory* (London: J. Flesher).

Van Selms, A. 1974. *Jeremia deel III en Klaagliederen* (Nijkerk: Callenbach).

Vermigli, P. M. 1629. *In Lamentationes Sanctissimi Ieremiae Prophetae Commentarium* (Zürich). Eng. tran: *Commentary on the Lamentations of the Prophet Jeremiah by Peter Martyr* (Sixteenth Century Essays and Studies, 55; trans. and ed. by D. Shute; Kirksville, MO: Truman State University Press, 2002).

Webb, B. G. 2000. *Five Festal Garments: Christian Reflections on the Song of Songs, Ruth, Lamentations, Ecclesiastes and Esther* (New Studies in Biblical Theology, 10; Leicester: Apollos).

Weems, R. J. 1995. *Battered Love: Marriage, Sex, and Violence in the Hebrew Prophets* (OBT; Minneapolis, MN: Fortress).

Wenthe, D. O. 2009. *Jeremiah, Lamentations* (Ancient Christian Commentary on Scripture, Old Testament, 12; Downers Grove, IL: InterVarsity Press).

Westermann, C. 1994. *Lamentations: Issues and Interpretation* (Minneapolis, MN: Augsburg Fortress; Edinburgh: T. & T. Clark).

Wilcox, P. 2011. 'John Calvin's Interpretation of Lamentations', in Parry and Thomas 2011; 125–30.

Wiles, J. P. 1908. *Half-hours with the Minor Prophets and the Lamentations* (London: Morgan and Scott).

Wiles, M. F. 2003. *Scholarship and Faith: A Tale of Two Grandfathers* (Cambridge: Cambridge University Press).

Willey, P. T. 1997. *Remember the Former Things: The Recollection of Previous Texts in Isaiah 40–55* (SBL Dissertation Series, 161; Atlanta, GA: Scholars Press).

Williamson, H. G. M. 1994. *The Book Called Isaiah: Deutero-Isaiah's Role in Composition and Redaction* (Oxford: Clarendon; New York: Oxford University Press).

Young, F. M. 1993. 'Allegory and the Ethics of Reading', in *The Open Text: New Directions for Biblical Studies?* (ed. F. B. Watson; London: SCM Press) 103–20.

Author Index

Lamentations Through the Centuries, First Edition. Paul M. Joyce and Diana Lipton.
© 2013 Paul M. Joyce and Diana Lipton. Published 2020 by John Wiley & Sons Ltd.